Arab
Industrialization
in Israel

Arab Industrialization in Israel

Ethnic Entrepreneurship in the Periphery

Izhak Schnell, Michael Sofer, and
Israel Drori

Westport, Connecticut
London

Library of Congress Cataloging-in-Publication Data

Schnell, Izhak.
    Arab industrialization in Israel : ethnic entrepreneurship in the
periphery / by Izhak Schnell, Michael Sofer, Israel Drori.
        p.   cm.
    Includes bibliographical references and index.
    ISBN 0–275–94856–0 (alk. paper)
    1. Palestinian Arab business enterprises—Israel.   2. Factories—
Location—Israel.   3. Minority business enterprises—Government
policy—Israel.   I. Sofer, Michael.   II. Drori, Israel.
III. Title.
HD2346.I75S56   1995
338′.04′089927405694—dc20   95–13916

British Library Cataloguing in Publication Data is available.

Library of Congress Catalog Card Number: 95–13916
ISBN: 0–275–94856–0

First published in 1995

Praeger Publishers, 88 Post Road West, Westport, CT 06881
An imprint of Greenwood Publishing Group, Inc.

Printed in the United States of America

The paper used in this book complies with the
Permanent Paper Standard issued by the National
Information Standards Organization (Z39.48–1984).

10 9 8 7 6 5 4 3 2 1

Contents

Figures and Tables

TABLES

Preface

Previous studies of industrial activity in Arab settlements in Israel have been less than comprehensive. We believe that the lack of interest and data on Arab industry stems from the fact that no real effort has ever been made to further the economic development of these settlements in general and their industrial development in particular. For their economic base, the majority of Arab settlements continue to rely largely on commuting to Jewish employment centers. Nevertheless, over time, industrial entrepreneurship has emerged in Arab settlements. It is against this background that the importance of our work can be seen, for it presents, for the first time and at first hand, a thorough analysis of entrepreneurship and industrialization in the Arab sector in Israel.

Arab industrial entrepreneurship in Israel is a unique phenomenon. Most previous studies have examined entrepreneurship among the ethnic minorities which, in recent years, have migrated to the metropolitan centers of developed countries. Israeli Arabs constitute an endogenous ethnic minority which is in transition from a traditional culture, based on a domestic economy, to a modern culture, which is becoming integrated into an advanced capitalist system dominated by a Jewish majority. Moreover, they inhabit highly homogeneous and segregated regions in the national periphery. They are therefore forced to overcome three complementary sets of obstacles in their integration into the larger economy and their attempt to industrialize: lack of experience and expertise in advanced forms of production and marketing; ethnic marginality; and socio-spatial peripherality.

We believe the contribution of this book to be fourfold: (1) It is based on a unique case study which may expand the range of case studies available for comparative cross-cultural research; (2) it presents new theoretical formulations regarding issues that remain unresolved in the current literature on ethnic entrepreneurship; (3) it is grounded in intensive field research; and (4) it offers possible guidelines for constructive policy.

It is particularly significant that the Institute of Israeli Arab Studies took it upon itself to promote this study. We are grateful to the heads of this institute, Prof. Shaul Mishal and Dr. Yitzhak Reiter, for giving us a roof under which to conduct our research, and to the Ministry of Science and Technology for providing the funding for it. We would also like to thank Mr. Aas Atrash, who directed the field work carried out by a team of canvassers; Ms. Sara Kitai, who undertook the demanding task of preparing the English edition of the book; and at the Geography Department of Tel Aviv University, Dr. Ya'akov Dorfman, who drew the graphs and maps, and Dr. Itzhak Benenson and Mr. Itzhak Omer, who assisted in analyzing the data. Above all, our thanks go to the hundreds of Arab entrepreneurs who willingly cooperated with us and completed our lengthy and time-consuming questionnaire. We hope this study will provide them with relevant information and aid them in overcoming the day-to-day obstacles they encounter and in promoting their enterprises. It is our hope that this book will help advance Arab industrial entrepreneurship in Israel, enhance the status of Arab industry, and add to the body of knowledge concerning the industrial entrepreneurship of ethnic minorities at large. This will then be our reward.

Dr. Izhak Schnell, Department of Geography
Dr. Michael Sofer, Department of Geography
Dr. Israel Drori, Public Policy Program
Tel Aviv University, December, 1994

Arab
Industrialization
in Israel

PART I

BACKGROUND

Chapter 1

Introduction

BACKGROUND AND AIMS

The economic development of the Arab sector and its full integration into the Israeli economy is a major challenge for both Arabs and Jews. Such development is an important factor in increasing the efficiency of the Israeli economy as a whole, in reducing the gaps between the haves and the have-nots, and in strengthening the social cohesion of Israel in terms of Jewish-Arab coexistence. In this context, the study of economic growth as reflected by industrialization is of particular significance. For one thing, industrialization plays a major role in furthering regional development, and industrial entrepreneurship is a relatively complex matter placing serious challenges in the path of those who seek to undertake it. Consequently, the emergence of industrial entrepreneurship attests to the high level of a society's economic development and the degree of its integration into the national economy.

Beginning in the 1970s, Arab industry was launched into rapid expansion. The number of factories and the capital invested in them grew at an impressive rate, although most of the plants were still small. At the same time, there was an increase in the number of those employed in industry. Nevertheless, this sector has received little attention from researchers. Exceptions include the study by Meyer-Brodnitz and Czamanski (1986a), which presents an early picture of Arab industry in the 1980s. Here it is clearly shown to be laboring both under the restrictions imposed on it by Israeli realities and under the weight of its own traditions. Arab plants at that time were typically small-scale operations that relied on the simplest machinery, guaranteed local markets, and manpower drawn from the adjacent Arab community. A study conducted by the Jaffa Research Center in 1990 (Atrash, 1992) and additional studies by Bar-El (1993) and Haidar (1993) demonstrate a certain development in the structure of Arab industry in the early 1990s and emphasize marginalization forces in Israeli economy and government policies. Nonetheless, there would still seem to be a need for a comprehensive survey examining the features of industrial entrepreneurship and entrepreneurial culture, on the one hand, and the degree and patterns of the integration of Arab industry into the Israeli economy and the marginalization processes affecting Arab industrialization, on the other.

It is our aim in this volume to describe and analyze industrial entrepreneurship and the structure and features of Arab industry in the early 1990s, with reference to the quantitative and qualitative changes that have taken place during the 1980s. As we see it, the growth of industry is impelled by the industrial entrepreneurship that exists in a given structured environment. The Arab entrepreneur operates in a complex environment influenced by the interplay of three structural features. First, he operates on the margins of the national economy, where the role of large corporations enjoying substantial government aid and protection is extremely significant. Second, he belongs to an ethnic minority which is discriminated against by a socio-economic policy that does not provide an institutional framework for the encouragement of economic growth in the Arab sector. Third, he operates within a society undergoing changes that might be defined as the transition from a traditional society characterized by nonmodern economic activity to integration into a modern society based on a competitive market economy.

Each of these three components was largely affected by historical events and changes within the Israeli economy. In this context, restrictions imposed on the Arab work force as a result of the war of independence in 1948 prevented Arabs from seeking work in Jewish towns. Lifting the restrictions affected their employment patterns and income levels. Similarly, government policy which encouraged industrialization of the new development towns by erecting industrial zones did not assist industrial development in Arab settlements. In addition, restructuring of the Israeli economy, from being spurred by means of intense government involvement in all aspects of economic activity toward corporate capitalism controlling major shares of the national market and dictating the direction of industrial development, has influenced the development pattern of Arab industry. Consequently, the historical background and the changing political-economic environment conditioned the industrial initiatives in Arab settlements and their form and pattern of industrialization.

This study focuses on the structural aspects which mold the development of Arab regions in the Israeli socio-economic space. Industrial entrepreneurship draws its economic, technological, social, and political resources both from the entrepreneurial environment in which it operates and from the socio-economic structure of the Israeli economy as a whole. In turn, the entrepreneurs, as major agents operating within the economic system, themselves contribute to the restructuring of the Israeli economy.

Under present circumstances, Arab entrepreneur have become primary agents of economic advancement and growth. To a certain degree, they might be compared to the Roman god Janus, with his two faces—one looking to the East and the other to the West. Janus was afforded the high status of guardian of the gates. As a major force in Roman mythology, he was considered the God of good beginnings of all types, from the rising of spring waters, through the start of the new year, to the beginning of the universe itself. When Janus arrived from Thessaly, he released the Romans from their ignorance by bringing them security and progress. In a similar fashion, Arab entrepreneurs are asked to release the Arab economy both from the inferiority and discrimination it suffers within the Israeli economy and from the shackles of traditional Arab society. They are forced to make their way between these two worlds, identifying opportunities and obstacles, to pave a path for themselves, as well as for the Arab sector toward development, growth, and integration into the larger Israeli economy.

At present, on the eve of peace with the Arab countries and the establishment of Palestinian autonomy in the territories which have been occupied by Israel since 1967, the Arab entrepreneur will be asked to cope with new realities. The anticipated investments in the economic development of the autonomous Palestinian regions, along with open borders with the Israeli economy, are apt to create unfair competition for the Arab entrepreneur. On the other hand, access of the Israeli economy to markets in the Arab world may open new windows of opportunity for Arab entrepreneurs in Israel. An understanding of the potential for entrepreneurship and growth in Arab industry is now that much more important as an aid in preparing to meet these new challenges.

ENTREPRENEURSHIP

Our assumption of a key role for entrepreneurship in industrialization and regional development has been demonstrated in numerous studies. It is frequently argued that the extent and forms of entrepreneurship follow certain regular principles in time and space, subject to the particular structural conditions under which entrepreneurs operate in given regions (Armington & Odle, 1982). In addition, it has been claimed that entrepreneurship in general and industrial entrepreneurship in particular are major factors in regional development (Czamanski & Taylor, 1986). There are several common definitions of entrepreneurship. In the broadest sense, it is defined as the use of different sets of resources to produce outputs for which there is a demand and which are of commercial economic value (Bird, 1989). Thus, the opening of a new manufacturing plant would be considered an entrepreneurial action. This definition, however, does not distinguish between enterprises which merely increase the volume of industrial activity in the economy and those which contribute to qualitative changes that improve the economy's ability to compete. The more detailed definitions, which attempt to allow for this distinction, can be divided into three groups (Halbert & Link, 1982).

The first group of definitions underlines the entrepreneur's commitments to establish the plant and manage it throughout the cycle of commercial activity (Bird, 1989; Cole, 1959; Meir, 1970). Entrepreneurs are seen as the initiators and founders of organizations that mobilize others and channel social and financial efforts toward the furthering of economic aims. They are therefore the catalysts of socio-economic change and regional development. The primary conclusion to be drawn from this sort of definition is that entrepreneurship, like labor, raw materials and capital, is perceived as an economic resource to be exploited to the fullest in order to expose and actualize a new set of opportunities for financial investment (Brockhanse, 1982; Harrison & Myers, 1959).

The second group of definitions emphasizes the element of risk taking under conditions of uncertainty (Aldrich & Auster, 1986). Entrepreneurs must be willing to risk their savings, job, security, health, and social and family relations for the sake of their commitment to establish an industrial enterprise (Burch, 1986). The degree of willingness to take these risks is affected by the size of the investment required, the amount of anticipated profit, the degree of the entrepreneur's determination and personal commitment, and his ability to salvage investments in the case of failure and to channel his capital in alternative directions (Kenneth & van Voorish, 1980; Webber, 1984). Therefore, industrial entrepreneurship is encouraged by the existence of effective risk-reducing institutions and deterred by their absence (Grossman, 1984). Other researchers attribute less importance to risk taking in defining entrepreneurship, claiming that most developed economies are replete with risk-reducing mechanisms, such as insurance companies, credit, bank guarantees, and government aid (Chamley, 1983).

The third group of definitions stresses the introduction of new and innovative elements into industry in the entrepreneurial environment. These elements can refer to any economic action that breaks with accepted practice in any aspect of business activity (Druker, 1985; Mathot, 1982; Schumpeter, 1934): the introduction of technology into the production process; new products; entrance into new markets; the use of new resources; the adoption of new management techniques; or the organization of business activity in a new fashion. Any or all of these might be considered instances of the introduction of new elements into industry and thus be defined as entrepreneurship (Burch, 1986). The adoption and application of new methods best explains how entrepreneurship can contribute to structural changes in the economy and to a significant increase in the volume of industrial production (Meyer-Brodnitz & Czamanski, 1986b; Vesper, 1980). Indeed, the element of risk taking discussed earlier derives to a large extent from the introduction of new and unconventional approaches into economic processes. Any such endeavor to alter existing economic structures inherently entails a considerable investment of energy and high risk (Aldrich & Waldinger, 1990; Deek, 1976).

For the present analysis, we chose a definition that combines elements borrowed from all three groups. First, the foundation of a new industrial plant is defined as an entrepreneurial action involving risk taking. Second, any incident in which a new pattern of economic activity altering accepted practices of industrial activity in the environment in which the entrepreneur operates is also defined as entrepreneurship (Aldrich & Waldinger, 1990; Shapiro & Stokols, 1982). It thus follows that it is possible to identify a scale of entrepreneurship. At the top are factories adopting significantly new methods in terms of the patterns of industrial activity; at the bottom are plants following the relatively simple traditional patterns of production that evolved in the Arab economy. In view of the lack of risk-reducing mechanisms, which is typical of economies undergoing the transition from the traditional to the modern, the risk accompanying entrepreneurship is seen as a deterrent to potential entrepreneurs. Hence, our interest in the risk entailed in entrepreneurship is primarily part of our examination of the impeding mechanisms.

METHODOLOGY

The information presented herein is based on an intensive field study conducted largely in 1992. Data were collected from three primary sources. The first source was open-ended interviews with 70 Arab industrial entrepreneurs who had founded plants in Arab settlements. They represent different generations, a range of industrial branches, factories of varying sizes, and a broad cross-section of settlements. In these interviews, we sought to examine the motives behind the nature of activity undertaken by these people and their views regarding the future of their enterprise and the direction of its development within the Israeli economy. In addition, we attempted to identify the difficulties encountered by the entrepreneurs over the years and the reasons underlying the way in which they perceived these obstacles.

Our second source was a questionnaire addressed to the heads or secretaries of local Arab councils within whose jurisdiction the industrial survey of 1990 (Jaffa Research Center, 1991) had found industrial plants. The questionnaire, mailed to all 60 settlements in which at least one industrial plant was established, was completed by only 27 local councils, including most of the larger and medium-sized settlements (over 10,000 residents) as well as a number of smaller ones. The questionnaire emphasized issues of town planning, infrastructure, and municipal services provided to the local factories. Questions were related to the year in which the settlement was connected to physical infrastructure systems—electricity, water, roads, telephones, etc.—as well as to the provision for industrial zones in town plans, the level of taxation, the policies of the local council for encouraging industrialization, and the difficulties confronting industrialization as perceived by the heads of the local authority.

The bulk of the quantitative data concerning the nature of Arab industry were drawn from the responses to a factory questionnaire addressed to the owners and managers of 514 industrial plants in Arab settlements. These factories are located in 35 settlements in Upper and Lower Galilee, the Carmel, and what is known as the Little Triangle (an area of Arab villages between the coastal plain and the West Bank) and represent 57 percent of all Arab plants in Arab settlements and mixed cities within Israel. The survey included about 80 percent of factories in all settlements with a population over 10,000 at the time of the survey, along with a random sample of smaller settlements. A factory was defined as a production unit with at least three workers that yields products or other outputs. The comprehensive questionnaire included items relating to the location of the plant; features of the land and infrastructure; the nature of organization and management; sources of manpower, capital, and technology; and relations with suppliers and purchasing agents in the market. Other items concerned the attitudes of factory owners regarding obstacles to plant development in the present and future.

The questionnaire was administered to the plant owners and managers during July-August 1992 by five Arab research assistants after a pilot survey of 20 questionnaires, conducted by the authors, had been tested and found appropriate, with minor modifications. The reliability of the large sample was determined by comparing it with the results of the survey of Arab plants conducted by the Jaffa Research Center in 1990. For the purposes of this comparison, new plants established between 1990 and 1992 were eliminated from the analysis. Comparison of the distribution of the variables of size and economic branch revealed significant similarity between the two studies. The one exception that stands out in the present study is the subsample of textile and clothing plants. Our sample included some 38 percent of all textile and clothing factories in the Arab sector, rather than the 57 percent dictated by the size of the sample as a whole. In the Jaffa Research Center study, the textile and clothing industry represented 27 percent of all plants, while in the present study it constitutes only 14 percent. Accordingly, data were adjusted wherever it was felt that the low representation of textile and clothing factories might affect the results.

The sample was devised to make it also possible to draw valid conclusions from a comparison of the different geographical regions of industrial activity in the Arab sector with the exception of several marginal regions, such as the Bedouin settlements in the Negev; Arab settlements in the Jezreel Valley, Ramat Cochav, and the coastal plain; and mixed cities. Although some regions were slightly underrepresented in relation to others, analyses for which geographical aspects were relevant were adjusted for these differences. One weakness remained in the geographical representation of the sample. Only 20 percent of the plants in Upper Galilee were surveyed, so even after adjustment, the reliability of the sample in this region, with its small number of factories, may be questioned.

The data were processed by means of a combination of qualitative and quantitative methods. The qualitative methods were of two types. First and foremost was an anthropological study based on participant observation, open-ended interviews with entrepreneurs and senior employees of the plants, and participation in consulting for Arab factories. Using these techniques, we uncovered the central features of the entrepreneurial culture that has evolved in Arab society. Second, the Q test (Atkin, 1974, 1981) was used to analyze the structures of the entrepreneurial infrastructures which are a prerequisite for plant expansion and the adoption of more advanced work methods. Q analysis is a language designed to define complex structural questions in an explicit, accurate, and operational way without any pregiven assumptions.   It is based on a topological algebra in which interrelations among elements in rigorously defined sets are presented.   The analyzed concepts are systematically defined while their internal structures are investigated.   The degree of fragmentation in the structure of infrastructural elements and the degree of obstruction to changes in degree of entrepreneurship at various dimensions are analyzed (Gaspar & Gould, 1981).   The quantitative methods employed accepted statistical procedures and mathematical models explaining the behavior of phenomena in space.

The book is divided into four parts.   The first two chapters lay down the theoretical basis.   The second part describes the nature of the Israeli Arab population and examines the development, branch structure, and spatial dispersion of Arab industry.   The third part analyzes the nature of industrial entrepreneurship and discusses the patterns of exploitation of production factors: manpower, capital, technology, management, and land.   The fourth part portrays the entrepreneurial culture of the Arab society and discusses the Israeli economic milieu in which the Arab economy is molded and the underlying mechanisms affecting the current development of Arab industry.   In this part, we focus on the Israeli economy, which affords advantages to large concerns supported by elite political and economic groups in Israeli society while discriminating against Arab entrepreneurs.   The book concludes by suggesting a comprehensive framework within which it is possible to assess the obstacles and opportunities confronting industrialization of the Arab economy, as an example for an ethnic-peripheral minority.   Both the obstacles and the opportunities are influenced above all by the structure of the two entrepreneurial environments in which Arab entrepreneurs operate: the national Israeli and the sectorial Arab.

Chapter 2

Theory and Concepts

THE STUDY OF ISRAELI ARABS

Studies of the status of the Arab economy within the Israeli state have followed paradigms of three major sorts: cultural, pluralistic, and class conflict (Lewin-Epstein & Semyonov, 1993). Theoretically, ethnicity as the source of divergent cultures is considered disruptive to social integration. In this context, Ben-Rafael (1982) describes Jewish-Arab relations in Israel in terms of cultural dominance and subordination. Rather than promoting assimilation, interethnic encounters reinforce the boundaries of mutual exclusivity. According to Smoocha (1989), the fact that Jewish-Arab conflicts are not only ethnic but also religious and national in nature intensifies the magnitude of the conflict. Moreover, the refusal of many Jews to legitimize Israeli Arabs' national identity strengthens the salience of their Palestinian identity. Consequently, antagonism between the two communities is heightened (Schnell, 1994b; Shamas, 1987). Ethnicity is also expressed spatially, with the Arabs in Israel segregated in separate regions, mostly in the national periphery, but also in Arab neighborhoods in mixed cities (Kipnis & Schnell, 1978; Soffer, 1983). Spatial segregation and social-ethnic antagonism may reinforce each other, creating areas of economic and social activities of mutual exclusivity.

A basic premise of the pluralistic approach is the argument that sources of conflict are exogenous to relations between ethnic communities. Rather than stemming from the differences between the groups, conflict originates in competition over scarce resources (Lewin-Epstein & Semyonov, 1993). Pluralism also emphasizes the predominance of the polity as the arena in which ethnic groups struggle for control (Smoocha, 1978, 1984). According to Lustick (1980, pp. 25-26), the concept of control, particularly political control, is essential for understanding the relations between the Jewish majority and the Arab minority. The economic and political control of the Jewish majority, through which resources are extracted and independent organization is limited, operates on the basis of three principles: segmentation, dependence, and co-optation. Segmentation refers to the exclusion of Arabs from the political and economic core of the Israeli state; dependence refers to the enforced reliance of Arabs on Jewish resources and decision making; and co-optation refers to the use of payments on the side to the perceived Arab elite for purposes of surveillance and resource extraction.

Class conflict is the most frequent paradigm employed in the analysis of Jewish-Arab relations in Israel and derives from the Marxist and dependency paradigms. Indeed, few scholars advance the importance of politics in perpetuating class disparities. According to Rosenfeld (1964, 1978), the central factors responsible for the class situation of Arabs in Israel are the Zionist ideology of the Jewish nation and state control of the economy. Arab dependency is reflected in the manipulation of the Arab labor force into Jewish-owned firms and seasonal labor markets, while restrictions imposed by the state inhibit development of Arab enterprises. The idea of internal colonialism, in which allocation of resources is selective and in line with the interests of the Jewish majority as a colonial regime, was advanced by Zureik (1979). He offers the historical exposition of a capitalist economy imposed on a traditional agrarian system. The primary mechanisms at work in this process are the proletarization of the peasant labor force, ecological separation (which permits clear identification of core and periphery), and superordinate-subordinate relations. In other words, the expansion and development of the Jewish economy has required cheap labor, which is provided by the Arab sector.

Gottheil (1972) analyzed the economy of the Arab settlements along similar lines, emphasizing the transformation from an economy based largely on subsistence agriculture into a consumer society integrated into the national economy primarily through the exportation of wage labor, a pattern demonstrated earlier by Zarhi and Achiezra (1966). While some may regard this integration as a form of exploitation (Gottheil, 1972), others may view it as a stage in the process of economic development (Arnon & Raviv, 1980). As a result of increasing contact with the Jewish sector, the traditional, less developed Arab society has undergone rapid changes, which may be seen either as modernization and urbanization (Bar-Gal & Soffer, 1976) or as peripheralization and latent urbanization (Meyer-Brodnitz, 1969; Schnell, 1990, 1994b).

An analytical framework suggested by Khalidi (1988) is based on four aspects of economic status which serve to peripheralize Arabs in Israel: (1) selective state policies and popular attitudes; (2) Arab concentration in areas remote from the center; (3) unique cultural and social structure; and (4) differentiation along ethnic lines in the economic, political, and social spheres. Khalidi proposed analyzing the Arab space as a region operating in the larger context of the state and examining the effect of state policy on the Arab population.

Implicit in all three paradigms is the pervasive division of Israeli society into Jewish and Arab sectors in a wide array of aspects: ethnic, political, economic, cultural, and spatial. Three aspects appear crucial for understanding Jewish-Arab relations. First is the political economy in which Arabs are peripheralized economically and spatially. Second is the ethnicity which divides the two groups into mutually exclusive communities, in cultural and spatial terms. Third is the historical process that, since the 1950s, has forced Arab peasant society to integrate into the Jewish-dominated capitalist economy, state managed in the early years and more recently corporate managed. Here, proponents of the political-economic and the cultural approaches may disagree. The cultural approach would hold that modernization processes which rely on the adoption of new technology may encourage social assimilation and close socio-economic gaps (Eisenstadt, 1981). Yet even Ben-Rafael (1982) admits that certain control mechanisms, which are analyzed further by the political-economic approach, continue to preserve ethnic and economic disparities in Israel even where modernization has taken place.

PERIPHERALIZATION AND INDUSTRIAL CHANGE

Peripheral areas are known to share several industrial features (Nanjundan, 1987; Segre, 1986): the dispersed existence of small and medium-sized firms; a substantial specialization in branches considered to be backward; high rates of business turnover (the opening and closing of plants); and high labor mobility. The prospect for real industrial progress in peripheral areas has been questioned in a number of case studies (Hamilton, 1986). Experience has shown that confused government policy, state attitudes, regional problems of social structure, and bad local management lessen the positive impact that externally controlled enterprises might have, for all their failings and negative ramifications. The central idea is that the survival, and even growth, of industry in peripheral areas results from their comparative advantages in low-technology and high-labor-intensive branches. Continued industrialization exploiting these advantages leads to concentration in old (declining) industries, many of which have been forced out of core areas.

In general, spatial peripheralization is a matter of the distribution of the dynamic sectors of the economy and the result of their impact on activities within the nondynamic sectors outside the (industrial) core areas. Thus, when considering industrial development, it is important to analyze the impact of peripheralization both on the location of industries and on other sectors in the national economy. Differential location patterns emerge, whereby the more advanced and dynamic branches, characterized by a high level of research and development and relatively high returns on investments, are concentrated in and around core metropolitan areas, where they enjoy the economies of scale typical of capital-intensive technologies as well as agglomeration advantages. The possibility of regional dispersal for these branches is limited to isolated localities. Moreover, local labor-intensive industries may be negatively affected by the particular pattern of industrialization (Rauch, 1988). Indigenous manufacturing sectors become marginalized, or even eliminated, due to the competitive advantage of modern technology and government bias in its favor. In addition, the dynamic sectors are strongly orientated toward external supply—from metropolitan areas or from abroad—so that linkages with local industries are limited. Peripheralization, however, is not only a spatial phenomenon. In terms of industrial development, it may appear in other forms as well, such as the consequences of relations between large and small enterprises, between workers and management within any particular firm (Linge, 1988), or even between people associated with new types of jobs and occupations and those still working at traditional ones (Obregon, 1974; Sunkel, 1973).

It is generally agreed that as part of capitalist development, the survival of industrial production requires a constant search for ways to reduce production costs. Labor costs naturally come under scrutiny, and the desire to find cheaper labor may shift some stages of production into peripheral areas, seen merely as additional sources of labor. The expansion of industrial production into new labor reserves in the periphery, which in many cases also means new locations, serves to lower the cost of labor, to assist in maintaining acceptable profit rates, and to change the social space by creating social hierarchies linked to the stages of production. The idea that spatial change is the outcome of production change was strongly advanced in the 1970s (Massey & Meegan, 1978, 1979). It was later expanded so as not to ignore the crucial impact of spatially organized locational opportunities and the role of distance and spatial separation (Massey, 1985). The affinity between the changing spatial organization of production and that of occupation, reflected in the spatial differentiation of occupational structures within firms, is also significant to the peripheralization process. In some instances, it accompanies the separation of the different stages of production; in others it is organized around the "product-cycle" hierarchies of plants; and in still others it is simply a case of large numbers of plants each producing the same commodity (Massey, 1984). The plants relocated in the periphery are engaged in routine standardized production, require cheap labor, and produce large volumes. The result is a correlation between the social and spatial hierarchies, along the scale from the strategic to the routine. This correlation is paralleled by the level of management and skill of labor.

The capitalist theory of regional location holds that private enterprise will adopt a cost-minimization strategy in choosing the location for new ventures. After gathering information about the structure of costs and benefits, entrepreneurs may decide to locate in areas of high labor availability and low labor costs, if the savings at least offset the additional transport costs to main markets. Inversely, this theory maintains that labor mobility between regions, either by migration or commuting, is a response to differences in employment prospects and income levels (Sjaastad, 1962). Seen from the viewpoint of neoclassical economics, labor mobility plays a role in narrowing spatial differences in income, thus serving as an equilibration mechanism. The outward mobility of labor from regions of high unemployment and low income is complemented by a reverse flow of capital into the regions of labor sources. In reality, the regional imbalance continues due to the fact that unequal development is inherent in capitalist economic growth. Thus, from a structural perspective, labor mobility is regarded as a mechanism by which capital controls labor within a capitalist state, and hence labor is intrinsically tied to capitalist expansion. Consequently, the labor reserves of the less developed regions become the lever for new capital accumulation over the long term in the more developed regions (Holland, 1976). In this context, the commuting of Arab labor in Israel as a mechanism for industrial growth within the Jewish sector in Israel has been discussed by Yiftachel (1991).

Different types of peripheries tend to respond in different ways to the current global processes (Massey, 1984), as has been demonstrated by a number of studies (van Geenhuizen & Nijkamp, 1993). Distinct in the Israeli context is the disparity between the Jewish periphery and the Arab periphery. Development towns, which represent Jewish periphery and which receive government support in the form of subsidies and investment in infrastructure, have benefited from the establishment of factories, mainly those engaged in the routine production stages. This is not the case in the Arab periphery, where there is a high concentration of cheap labor, an appropriate infrastructure does not usually exist, and government subsidies are not generally available. Arab labor commutes to Jewish centers of industrial production. Recently, the only industrial change in this sector has been the expansion of the textile and clothing industry, which has brought merely limited benefits to the periphery.

ETHNICITY AND INDUSTRIALIZATION

An argument frequently raised by dependency theoreticians since the time of Myrdal's seminal argument (1944) is that discrimination by a dominant majority prevents minorities from realizing socio-economic mobility. Myrdal maintained that the lack of such mobility reinforced prejudices against the dependent minority, which in turn created a vicious circle by which socio-economic mobility was further reduced. Lieberson (1980) rejects this deterministic approach, which claims that disparities are perpetuated, and argues that interethnic competition increases interethnic hostility and the salience of cultural differences. In what is regarded as a dynamic model of interethnic relations, ethnic minorities may find certain niches and room for maneuver in the majority-dominated economy which allow ethnic entrepreneurship to thrive and socio-economic mobility to occur. Jiobu (1988), for example, showed how Japanese immigrants in the United States succeeded in overcoming strong economic and social discrimination.

Subordinate ethnic groups may respond to their situation by using ethnic resources for their own benefit. In this context, the most frequently mentioned theoretical formulation is the ethnic enclave theory. Most research on ethnic enclaves has proceeded on the premise that enclave labor markets shelter minority members from economic discrimination. Within the ethnic enclave, minority members may enjoy economic opportunities that are usually monopolized by members of the dominant community (Semyonov, 1988; Waldinger, 1986). In ethnically segregated areas, internal markets are relatively free from interethnic competition, and this may therefore promote the tendency to use enclave strategies in the economic sphere, particularly through the creation of white-collar jobs and small enterprises (Light & Bonachich, 1988). The Israeli example confirms these findings, as shown in several studies of the Arab labor market in Israel (Lewin-Epstein & Semyonov, 1986, 1993, 1994; Shavit, 1992). Most particularly, these investigations have demonstrated the advantages of an intraethnic labor market in regard to white-collar jobs.

Several studies have proposed that the ethnic enclave strategy may benefit both workers and employers. Workers have unique opportunities to acquire skills on the job through ethnic networks (Light, 1972; Wilson & Portes, 1980). Such networks reduce the risk involved in skill acquisition not only for employees, but also for entrepreneurs in their capacity as employers (Baily & Waldinger, 1991). Furthermore, Portes and Bach (1985) suggest that ethnic solidarity in skill training is a major route to self-employment and entrepreneurship. Most recent research, however, indicates that the advantages of the enclave are not that clear. In many cases, the returns on work experience in the enclave and outside do not differ significantly (Portes & Jensen, 1989; Sanders & Nee, 1987), though business owners, unlike workers, do seem to gain higher benefits from operating within the ethnic enclave (Sanders & Nee, 1987).

In recent years, there has been an increasing number of appeals to reconcile the authority dependency and ethnic enclave theories and apply them in a more flexible manner. Dependent ethnic groups might identify and exploit appropriate niches in the national economy to develop ethnic hegemony in specific economic sectors (Jiobu, 1988) or to integrate themselves better into the national economy. While using ethnic resources to minimize entrepreneurial risks, they might also take advantage of windows of opportunity in the economic sectors dominated by the majority. Accordingly, ethnic entrepreneurs may be perceived as key factors in the development and advancement of the ethnic minority. They are required to use flexible and sophisticated strategies to exploit limited opportunities, either those that are relatively safe but limited in scope in the ethnic enclave or the riskier and less assured windows of opportunity in the larger economy.

STAGES OF INDUSTRIAL INTEGRATION

Both theory and empirical studies have indicated that in the course of economic integration, manufacturing enterprises go through three broad yet distinct phases in terms of structure, pattern, and size (Nanjundan, 1987). The first phase is dominated by household and shop enterprises. The predominantly rural and agricultural character of the economy supports non farm enterprises in rural and semi urban economic environments. Production in a cottage industry is labor intensive and encouraged by fragmented markets, insufficient infrastructure, and a low level of technology. In the second phase, household manufacturing is replaced by small workshops and factories located in urban centers and employing modern technology and equipment. The markets of these businesses are wider, and their integration into the economic environment is greater. The third phase is marked by the growth of infrastructure, technology, and urbanization. Large-scale production tends to dominate and replace not only most household and cottage manufacturing but a significant proportion of small-scale enterprises as well.

Roberts (1978) adds the dimension of marketing to the model of industrial development. He argues that in the early stages of integration, industrial plants tend to interact more intensively with the traditional sector, while in later stages they gradually penetrate the large-scale economy. In the early stages, plants generally adopt informal methods of management, production, and marketing, while in later stages, they are gradually required to incorporate more formal methods.

Although most Arab enterprises employ relatively low technology, the basic stages of the Vernon (1966) model may be applicable to the current discussion. According to Vernon, enterprises develop in four stages: the prelaunch stage, in which the idea is formulated; the start-up stage, in which the challenges of raising capital, enlisting labor, and finding premises must be met; the sustainable stage, in which production and marketing are consolidated by improving control methods; and, finally, the expansion stage, in which the plant is fully integrated into the national economy. The Vernon model makes explicit the challenges that entrepreneurs must face in each of the stages of integration suggested by Nanjundan's (1987) model. Its weakness lies in its deterministic approach. In particular, because of the constrained circumstances of Arab industry, the road to integration in the national economy may not be quite as smooth as is implied in the model.

In the Arab sector in Israel, as in other developed and developing economies, enterprises of different size and production characteristics coexist. Thus, the phases of growth tend to overlap, with household production operating side by side with larger scale enterprises. In terms of Nanjundan's (1987) model, in its current stage of development the Arab industry seems to be undergoing transition from the first to the second phase. Household production and informal subcontracting activities exist simultaneously with an increasing number of workshops and factories and even a very small number of recently developed large-scale enterprises. All these plants are integrated into the market economy in a more or less formal manner. In light of these factors, a nondeterministic approach is adopted here to depict the structure and development of industrial entrepreneurship among Israeli Arabs without any pregiven assumptions.

ENTREPRENEURSHIP UNDER DEPENDENCY

Israeli Arab entrepreneurs have to overcome the difficulties that stem from their peripheral, ethnic, and traditional circumstances. In the Israeli economic milieu, they are forced to cope with forces of three major types—political-economic, ethnic, and intrasectoral—representing barriers which together marginalize them into ethnically segregated enclaves in the national periphery. Development within these enclaves was dominated by a state-managed economy during the 1950s and 1960s and by what has increasingly become a corporate-dominated economy since the 1970s.

Peripheriality may affect the set of industrial development opportunities in several ways. Geographical distance from the cores of economic activity in terms of markets, financing, management, and so on diminishes the location advantages of industrial plants in the periphery. Furthermore, the fact that communities in the periphery are characterized by lower consumer power and backward communications infrastructure has an impact on local demand for goods and services, on the availability of productive capital, and on manpower resources. Distance from the core primarily inhibits the ability of entrepreneurs to evaluate appropriately the potential of economic opportunities. Local factories are typically small and make limited use of capital and technology. Such enterprises have difficulty in applying to government subsidy programs due to the high cost of dealing with a large and established bureaucracy (Bergmann, 1971). Capital markets are likely to be less responsive to small peripheral factories as well (Hornbeck, 1989). In Israel, banks operate on a national scale and tend not to be flexible in responding to the capital needs of small firms and to the high risks involved in such loans (Tamari, 1991). Consequently, there is only limited interaction between the large-scale economic activities that, although operating in the periphery, are linked to the core and small-scale firms operating in regional markets within the periphery (Felsenstein & Schwartz, 1993).

Moreover, the existence of ethnic subeconomies in the periphery works against the location advantages of the ethnic minority even further. Ethnic boundaries which discourage collective experiences and routines may increase entrepreneurial uncertainty and risk, thus undermining the development of the ethnic group's economy (Camagni, 1991; van Geenhuizen & Nijkamp, 1993; Ratti, 1992). In the context of peripheral and ethnic deprivation, discriminative governmental policies may be even more harmful to the development of peripheral ethnic regions. In the absence of risk-reducing institutions, potential entrepreneurs may avoid risk, limiting their decisions to mimicking strategies (Czamanski & Taylor, 1986).

Israeli Arabs began their transition and integration into the national economy at the end of the 1950s, when the Jewish economy was in an advanced stage of organization under a state-managed capitalist system. In the Arab sector, capital accumulation processes, accumulated experience in the labor market, and the construction of basic infrastructures took place during the 1970s, when the Jewish economy was shifting toward a corporate capital economy. This form of development forced small Arab entrepreneurs to compete with national monopolies for national markets. During the first phase—in the 1950s and 1960s—Arab industrialists responded to these constraints mainly by emphasizing consumption (Schnell, 1994b). During the next phase—in the 1970s and 1980s—Arab industry in Israel seems to have developed according to its own internal dynamic, despite the constraints imposed on it (Atrash, 1992; Meyer-Brodnitz & Czamanski, 1986b).

These new beginnings of industrialization raise the question of whether Israeli Arab entrepreneurs have succeeded in finding suitable economic niches in the larger Israeli economy or whether they have remained within the limited markets of the ethnic enclave. Have they found ways to overcome their initial constraints, and is it possible to identify a new set of constraints now imposed on them? To what extent does the ethnic cultural milieu encourage or inhibit industrial entrepreneurship given these particular constraining circumstances? The following chapters will attempt to answer these questions.

PART II

ARAB INDUSTRY

Chapter 3

The Israeli Arabs

This chapter presents the broader contexts within which the patterns of Arab industrial entrepreneurship and industrial development in Israel must be viewed. They include the major features of Arab society and economy and the historical events which led to the peripheralization of the Israeli Arabs in terms of society, political economy, and the Israeli space. These circumstances represent major factors in defining the range of opportunities for industrial entrepreneurship and development.

HISTORICAL PERSPECTIVE

As the first Zionist settlements appeared in Palestine in the late nineteenth century, the Arab economy, just starting out on a slow path to modernization, found itself confronting a Jewish community which brought with it to the region modern Western patterns of activity steeped in Zionist and Socialist ideology. The first encounters between Arabs and Jews centered primarily around the sale of land. The Arabs preferred to sell the Jews plots in the valleys and coastal plain, land they considered marginal after the failed attempts by local landlords (*effendis*) to cultivate it by means of tenant farmers (Kanu, 1983). These sales affected Arab society in two ways. First, against Arab tradition, the Jews evicted the tenant farmers from their newly purchased land. The farmers were thus forced to seek work as wage laborers. Second, the sales injected a large amount of capital into the Arab economy, thereby spurring development and growth along with urbanization and industrialization, primarily in the coastal towns of Acre, Haifa, Jaffa, and Gaza. In 1918, Palestine was largely an agricultural country with a population of some 750,000, 89 percent of which was Arab. Over two thirds of the work force were farmers. The new spate of development, as well as measures taken by the British Mandatory Government since 1922, led to a dramatic change in the structure of the Arab economy. The population of Palestine increased to 1.5 million in 1939, some two thirds of which was Arab. The proportion of farmers in the Arab population fell to 53 percent, while the proportion employed in services and commerce rose to 35 percent and those working in industry rose to 12 percent.

Despite these changes, the gaps between the two economies grew consistently wider, from a ratio of 1:7 in per capita production in 1922 to 2.6 in 1939 and 6:5 in 1943 (Kimmerling, 1983). The Jewish economy remained primarily urban, with a higher tendency to engage in industry, and refrained from hiring Arab workers for ideological reasons. Arabs accounted for only some 15 percent of the work force in the Jewish sector, representing 2.5 percent of the total Arab work force in Palestine (Kimmerling, 1983). These workers were to be found mainly in agriculture and to a certain extent in the ports and transportation. The rift between the sectors widened with each new wave of violence, culminating in the War of Independence in 1948, when the defeat of the Arabs spelled disaster for their economy.

The events which turned some 700,000 Palestinians into refugees have been discussed elsewhere and are not our province here (Morris, 1987). The fact is that following the armistice agreements of 1948, around 165,000 Arabs remained within the territory of the State of Israel, concentrated in three regions: the Galilee hills, the Little Triangle, and the Negev (Figure 3.1). The social, economic, and cultural elite abandoned the country en masse, leaving behind traditional farming villages located in several peripheral regions of the country. Nearly all of the Arab population remaining in the country lived in settlements that lacked even a minimal modern infrastructure, with the exception of Nazareth and Shefar'am, which had been incorporated as cities during the British Mandate. Almost the entire population lacked basic formal education. Such conditions alone would have made it difficult for the Arab economy to develop, but Israeli government policy, at least until the late 1960s, placed even more obstacles in its path.

The government of Israel, fearing the loss of Jewish control over the territory of the young state, adopted a series of measures designed, on the one hand, to integrate the Israeli Arabs into the Israeli society and economy while, on the other hand, relegating them to a marginal position. The most prominent of these measures were the imposition of security regulations, the appropriation of property, and a discriminatory development policy.

As soon as the fighting ceased, Israeli Arabs were placed under martial law, which confined them to their villages and thus isolated them both from Israeli society and from the rest of the Arab world. Until 1954, Israeli Arabs were under total closure, prevented from contact even with other villages in the country. This was accompanied by massive appropriations of lands belonging to refugees now in Arab countries or in other settlements in Israel, as well as those of Arab residents prohibited from working their land by order of the military authorities. All in all, some 60 to 70 percent of the lands owned by Arabs before 1947 were appropriated, including around 1.2 million dunams owned by Arabs still in the

Figure 3.1
Location Map of Israeli Arab Settlements

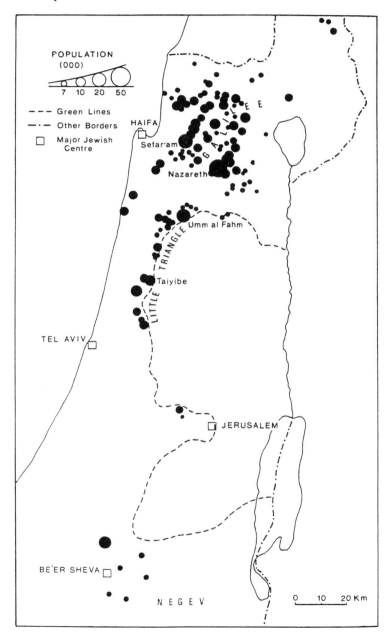

country (Cohen, 1964; Rekhess, 1977). This loss of land became the most painful wound afflicting relations between Arabs and Jews in Israel. Indirectly, however, from the mid-1950s, these appropriations encouraged the Israeli Arabs to abandon agriculture and adopt an alternative economic base.

When it became clear to the government that the traditional economy was unable to support the Arab population, the military authorities began to issue work permits enabling residents to work as wage laborers in the Jewish sector. As a result, over one half of the Arab work force shifted from peasantry to urban proletariat (Rosenfeld, 1978). In the 1950s and 1960s, these Arabs worked as migrant workers with no permanent status or social benefits, employed primarily in the branches of construction, agriculture, and services (Schnell, 1986). To this day, most Arab workers continue to commute daily to their jobs, although there has been a certain change in their status. The most striking change occurred in the late 1960s, with the transition to jobs affording permanent status and social benefits, while the market for migrant workers was taken over by Arab laborers from the West Bank and Gaza Strip. Nevertheless, the majority of Arab workers, particularly those employed in the Jewish sector, have remained in blue-collar jobs. As for white- collar workers, 70 to 80 percent are compelled to find employment in the small Arab labor market, since the range of opportunities offered them in the Jewish sector is extremely limited (Lewin-Epstein & Semyonov, 1994; Schnell, 1986).

LABOR FORCE CHARACTERISTICS

The Arab work force can be divided into three groups. The most privileged are employed in the Arab settlements themselves. Here the workers enjoy the relative advantages stemming from ethnic solidarity and from the fact that the market operates according to Arab norms. This realm offers the greatest number of opportunities for white-collar jobs, whether as employees of the local authority and school system or as academic or self-employed professionals. The second group is employed in the Jewish labor market, which means they must commute for long distances to work under conditions inferior to those of their Jewish counterparts. The third group is employed in the markets in which Arab workers suffer most from severe competition—in mixed cities (Lewin-Epstein & Semyonov, 1993). Yet the lack of development in Arab settlements along with limited employment opportunities compel most Arab workers to enter the mixed labor market of these latter two groups. In addition, the offer of privileged positions to the more highly educated has become a co-optation instrument for mobilizing the support of the new Arab elite (Lustick, 1980).

Further changes in the economic activity of Israeli Arabs occurred in the degree of their involvement in the different branches and occupations in the market. As shown in Table 3.1, with respect to Arab employment, the branches of the economy can be divided into three groups. The first consists of the branches of transportation and storage, commerce and sales, industry, and personal services, where Arab workers have achieved a weight in the Israeli economy appropriate to their relative weight in the work force. In transportation and commerce, this level was already achieved by the 1970s, while in industry and personal services, it was attained in the 1980s. The second group represents the most privileged employment both for the working class and the middle class and includes the branches of public and community services, electricity and water, and financial and commercial services. Although intensive integration of Israeli Arabs into the branch of public and community services began in the 1980s, there is still a gap

Table 3.1
Distribution of Arab Workers by Economic Branch, 1972-1990

Economic Branch	Percent of Total Arab Work Force			Ratio of Arabs to Jews		
	1972	1986	1990	1972	1986	1990
Agriculture	19.1	8.3	7.2	2.8	1.6	1.5
Construction	26.6	15.6	17.5	3.5	3.5	3.6
Transport & Storage	7.8	7.1	5.3	1.1	1.1	0.8
Commerce & Sales	15.1	15.1	14.6	1.1	1.2	1.0
Industry	12.5	24.9	23.1	0.5	1.1	1.1
Personal services	5.1	6.6	8.6	0.7	1.0	1.2
Public & community services	13.5	19.2	19.7	0.2	0.6	0.7
Electricity & water	0.3	0.5	0.5	0.3	0.5	0.5
Financial & commercial services	0.8	2.7	3.5	0.1	0.3	0.3

Sources: Central Bureau of Statistics, 1973, 1987, 1991.

of 30 percent with respect to their relative weight. In the case of electricity and water and financial and commercial services, the proportion of Arab workers remains extremely small, although there has been a modest increase in their relative weight here too. The third group consists of the branches of construction and agriculture, characterized by high mobility and low prestige, where the proportion of Arab workers has remained high throughout the past 20 years. While there has been a drop in the number of Arab workers in agriculture during this period, in construction they have maintained a proportion 3.5 times that of Jewish workers in this branch.

Table 3.1 indicates that Arab workers have found jobs in a wider range of economic branches over the years. Although they remain highly concentrated in construction and agriculture, their involvement in these less privileged branches of the economy has been decreasing steadily.

Examination of the status of Arab occupations indicates a more limited degree of social integration. As can be seen from Table 3.2, the weight of Arab workers in white-collar professions is only about one third that of Jewish workers in the same branches, and this ratio remained virtually unchanged throughout the 1970s and 1980s. Most striking is the gap in the percentage of Arab workers in management and in the scientific and technical professions. In mid-level occupations, such as sales, agencies, and services, the weight of Arab workers is approaching that of Jews employed in the same fields, with the exception of agriculture (where, as we have seen, the proportion of Arab workers is still high). In contrast, the relatively high rate of Arab workers in blue-collar occupations is still quite apparent. They represent more than twice the number of Jewish workers in the skilled professions and 4.6 times more in the unskilled. Their relative weight in these two groups almost doubled in the 1970s and 1980s, when the Jewish work force was shifting toward middle-class occupations, while Arab workers were changing their status from that of migrant workers to that of organized labor yet still commuting to the Jewish centers. Nevertheless, skilled laborers today account for about one half of the Arab work force.

Employment in the Jewish sector, along with the increasing professionalism of the Arab work force that began in the 1960s, created reserves of skilled laborers with the potential to undertake entrepreneurship in a variety of fields. The diffusion of agricultural technology from Jewish farming settlements to Arab villages via the Arabs employed in the Jewish settlements proved to be highly efficient (Schnell, 1980). A similar process took place in the construction branch. Beginning in the 1960s, Arab society entered an era of intensive residential rebuilding. Construction workers adopted the new skills and norms learned in the Jewish sector in building their own homes. Another reason behind the development of this branch was the growing demand for additional housing units in the Arab sector.

Table 3.2
Distribution of Arab Workers by Occupation, 1972-1990

Occupation	Percent of Workers			Ratio to Jews		
	1972	1986	1990	1972	1986	1990
Blue-collar						
Unskilled & semi skilled workers	11.8	11.9	10.5	1.8	3.6	4.6
Skilled workers	41.9	39.8	41.9	1.4	1.7	2.1
Agriculture	16.2	8.7	7.7	2.3	1.9	2.3
Gray-collar						
Services	9.7	13.1	13.6	0.8	1.0	1.0
Sales	7.1	7.9	6.7	0.9	1.0	0.9
White-collar						
Clerks	4.3	6.3	5.6	0.3	0.4	0.3
Managers	0.4	0.7	1.5	0.1	0.1	0.2
Professional occupation	7.4	8.4	9.5	0.6	0.5	0.6
Scientific & technical professions	1.2	2.3	3.0	0.2	0.3	0.3

Sources: Central Bureau of Statistics, 1973, 1987, 1991.

DEMOGRAPHY AND SETTLEMENTS

One of the most marked implications of the economic mobility of Israeli Arabs in the 1950s and 1960s was a demographic explosion. The total fertility rate of Muslim women, representing some 80 percent of all Arab women, rose from around seven children per woman of reproductive age to nearly ten. With no emigration to speak of and a low mortality rate, this led to a population growth of over 4 percent a year (Schnell, 1994b). It was only in the late 1960s, when the generation of women born after establishment of the State of Israel reached reproductive age, that the overall birth rate began to fall, settling at just under five children per woman in the 1990s. The rapid population growth had significant ramifications for the nature of development and urbanization of Arab settlements. Arabs do not tend not to migrate out of their own villages, where they enjoy the far-reaching support of their extended family and a legacy that includes a plot of land. Moreover, the urban centers, with their Jewish majority, are within commuting distance. As a result, most villages grew at a similar rate, from several hundred to a few thousand residents in the early 1950s to townships of 5,000 to 30,000 residents in the 1990s. Since hubs of economic activity did not develop within the settlements themselves, most workers are still forced to commute to the Jewish centers.

The lack of economic development in the towns led to latent urbanization (Meyer-Brodnitz, 1969; Schnell, 1994b). While encouraging Arab workers to commute to jobs in the Jewish sector, the government also assisted Arab villages in laying a basic infrastructure. Between the mid-1950s and the late 1960s, nearly all Arab settlements were connected to road, electricity, and water systems. In addition, in most settlements school systems were built from the ground up, along with municipal frameworks. These measures created jobs for the young generation of educated Arabs who began to graduate from Israeli schools in the 1960s.

In contrast to its success in building an infrastructure, the government failed in the application of planning and construction regulations to Arab settlements. By the end of the 1980s, only a very few town plans had been approved, and only some of these included the allocation of areas for industrial zones (Khamaisi, 1986). This situation placed the Arab settlements at a disadvantage in relation to the new towns erected in peripheral regions of the country. Here the government built modern industrial zones to promote industrialization. In the 1950s and 1960s, the government encouraged plants to shift into these industrial zones, to ensure full employment in the new development towns. In consequence, during the recession of 1965-1967, Arab villages suffered from the highest unemployment rate in the country, while the neighboring development towns enjoyed a relatively low rate of unemployment. It thus seems apparent that in the absence of supportive government policy, infrastructure, and professional training, the Israeli Arabs were limited in or incapable of developing industrial plants beyond the scale of small workshops before the 1970s, and even then they had to compete with their Jewish neighbors from a position of inferiority.

In view of the sparse opportunities for investment in production enterprises, most of the funds saved by wage earners went into housing. The Arab economy financed a highly impressive housing project in which nearly all traditional homes were replaced, extended family households were able to split into nuclear family households, and housing was provided for the many young couples, as the children born during the baby boom grew up and married (Shmueli, Schnell, & Soffer,

1986). As a result, the built-up areas of most Arab settlements grew tenfold larger or more, and aggregates of settlements establishing mutual economic relations began to evolve (Schnell, 1987; Shmueli & Schnell, 1980; Soffer, 1983). Nine such regional settlement systems can be identified in the Israeli space, six in the Galilee hills and three in the center of the country on the border between the Jewish coastal plain and the Palestinian West Bank (see Figure 3.2). These settlement systems represent regional units characterized by territorial continuity, the development of a single residential area, increasing spatial and regional awareness, and the emergence of the first signs of functional interrelations among the settlements. The infrequency of such relations derives from the relatively low level of development as well as from dependency on the Jewish urban centers (Schnell, 1987).

Distinct differences can be seen between the various regional settlement systems. That centered around Nazareth is the largest, with some 130,000 residents in about 16 settlements. Nazareth serves as a central core for these settlements and to a certain extent for other villages outside the system as well. Although the majority of the population in this region is Muslim, there is also a relatively large Christian community.

In contrast, the regional settlement systems in the central region feature a homogeneous population. A complex of settlements with a total population of some 60,000 took shape in Wadi Ara around Umm al Fahm. Although Umm al Fahm became the central hub for the smaller surrounding villages, a secondary economic hub evolved around Kafr Qari, both because of *hamula* rivalries and because of its geographic proximity to Ara and Arara. Secondary hubs also developed in the region of the Little Triangle around Taiyibe and Baqa al Gharbiya.

The other regional settlement systems in Galilee are more heterogeneous in terms of population. A large majority of the population of Central Upper Galilee is Druze or Christian, while in Western Upper Galilee there is a distinct Druze majority and a smaller, but significant, Christian minority. In the settlement system in Western Lower Galilee, the population, numbering close to 60,000 residents, is also mixed, with all three ethnic groups represented, but here the Muslims constitute a clear majority.

The ethnic structure of these regions is of considerable importance in understanding their industrialization. The Christians are the most highly educated ethnic group in the Arab sector, and their birth rate is similar to that of the Jewish population. It is therefore easier for them to accumulate the capital needed for higher development. Since the Druze serve in the Israeli army and profess total loyalty to the country, they receive government assistance and more financial incentives than the other ethnic groups and thus have a greater development potential, even though their social and demographic features are most similar to those of the Muslims. The Bedouin population, unlike the other groups, is still in the first stages of sedentarization in permanent townships. Moreover, the Bedouins have a relatively low level of education and particularly high birth rate.

Figure 3.2
Arab Regional Settlement Systems in Israel

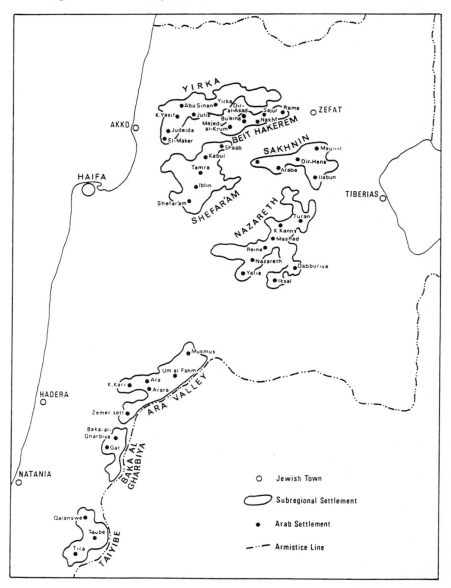

As a result, the development potential of the Bedouin townships scattered throughout the northern part of the country is extremely low. In the Bedouin areas of the Be'er Sheva heights the level of development is so low that there are virtually no industrial enterprises in these townships.

A further ramification of the economic changes in the Arab sector is social in nature. Traditional kinship relations have undergone a striking alteration over the past 40 years. The Arab family in the past was patrilineal, patriarchal, and patrilocal. The father controlled the subsistence economy while making intensive use of family manpower. The household included all members of the families of the father and his sons. This arrangement developed hierarchically from the patriarchal extended family household to the *hamula* and the ethnic group (Avitzur, 1986; Ginat, 1983; Habash, 1973). The power of the extended family was further enhanced by the endogamous marriages that characterized the Arab kinship system. The extended family constituted the dominant economic unit, with the *hamula* as the dominant political unit.

In modern reality, extended family households have broken up into households of nuclear families living in close proximity to one another. As the nuclear families became self-supporting, they were no longer financially dependent on the father (Rosenfeld, 1964). More people were now involved in decision making, and it became common for the father to divide the family land among his sons during his own lifetime.

The fact that children educated in Israel were able to achieve higher positions in the Israeli labor market than their parents frequently made the older generation financially dependent on the younger. Despite these upheavals, however, kinship relations did not disintegrate entirely. In many cases, they contributed to the processes of urbanization and modernization. The extended family became the major source for its members in regard to financing, investment, residential construction, and moral support (Meyer-Brodnitz, 1983; Schnell, 1994b). In the absence of government aid for development, the extended family served as the major factor supporting social change and economic growth. The *hamula*, on the other hand, derived its power from control of the local authority. It thus continued to provide for its members' land needs by means of larger allocations for construction, town planning, the erection of public institutions, the laying of infrastructure, and so on.

In sum, Arab society has been undergoing rapid transition from a traditional to a more modern society, a change spurred by new economic opportunities and the adoption of Western societal patterns. While modernization is impelled by close contact with Jewish society, it is also supported by traditional institutions encouraging the introduction of change (Berler, 1974; Schnell, 1980). In the process, Israeli Arabs have been peripheralized in the socio-economic space of Israel. It is under these circumstances that Arab industrial entrepreneurship has evolved and developed.

Chapter 4

The Development of Arab Industry

Although for many years Israeli Arabs had not been strangers to the world of the trades and industry, the level of modernization and extent of industrial activity remained extremely limited. In the 1970s, conditions became ripe for the development of industrial enterprises which could establish themselves within the modern Israeli economy. An understanding of the changes undertaken by Arab entrepreneurs with regard to the trades and industry demands a look at both quantitative changes—the number of industrial start-ups and employees of industrial plants—and qualitative changes in the nature of the activities of both the entrepreneurs and the plants themselves. Unfortunately, there is a lack of continuous data over a prolonged period of time, and existing data regarding the distant past are far from complete and are not necessarily comparable. This makes it difficult to present a systematic quantitative analysis of the industrialization process and the changes it has seen. Nonetheless, four stages characterizing different periods on the road to the industrialization of the Arab economy can be identified: the traditional stage; the imitation stage; the dependency stage; and the stage of latent integration into the Israeli economy (Schnell, 1994b).

THE TRADITIONAL STAGE—UP TO THE EARLY 1950s

During the British Mandate in Israel (1920-1948), Arab industry developed in two regional systems. The first was centered around the coastal cities—both Arab (Gaza and Acre) and mixed (Jaffa and Haifa)—and was spurred by the processes of urbanization and modernization, which began as a result of British involvement in the economy, as well as by economic links with the developing Jewish economy. This urban system collapsed, however, in the wake of the War of Independence. The second region of industrial development was in the provincial towns and outlying villages. Here local industrial initiatives complemented the traditional economy based on agricultural produce intended primarily to supply the needs of the rural household. As a result, manpower for the plants, like that for agriculture, was recruited intensively from the household or extended family, while both the capital investment and level of technology were low. This approach derived from the economic strategy of risk reduction rather than from a desire to maximize profit. In some of the larger villages, plants were set up in branches, such as coal or lime production, stone quarrying, oil pressing, and pottery. Toward the late 1920s, prodded by the British mandatory authorities, machinery was introduced into a small number of oil presses and flour mills, with diesel engines replacing the sources of power that had been in use since the time of the Ottoman Empire. In addition to the plants within settlements, tradesmen wandered from village to village offering their services as tinsmiths, shoemakers, blacksmiths, etc. In contrast, in certain trades entrepreneurs achieved a larger output by marketing their products beyond the borders of their own village or district.

One example of industrial activity from this period is the mat and basket weaving plant in Taiyibe (Golani, 1967), which was begun by Egyptian immigrants who had arrived in Palestine around 1832 and produced mainly floor mats, baskets for olive pressing, and storage baskets. The raw materials for this plant were reeds transported on camel back from the edges of local marshes. The baskets were woven in part by groups of men working together and in part by women during the seasons when they were not needed for agricultural work. After several years, the industry became a monopoly owned by a wealthy merchant of the Masrawe family, originally from Egypt. He provided the craftsmen with food and clothing on credit in exchange for the future baskets they would weave, thereby both gaining control of their work and installing them as his tenants. As the settlement merchant grew richer, he bought up much land in Taiyibe, one of the larger villages in the coastal plain, and his goods were sold as far away as Damascus and Beirut. As the marshlands throughout Palestine, and particularly along the coastal plain, shrank, the industry was forced to reduce production until it was closed down in the 1960s.

It is important to remember that industrial activity played only a small role in the traditional economy. Even after 1948, it grew at a very slow pace, and in 1950 the number of employees in the industrial sector was estimated at only 10 percent of the total population of Arab workers, a proportion that had not changed since the census of 1931 (Zarhi & Achiezra, 1966). The 1950s left the Israeli Arabs in particularly poor shape and provided little opportunity for the development of industry. The 165,000 Arab residents who remained within the State of Israel were placed under military rule, with restrictions that discouraged them from moving out of their villages or creating communication networks extending beyond the village borders. The remaining village population was relatively small (excepting Nazareth and Shefar'am) and for some time continued to practice traditional agriculture. Most of these farmers had little formal education and lacked any experience in running a modern farm. Significant economic development at this time would have required, above all, the implementation of government policies allowing for Arab integration into the developing Israeli economy.

THE IMITATION STAGE—FROM THE MID-1950s TO 1970

The imitation stage began in the mid-1950s with the cancellation of the closure imposed by military rule on the residents of Arab settlements in 1948. Now about half of the Arab work force was available for employment as wage laborers in Jewish towns. As Arabs left their villages, there was a relatively sharp rise in the number employed in industry, from 5,700 in 1955 to 10,900 in 1963. This latter figure represented 5.3 percent of all industrial workers in Israel in that year. Most of these Arabs worked as salaried workers in Jewish-owned plants. In 1962, some 3,500 Arabs were employed in Arab-owned industries, around 2,000 of them as salaried workers. It is estimated that in this year Arab industries employed approximately 1.8 percent of the industrial work force in Israel (Zarhi & Achiezra, 1966).

Within four years, employment in the Jewish economy led to a fivefold increase in the average wage per worker. However, the possibilities for industrial entrepreneurship in the Arab sector remained severely limited, for several reasons: a lack of capital and professional skills, a lack of experience in a market economy, and, most particularly, the absence of basic physical infrastructure in Arab communities. Accumulated capital in Arab hands was invested primarily in expanding construction projects in which new housing units were built for an ever-growing number of young couples (Schnell, 1994b).

The imitation stage reached its height in the 1960s and continued on into the 1970s, with Arab industry still developing along lines that ensured reduced risk. According to Czamanski and Taylor (1986), the development of Arab enterprise at this time was based on mimicking behavior, with the tendency to choose low-risk enterprises built into it. As they see it, the lack of risk-reducing institutions, such as those providing communication networks or managerial, professional, and marketing information, made it difficult for potential entrepreneurs to operate efficiently or make proper decisions. Having no such bodies to supply them with tools for risk assessment, the entrepreneurs tended to draw on the experience of others like them for the information they needed. Consequently, they generally imitated enterprises that had proven successful in the same entrepreneurial environment in which they operated, and they refrained from investing in areas in which others had failed.

The strategies of mimicking behavior encouraged enterprises in the two fields that had already begun to develop in the 1950s: food and building materials. These plants made intensive use of ethnic enclave strategies in relying on extended family resources as well as on local, relatively secure markets. The plants in the food industry relied on a combination of traditional knowledge, with local markets catering to the taste of the Arab consumer, and small-scale mechanization. When, in 1948, military restrictions cut off the rural communities from the oil presses, flour mills, and other food processing plants located primarily in the Arab cities, there was added incentive to establish plants for the processing of agricultural products in the smaller settlements. The plants producing building materials relied on the increasing demand for these products deriving from the continued growth in the demand for new housing. This stemmed from a rapid population increase in the 1950s and 1960s, when the total fertility rate rose from 7 to 10 per adult female while the mortality rate continued to drop steadily. Furthermore, the custom of erecting a house for the future family as a condition for marriage spurred the construction industry even more. As a result, and in line with the mimicking process, new plants producing concrete and concrete blocks were established in Arab villages to supply the needs of the local community. The increasing demand for building materials created a range of opportunities for economic enterprises in other fields as well, such as iron and wood, which supplied raw materials and finished products to the construction industry.

This early industrialization of the Arab villages began slowly. The 1950s saw the establishment of only a small number of plants, each employing an average of two or three workers. Figure 4.1 presents the number of plants existing in 1992 by year of foundation. Although it is impossible to know how many plants were founded in the 1950s and later closed down, the figure confirms the relatively small number established in that decade. In the traditional branches, electrically operated oil presses and flour mills were erected and produced a considerably larger output than was previously the case. At the same time, concrete block plants and carpentry and metalworking shops were established and constituted some 80 percent of the total number of workshops and plants at the time (Shmueli, Schnell, & Soffer, 1985). The testimony of elderly residents of the settlements in the region known as the "Little Triangle" (a strip of Arab villages along the border between the Jewish coastal plain and the Arab West Bank) and several Galilean villages indicates that in 1950 there were approximately 10 workshops in new economic branches in the Little Triangle and around 40 in Arab settlements. The rate of new industries rose in the 1960s as compared to the 1950s (Figure 4.1), until in 1970 the average number of plants per 1,000 residents in all Arab settlements reached around 0.5, approaching 1 plant per 1,000 residents only in Baqa al Gharbiya and Tira. Nevertheless, the lack of a minimal infrastructure restricted the establishment of new plants largely to those settlements connected to the electricity grid and water pipelines, and to a certain extent to the road system as well. Accordingly, industrial plants were obviously concentrated in the larger villages.

During the imitation stage, Arab industry continued to rely on family resources. The members of the extended family were expected to share in financing the factory, which was usually run by the eldest brother. The manager's obligation to his extended family was expressed in the employment of the younger brothers and responsibility for their financial well-being. For its part, the extended family,

Figure 4.1
Number of Existing Plants by Year of Establishment

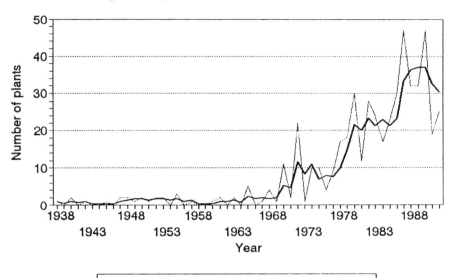

and even the entire *hamula* (clan), was obliged, through a system of informal relations, to purchase the products produced by the plant. Despite technological advances and the acquisition of modern equipment, the plant maintained its traditional character in terms of the organization of production and labor, and professional training of the workers remained minimal.

Only a few enterprises in the 1960s managed to grow beyond the range of 10 or more employees or to rely on markets outside the *hamula*. The best known of these are the cigarette factory in Nazareth and the pickle factory in Baqa al Gharbiya owned by Fares Hamdan in partnership with Jewish investors (Watad, 1966). Both plants reached proportions that threatened the market shares of monopolistic concerns in the Jewish sector. During this period, there was considerable governmental protection of industry, which derived from the policy to encourage the industrialization of the Jewish economy. Both of the aforementioned plants were eventually forced to close down because of their inability to compete with Jewish-owned competitors. They were undone by their success in growing to such a size that they had become a threat to large factories in the Jewish sector. The failure of the Baqa al Gharbiya pickle factory in particular had repercussions, since its owner, Fares Hamdan, was a member of Knesset representing the Communist party. Throughout the Arab community, it was rumored that government policy designed specifically to discriminate against the Arab sector had undermined the success of the plant. Today it is no easy matter to reconstruct the real reasons behind the failure of these Arab industrial enterprises. Nevertheless, a study carried out in the early 1980s among potential entrepreneurs in the Little Triangle (Shmueli, Schnell, & Soffer, 1986) suggests that these failures continued to discourage future entrepreneurs. Many stated that they were reluctant to undertake the risk of investing in industry, even in the 1980s, because of their lack of faith in the willingness of the political system to assist them.

THE DEPENDENCY STAGE—FROM 1970 TO THE MID-1980s

Industrialization of the Arab settlements in the 1970s involved a combination of factors that had already emerged in the late 1960s. The economic boom that characterized the Israeli economy following the Six Day War created new opportunities for Arab entrepreneurs in the industrial sector. This was followed by the extension to most Arab settlements of the minimum infrastructure required to support industrial development. In 1952 only the city of Nazareth was connected to the national electricity grid; by 1966 some 22 percent of the Arab settlements had been connected; and by 1970 nearly all of the settlements of 5,000 residents or more were hooked up to the grid. A similar process occurred regarding the connection of these settlements to the water and road systems. Moreover, the Arab work force had gained experience and skill in the various industrial branches, particularly those related to construction. Accumulated capital saved from wages, along with this increased experience in industry, enabled potential entrepreneurs to undertake small economic enterprises.

The impact of two major phenomena was felt from the 1970s to the mid-1980s. The first was the development of the textile and clothing industry, whose factories operated as subcontractors for companies in the major urban centers of the country. The second was the rapid rate of growth in the number of new plants in the food and construction sectors, which relied primarily on local markets. These phenomena combined with the emergence of regrouping and amalgamation processes affecting the dispersion pattern of industrial production in the country. This is typical of relatively developed countries, in which private capital tends to be concentrated in a small number of large companies, as has been happening in Israel over the past two decades. The spatial pattern of industrial production began to be characterized by the concentration of plant managements, research and development, the more sophisticated stages of production, and marketing management in the economic centers of the country. On the other hand, a significant number of old industries and standard production lines of large corporations were relocated to the industrial zones of peripheral settlements (Razin & Shachar, 1990). At the same time, small and medium-sized plants were established in the peripheral areas. Some of them became part of the production processes of the larger plants and others produced for nearby local markets (Felsenstein, 1992).

As part of the spatial reorganization of Israeli industrial capital, the large industrial corporations began to seek out inexpensive means of production and ways of obtaining government subsidies for their new plants. The newly established development towns of Israel thus became a desirable location for setting up these plants. Most offer a relatively well-developed industrial infrastructure as well as generous government subsidies, which may reach as high as 38 percent of the investment. In contrast, within the Arab sector there was a noticeable scarcity of available land for industry (see Chapter 9) and lack of national subsidies for Arab settlements, even those adjacent to the new towns. As a result, only in a very limited number of branches (mainly textiles and clothing) did Arab settlements have any chance of competing successfully against the development towns for entrepreneurs seeking sites outside the center of the country (Bar-El, 1993).

The dependency stage is exemplified by the textile and clothing industry. Dependency is reflected in the development in Arab settlements of production lines linked to Jewish-owned companies. This dependency is twofold: First, the local work force is dependent on textile and clothing plants for employment, and second, the plants are dependent on external sources for the sale of their output. The textile and clothing branch is characterized by a duality: on the one hand, inexpensive mass-produced items and, on the other, quality high-fashion apparel. For cheap items, low wages must be paid the workers. Moreover, due to the fluctuation in demand for the products, manufacturers prefer not to use expensive, sophisticated equipment to produce their total output. This production strategy is well suited to Arab settlements, which offer large reserves of women with low geographical mobility who seldom work outside their villages. These women represent a potential work force willing to work for low wages without permanent status or social benefits beyond the minimum required by law. Starting in the mid-1970s, these conditions spurred the establishment in Arab settlements of dozens of sewing shops devoted primarily to the simple and routine stages of production. Thus the textile and clothing industry became the prime employer of the local labor force. Design, cutting, quality control, and sewing on of the brand name, however, are generally carried out at the main factory located in an urban Jewish center. In most cases, the plant in the Arab settlement occupies part of the residence of the entrepreneur, who also finances purchase of the sewing machines, with the assistance of the main factory. At times, the core of the female work force employed in these sewing shops is trained at textile and clothing factories in the nearby development towns, where these women also work before their marriage.

In the other industrial branches, plants continued to develop in the 1970s along the same principles that had governed industrialization in the 1960s, with imitation remaining the primary guideline. In fact, except for those in the textile and clothing industry, only a small number of enterprises revealed a higher level of entrepreneurship, as expressed by the penetration of markets outside the settlement, the establishment of larger factories employing more than 10 workers, or financing from sources outside the family. Plants were located in some 60 Arab settlements, which represented the majority of those boasting a population of over 5,000 in the early 1980s. In contrast, the smaller settlements, with less than 3,000 residents, offered threshold conditions that were insufficient for industrial growth (Meyer-Brodnitz & Czamanski, 1986b; Shmueli, Schnell & Soffer, 1985). Entrepreneurs continued to draw on the resources of the extended family for both capital and work force. Some 60 percent of the capital came from private savings, primarily those of the entrepreneur himself, but also from members of his family. The extent of bank financing was only marginal (Schnell, 1994b).

According to Meyer-Brodnitz and Czamanski (1986b), the number of industrial plants in Arab settlements in 1983 is estimated at 410, which employed approximately 8,200 workers, 70 percent of whom were women employed mainly in textile and clothing factories. Some 85 percent of the plants were owned by local Arab entrepreneurs, with the remainder being mostly sewing shops that operated as subcontractors for Jewish-owned firms. Only one third of the plants, 90 percent of them in the textile and clothing industry, employed more than 10 workers, with another third defined as small-scale operations employing on the whole no more than three or four people. The large majority of the plants belonged to one of three branches: Some 40 percent supplied building materials, such as concrete blocks, floor tiles, stone, lime, and wood or iron for construction; around 36 percent were sewing shops performing the simplest sewing tasks as subcontractors; and some 15 percent were in the food industry. The remaining 11 percent were involved in a variety of other fields. A further characteristic of the changes taking place in the realm of industrialization was the entrance of Arab entrepreneurs into new branches of which they had no previous experience.

A striking feature of industrial development in the dependency stage was the rapid growth rate of new plants. Figure 4.1 indicates that, beginning in the early 1970s, there was a sharp increase in the rate of establishment of new factories. This process occurred in three major waves: The first began slowly in 1970 and continued until 1975; the second began in 1978 and continued until 1984; and the third occurred between 1986 and 1990. During each, more plants were founded than in the preceding wave, a trend that attests to the expansion of the industrialization process in Arab settlements.

The first wave of new plants benefited from Israel's economic prosperity following on the Six Day War. The second was most likely a reaction to the political upheaval of 1977, when the Likud rose to power, defeating the Labor party that had controlled the Israeli government since the establishment of the State. The new government revoked a long line of restrictions and protective measures that had previously made it difficult for small entrepreneurs to start new businesses. Furthermore, what was known as the "right economic policy" of then Finance Minister Yoram Aridor poured extensive capital into the economy and created an economic milieu that encouraged financial initiatives. This atmosphere prevailed until it was shattered by the economic crisis in 1984. The third wave of new factories, representing the start of the next stage, was fueled primarily by the outbreak of the *Intifada*, the civilian uprising in the occupied territories since 1967. In the wake of the disturbances, many factory owners, principally in the textile and clothing branch, pulled out of the West Bank and Gaza Strip and set up new plants in Arab settlements in the interior of Israel.

LATENT INTEGRATION—FROM THE MID-1980s

The 1980s and early 1990s were characterized by continued rapid growth in the rate of establishment of new plants, as seen in Figure 4.1. Between 1983 and 1990, the number of plants employing three or more workers doubled, reaching 831 (Atrash, 1992). By the end of 1992, the number of such factories was estimated at around 900 (Sofer, Schnell, & Drori, 1993). Nevertheless, Arab industry continues to be typified by a relatively large proportion (43 percent) of cottage industries (i.e., activity based on the household and the domestic labor force as a production unit). In addition, there are increasingly more small-scale and some medium-sized plants (56 percent) as well as a few large factories (1 percent). National figures indicate that in 1990 Arab industry represented nearly 6 percent of all Israeli factories employing five or more workers. In 1989, Arab workers accounted for some 4 percent of the total industrial work force in the country (Central Bureau of Statistics, 1992).

Dissimilar definitions of what constitutes a factory in the different surveys (Jaffa Research Center, 1991; Meyer-Brodnitz & Czamanski, 1986b) as well as inconsistent definitions of the various industrial branches make it difficult to formulate valid comparisons. Nonetheless, Table 4.1 indicates major trends in industrial development. The building materials branch (including wood) continued to maintain its leading position in Arab industry. The marked increase in the weight of this branch can be explained primarily by the fact that the 1983 survey did not include carpentry shops in its definition of industrial plants. Although there was no significant increase in the relative weight of plants in the food and drink industry, this branch shows a gain in terms of absolute numbers. One major reason for this is that oil presses were not included in the 1983 survey but do appear in that of 1990. Table 4.1 reveals a considerable drop in the relative weight of plants in the textile and clothing industry, deriving in part from the differing methodology of the two surveys but also from the relatively slow rate at which new textile and clothing plants were established. This rate can be divided into two stages: a slow increase at the start of the period due to the continuous establishment of textile and clothing plants in the West Bank and the Gaza Strip, at least until 1989; and a rapid rate of growth in the Arab settlements in the interior of Israel from 1989, as plants were relocated out of the areas of the *Intifada*. The most outstanding change in terms of both absolute numbers and

Table 4.1
Distribution of Industrial Plants by Main Branches, 1983 and 1990

Branch	Plants—number		Plants—percent	
	1983	1990	1983	1990
Food & beverages	74	156	18	19
Construction related materials	130	308	31	37
Metal & iron	46	81	11	10
Textiles & clothing	148	227	36	27
Others	17	55	4	7
Total	415	829	100	100

Sources: Jaffa Research Center (1991); Meyer-Brodnitz and Czamanski (1986a).

relative weight can be seen in the category "Others," which includes mainly chemicals, plastics, paper and printing, glass, jewelry, and electronics—all branches whose products are aimed at the larger Israeli market.

Figure 4.1, which presents the number of plants in operation today by year of foundation, does not indicate the number of factories that closed down before 1992. However, a comparison of the three surveys (Atrash, 1992; Meyer-Brodnitz & Czamanski, 1986a; Sofer, Schnell, & Drori, 1993) makes it possible to estimate the number of closures. Such an analysis reveals that between 60 and 70 percent of the plants are still in existence, and there seems to have been no notable change in the rate at which plants were closed during the different periods. This closure rate is low in comparison to the survival rate of small factories in Jewish development towns (Schwartz, 1986). This can be explained by the fact that Arab entrepreneurs embed a strategy of risk aversion into their operation. They depend to a large extent on family markets and resources and are willing to continue to operate even for low profits.

The surveys also indicate a change in the size of the plants. Between 1983 and 1990, the average number of workers per plant doubled, increasing from around 7 to approximately 14. In the building materials branch, where the number of workers per plant is relatively low, this figure rose from around 5 to 7; while in the leading textile and clothing industry, the average number of workers per factory reached approximately 36. In addition to the increased work force, it would seem that the factories have grown more sophisticated and complex.

Above all, the integration stage is characterized by changes in economic behavior on the part of the Arab entrepreneur. A new perception of the market and advanced marketing methods have led to increased penetration of Jewish markets and an expanded territory for the sale of industrial products (see Chapter 8). A carpenter from Jaljulya who wishes to sell to the Jewish market will employ a Jewish kitchen designer and a Jewish secretary, both of whom can bridge the gap between the needs of the Jewish customer and the plant's production capabilities. Entrance into Jewish markets and more successful integration into the Israeli economy are made possible by use of the mechanisms for financial planning and marketing commonly employed in the Jewish sector, along with the introduction of new technology and better quality control. The integration of Arab industry is also expressed in the growth of the food and building materials branches, which is in part a response to the rapid population increase in the Jewish sector resulting from the large wave of immigration in the late 1980s and early 1990s.

The analysis so far reveals that Israeli Arab industry fails to integrate fully into the larger economy. In spite of that situation, Israeli Arab industry has been developed along three qualitatively distinctive stages. During the 1950s, it had been mainly linked with the traditional peasant economy. Since then, almost every decade the Israeli Arab industry has developed in a process leading to a latent integration in the larger economy. Branch and spatial characteristics at the current stage of development are discussed in the following chapter; this leads to the more detailed restructuring processes that characterized industrial entrepreneurship and development, which are the core of the remaining chapters.

Chapter 5

Branch Structure and Spatial Distribution

This chapter describes the major features concerning branch structure and spatial distribution of Arab plants in Arab settlements in the early 1990s. The data in this chapter are based on a detailed survey of Arab industry conducted by the authors in 1992 and covering 514 plants. In some cases, data were supplemented by the full survey of Arab industry conducted by the Jaffa Research Center in 1990.

DISTRIBUTION OF PLANTS BY INDUSTRIAL BRANCH–1992

A detailed description of the distribution of plants in Arab settlements in the early 1990s by industrial branch indicates a continuing trend to concentrate on branches that had already existed and developed in the 1970s, with only a limited entrance into new fields. Industrial plants today can be divided broadly into two groups: (1) those in branches that were developed up to the 1970s and continue to produce mainly for local demand; and (2) those in new branches which have been introduced into the Arab sector since the 1970s. The factories in the first category may be further divided into two subgroups. The first consists of plants in the food and beverage industry, including, among others, bakeries, candy, coffee grinding, soft-drink concentrate, canned food factories, and olive oil presses. The second consists of plants related to the branch of building materials and housing, including concrete block, marble, iron and concrete factories, metalworking and carpentry shops, and plants producing window blinds. This subgroup includes most of the factories which appear in various sources under the headings nonmetallic minerals, metal and metal products, wood and wood products, rubber and plastics, and window blinds. The relatively new branches in the Arab sector belong primarily to the textile and clothing industry, represented by a growing number of sewing shops of various sizes. In addition, in recent years a small number of plants have been established in the branches of jewelry, electricity, electronics, chemicals, and machinery.

The distribution by branch of 514 factories, arranged by year of foundation, is presented in Table 5.1. About one quarter of all of these plants belong to the textile, clothing, and leather industry, and the overwhelming majority are sewing shops operating as subcontractors for Jewish factories. Over one third of the plants, including some of the wood, metalworking, and metal factories, supply products to the construction industry. The food industry accounts for another 20 percent of the enterprises. In fact, the three branches which appeared in earlier decades—food, wood, and building materials—with the addition of the textile and clothing industry today encompass some 80 percent of all Arab industrial plants, and the proportion of other branches remains limited.

The distribution of industrial branches by year of foundation reveals several major trends. The textile and clothing industry, which began to develop rapidly in the early 1970s, has maintained a fairly stable rate of growth over the past decade. A similar phenomenon characterizes the rate of establishment of new plants in the building materials industry, although its relative weight has dropped to only 17 percent of all plants. A somewhat different trend can be seen concerning metal, metalworking, and wood, which serve the construction branch. Here the rate at which new plants have been founded has slowed somewhat to 2.8 and 1.3 enterprises per year in the branches of wood and metal, respectively. The development of the food industry, however, followed a different pattern. Before the 1970s, this branch represented a considerable proportion of all plants. During the 1970s and early 1980s, there was a significant decline in the rate at which new food plants were established, even in comparison to other branches. In contrast, in recent years this branch has undergone renewed growth with the founding of bakeries and tehina, humus, and cheese factories. Although these plants still rely largely on Arab markets, they have recently begun to offer their products increasingly to Jewish markets.

Table 5.2 presents the distribution of employees by branch in the same 514 plants. The leading branch in terms of number of workers is the textile and clothing industry, which employs two thirds of all workers in Arab industry (mostly women). In addition, several hundred people are employed in the branches of building materials, food and wood. The number of workers in the other branches is relatively small. The average plant size by branch reveals that the textile and clothing factories employ three dozen workers, while in the other branches average plant size is less than 10 employees. Factories in the building materials industry have expanded relatively in recent years, so that the average plant size in this branch is two thirds larger than in the food, metal, or rubber and plastic industries. The print shops are particularly small in size, employing on the average less than four workers per plant. Plants under the heading "Others" constitute an exception in that they include the metalworks owned by Kadmani, which employs around 180 workers, thereby skewing the average size of plants

Table 5.1
Distribution of Industrial Plants by Branch, Year of Foundation, and Rate of Annual Plants Opening (percent)

Branch & N.P.Y.	Year Founded					Total %
	1938-1955	1956-1970	1971-1983	1984-1988	1989-1992	
Food	70.0	26.0	14.0	16.0	23.0	19.0
	3.9	1.7	1.1	3.2	5.8	
Textiles	–	14.0	27.0	31.0	29.0	26.0
& clothing	–	0.9	2.1	6.2	7.3	
Wood	20.0	21.0	18.0	17.0	11.0	17.0
	1.1	1.4	1.4	3.4	2.8	
Construction	5.0	10.0	20.0	15.0	15.0	17.0
materials	0.3	0.7	1.5	3.0	3.8	
Metal &	–	3.0	11.0	7.0	5.0	8.0
metalworking	–	0.2	0.8	1.4	1.3	
Printing	–	–	3.0	7.0	8.0	5.0
	–	–	0.2	1.4	2.0	
Rubber,	–	14.0	6.0	7.0	7.0	6.0
plastics, blinds	–	0.9	0.5	1.4	1.8	
Others	–	5.0	10.0	2.0	2.0	2.0
	0.3	0.7	0.2	0.4	0.5	
Total	100.0	100.0	100.0	100.0	100.0	100.0
%–period	3.9	5.4	37.7	29.0	23.9	100.0
Total–period	20	28	194	149	123	
N.P.Y.	1.1	1.9	14.9	29.8	30.8	

N.P.Y = New plants/year

Table 5.2
Distribution of Employees and Average Number of Employees per Plant by
Industrial Branch, Gender, and Total

Branch	Plants No.	Employees—No. & Average per Plant		
		Total	Males	Females
Food	97	563	533	30
		5.8	5.5	0.3
Textiles & clothing	139	5101	695	4406
		36.7	5.0	31.7
Wood	87	479	470	9
		5.5	5.4	0.1
Construction materials	88	898	854	44
		10.2	9.7	0.5
Metal & metalworking	42	260	244	16
		6.2	5.8	0.4
Printing	26	99	78	21
		3.8	3.0	0.7
Rubber, plastics, blinds	31	186	180	6
		6.0	5.8	0.2
Others	10	200	197	3
		20.0	19.7	0.3
Total	514	7786	3251	4535
		15.1	6.3	8.8

in this category upwards. Breakdown by gender reveals that some 60 percent of
those employed in Arab industrial enterprises are women. Eighty-eight percent
of these work in the textile and clothing industry, where they represent around 86
percent of all employees. In the other branches, some 95 percent of the workers
are men.

THE SPATIAL DISTRIBUTION OF ARAB INDUSTRY

In geographical terms, industrial activity in Arab settlements can be divided into eight primary and five secondary regions, with the latter being relatively small and isolated. This division is presented in Figure 5.1 and in Table 5.3.

Table 5.3 reveals that the region of Nazareth, home to the largest Arab population, also contains the greatest number of industrial plants. The regions along the coastal plain, adjacent to major Jewish centers, also stand out for the large number of Arab industrial enterprises, particularly those employing 10 workers or more, which do not display a significant presence in the region of the Little Triangle. The small number of factories in the Sakhnin and Beit Kerem Valley regions, and especially the scarcity of large-scale enterprises (also the case in Wadi Ara), can be explained geographically by their distance from the Jewish population centers of the coastal plain and the existence of other Arab regions, which function as "intervening opportunities" between them and the Jewish market. Among the secondary regions containing smaller Arab populations, the Negev and mixed cities show particularly few individuals employed in Arab industry. Whereas the Bedouin settlements in the Negev lack any internal economic infrastructure, Arabs in the mixed cities prefer to engage in commerce and services rather than industry.

On the level of the single settlement, five stand out as industrial centers, housing over one third of the total number of factories in their respective regions (Table 5.3). The large number of plants in Nazareth and Umm al Fahm stems from their status as the two largest Arab urban centers in Israel, each surrounded by numerous smaller settlements. Umm al Fahm, for example, has 15 ancillary villages. Baqa al Gharbiya is a growing urban settlement in the Little Triangle which serves as a commercial center even for the neighboring Jewish communities. The Druze township of Yirka enjoys government aid, which has promoted the development of the first significant industrial zone in an Arab settlement.

A more accurate measure of regional industrial level is the number of factories for every 1,000 residents in the population, as presented in Table 5.4. On the basis of these figures, it appears that the most highly industrialized areas are in Upper Galilee and in the Central and Western regions. These regions saw the greatest growth in the number of plants and the number of those employed in industry in the 1980s. The number of factories per 1,000 residents more than tripled in Western Upper Galilee between 1980 and 1990 and more than doubled in Central Upper Galilee during the same period. In contrast, the lowest growth rates for those years were recorded in the regions of Nazareth and the Sakhnin Valley, which were the most industrialized by 1980.

The various regions are distinguished not only by differences in strength of industrialization but also by differences in branch structure. Although the interregion variance is not significant, the tendency of certain regions to specialize

Figure 5.1
Primary Arab Industrial Regions in Israel

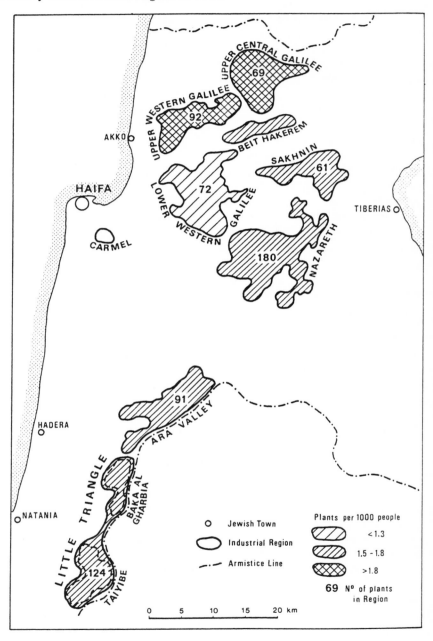

Table 5.3
Regional Distribution of Arab Industry in Israel

Region	No. of settlements	No. of plants	Plants with 10+ workers	Total employed in industry
Primary				
Nazareth	15	180	46	2258
Little Triangle	10	124	39	1342
Western Upper Galilee	7	92	33	2176
Ara Valley	9	91	15	1164
Western Lower Galilee	5	72	31	1136
Central Upper Galilee	12	69	28	2103
Sakhnin Valley	5	61	12	492
Beit Kerem Valley	6	51	15	397
Secondary				
Mixed cities*	5	37	6	226
Carmel	3	32	13	436
Negev	4	10	2	54
Jezreel Valley	5	7	1	130
Jerusalem Corridor	3	5	3	107

Table 5.3, continued

Leading Industrial Centers	Region	No. of plants	% of total plants in region	plants with 10+ workers
Nazareth	Nazareth	79	44	15
Umm al Fahm	Ara Valley	52	57	14
Baqa al Gharbiya	Little Triangle	48	39	18
Tamra	Western Lower Galilee	32	44	20
Yirka	Western Upper Galilee	30	33	19

* Mixed cities include Jaffa, Haifa, and Acre.

Source: Jaffa Research Center (1991).

in particular branches can be identified. This is shown in Figure 5.2 and Table 5.5, based on data derived from the Jaffa Research Center (1991), which systematically analyzed all Arab industrial enterprises. Both the table and the figure (which displays only the four largest branches in terms of number of workers) employ the concept of location quotient. Location quotient refers to the proportion of those employed in a branch in a given region as compared to the proportion of regional industrial workers of all industrial workers in Israel. A location quotient of 1.0 indicates that branch specialization in a region is equal to that region's share of all industrial workers. The higher the location quotient rises above 1.0, the greater the branch specialization.

According to the data in Figure 5.2 and Table 5.5, the Beit Kerem and Sakhnin Valley regions stand out for their specialization in the food industry. The Little Triangle most prominently specializes in construction materials (nonmetallic minerals). The villages in the Jezreel Valley seem to concentrate on woodworking, and the textile and clothing industry is favored in the regions of Jerusalem, Central Upper Galilee, and Western Lower Galilee. The strength of the textile industry in terms of number of employees (64 percent of all Arab

Table 5.4
Number of Plants per 1,000 Inhabitants in Arab Regions

Region	Population 1990	Plants No.	Plants per 1,000 pop. 1990	Plants per 1,000 pop. 1980
Central Upper Galilee	32,000	69	2.2	0.9
Belt Kerem Valley	35,000	51	1.4	0.8
Sakhnin Valley	50,000	61	1.2	1.1
Western Upper Galilee	40,000	92	2.3	0.7
Western Lower Galilee	61,000	72	1.2	0.7
Nazareth	125,000	180	1.4	1.0
Ara Valley	60,000	91	1.5	0.0
Little Triangle	90,000	124	1.4	0.0
Carmel	19,000	30	1.6	0.0
Negev	100,000	10	0.1	0.0

Sources: The figures for 1980 are derived from Meyer-Brodnitz and Czamanski (1986a) and Shmueli, Schnell, and Soffer (1985); the figures for 1990 are from the Jaffa Research Center (1991).

industrial workers) naturally affects the regional level of specialization in the other branches. In other words, a region specializing significantly in the textile and clothing industry will inevitably show low levels of specialization in other branches. By the same token, in a region where the textile and clothing industry is not strong, most other branches will show higher levels of specialization. The small proportion of the category "Others" makes it impossible to relate this category to any significant level of specialization.

Figure 5.2
Regional Location Quotients of Selected Branches

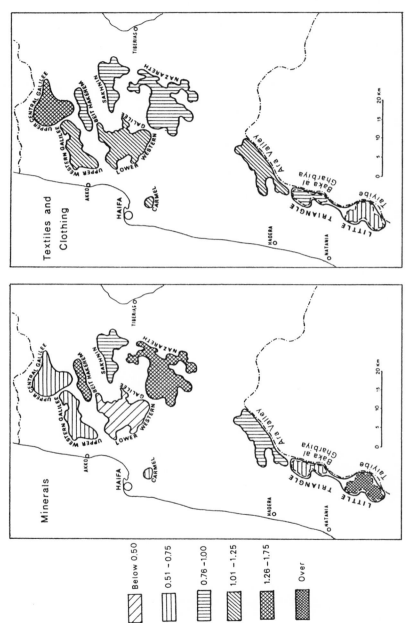

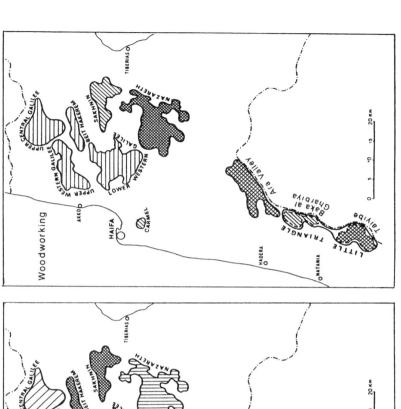

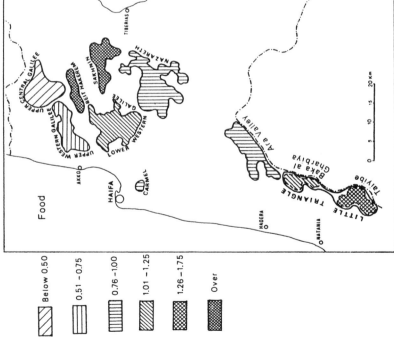

57

Table 5.5
Location Quotients of Workers in Arab Industry by Region, and Branch

Branch	Food	Textiles & clothing	Wood	Printing & paper	Rubber & plastics	Const. materials	Metals	Others
Region								
Western Upper Galilee	0.66	1.09	0.62	0.43	0.47	0.56	1.97	0.08
Central Upper Galilee	0.39	129	0.51	0.22	0.48	0.70	0.34	0.19
Beit Kerem	1.65	0.90	0.72	1.49	1.51	1.49	0.75	0
Sakhnin Valley	1.88	0.93	1.16	0.60	0.91	0.93	0.81	0.08
Nazareth	0.77	0.75	1.76	2.49	1.32	1.46	1.54	0.87
Western Lower Galilee	1.05	1.22	0.64	0.37	0.65	0.43	0.32	1.03
Carmel	0.81	1.02	1.10	0.99	1.44	0.54	0.43	6.11
Ara Valley	0.96	1.03	1.35	1.14	1.15	0.94	0.40	0.22
L. Triangle	1.39	0.63	1.31	1.85	1.40	2.15	1.36	3.96
Jezreel Vally	1.48	0.49	2.33	1.72	3.23	1.46	2.12	0
Negev	4.40	0.51	1.35	0	3.52	1.36	0.46	0
Jerusalem	0	1.37	0.10	0	3.61	0	0.39	0
Total	900	8038	1054	178	317	1119	870	137

The concentration of the various branches can also be examined by means of the Gini coefficient. This reveals the deviation of the spatial concentration of each branch from the national mean. In the Gini formula, $G = 1/2\sum_i |X_i - Y_i|$, where X_i refers to the number of workers in a given branch in a given region in relation to the number of workers in that branch in the whole country, and Y_i refers to the number of workers in all branches in that region in relation to the total number of workers in all branches in the whole country. The results are within the range of 0 to 100, where a coefficient of 0 indicates an exact correlation between regional distribution and the national mean (i.e., no concentration or grouping). Higher values indicate the greater concentration of a branch in a small number of regions. Thus the Gini coefficient highlights branch variance, while the location quotient highlights regional variance.

Figure 5.3 displays the Gini coefficient by means of a Lorenz curve, showing the cumulative percentages of all industrial workers plotted against the cumulative percentages of those in a given branch. Figure 5.3 reveals the textile and clothing industry $(G = 0.09)$ to be the least concentrated of all branches. Its spatial distribution corresponds to the weight of the region in all branches and to the proportion of the entire branch in the total number of industrial workers. Moderate concentration values are displayed by the branches of food $(G = 0.19)$, chemicals $(G = 0.21)$, and building materials $(G = 0.22)$, as well as iron and metals $(G = 0.29)$ and woodworking $(G = 0.29)$. Although the category showing the highest concentration is "Others," the Gini coefficient here is affected by sensitivity to branch and region size, thus making it difficult to draw any clear conclusions regarding this category and the branch of printing and paper.

CONCLUSIONS

The branch structure of Arab industry indicates preservation more than change. There has been no significant development of new branches along with the "constructive destruction" of long-standing branches which have ceased to grow. The textile and clothing industry did not replace other branches but rather emerged alongside them. There was no evolutionary development in which labor-intensive branches disappeared as capital-intensive and hi-tech industries emerged. On the contrary, the textile and clothing industry, increasingly gaining strength in Arab settlements since the mid-1970s, is, to a certain extent, being phased down in the Jewish economy, where it is perceived as an older branch with limited prospects for growth.

Some regions more than others have been the locus of Arab industrial development; the most prominent are the Upper Galilee and Nazareth. Additional regions containing several dozen factories in a variety of branches can also be identified. The most conspicuous branches in the Arab sector are textiles and clothing, construction-related industries, and food, all of which are distributed similarly in the major industrialized regions. These plants have developed most

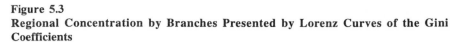

Figure 5.3
Regional Concentration by Branches Presented by Lorenz Curves of the Gini Coefficients

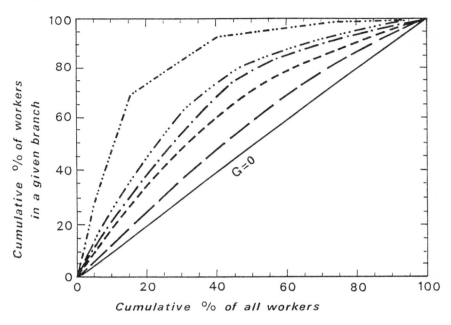

significantly since the 1970s, when the construction of a modern infrastructure in Arab settlements was completed and residents began to accumulate capital and professional know-how. Furthermore, the rise in the standard of living led to the expansion of the local markets that serve as the basis for local industry.

Arab industry owes its growth and the nature of its present branch and spatial structure above all to the rise of industrial entrepreneurship. Arab industrial entrepreneurship displays unique features and a particular developmental pattern. To understand the manner in which entrepreneurs operate and the factors affecting their ability to climb the entrepreneurship scale, one must first understand the specific aspects of Arab industrial entrepreneurship. This is the focus of our discussion in Part III.

Figure 5.4
A General View of Kafar Qasem

Figure 5.5
Wood Plant in the Residential Area

Figure 5.6
Construction Materials Plant in the Residential Area

Figure 5.7
The Industrial Area of Taiyibe

PART III

INDUSTRIAL ENTREPRENEURSHIP

Chapter 6

The Model of Industrial Entrepreneurship

INTRODUCTION

Attempts to analyze the developmental stages of industrial entrepreneurship have generated a series of deterministic models (Nanjundan, 1987; Norton & Rees, 1979; Utterback, 1979; Vernon, 1966). Vernon emphasizes four stages in the entrepreneurial process. The first begins with the conception and the mobilization of resources to start a factory; the second focuses on the start of operations; in the third the factory is concerned with establishing conditions for its survival; and in the fourth it develops and expands by entering wider markets, standardizing production, and so on. These models, however, have not received sufficient empirical confirmation (Taylor, 1987). In fact, in a historical survey of factories and their founders, it is difficult to find many cases of continuous and steady development in a given direction (Markusen, 1985).

Nanjundan (1987) describes the course of industrial growth in three broad yet distinct phases in terms of the structure, pattern, and size of manufacturing enterprises. In the first phase, household and cottage industries predominate. The essentially rural character of the economy supports nonfarm enterprises only in a rural or semiurban economic environment. Cottage industries are labor intensive and are the natural response to conditions of fragmented markets, insufficient infrastructure, and low technology. The beginning of the second phase is marked by replacing of household manufacturing by small workshops and factories located in urban centers and adopting modern technology and equipment. Their markets are wider and their integration into the economic milieu is greater. The third phase emerges with the growth of infrastructure, technology, and urbanization. Large-scale production, strongly interwoven in the local economy or external markets, tends to predominate, replacing most household and cottage manufacturing and a significant proportion of small-size enterprises as well.

Our study analyzes Arab entrepreneurship by identifying those entrepreneurial events that have led Arab industry to qualitative changes in its level of development. It avoids any commitment to pregiven stages or processes. Instead, an empirical model is adopted based on the analysis of both a relevant set of infrastructure indicators and the amount of capital invested. In this context, we describe the different levels of entrepreneurship existing in the Arab sector and the distribution of the factories on this scale. It is assumed that such an analysis will reveal the paths along which industrial initiatives develop in the Arab economy and that the resulting model will indeed reflect the range of opportunities and obstacles for industrial development in this sector without any preconceived notions. Furthermore, we analyze the conditions encouraging advancement to higher entrepreneurship levels. Here it is assumed that the foundation of factories adopting modern methods, or the introduction of such methods into existing plants, can only take place if there is a supporting system of physical, economic, social, and cultural infrastructures.

PRINCIPLES OF THE ANALYSIS

The following analysis is based on the principles of the structural approach. It is assumed that industrial growth is not a smooth and gradual process of the accumulation of capital but rather one in which structural thresholds exist. This means that without the development of human, social, and physical infrastructures, potential entrepreneurs have no chance of succeeding in their ventures. The reconstruction of the entrepreneurial environment is therefore a necessary condition for continued industrial development (Justman & Teubal, 1993). This notion derives from the conceptual approach of Schumpeter (1934), which underlines the connection between modernization—in the broadest sense—and the reconstruction of the institutions that form the social structure supporting entrepreneurship and economic growth. Market forces themselves do not guarantee that reconstruction will occur in such a way as to enable the continued, unhindered growth of industry. The following section therefore analyzes the structural thresholds of the various infrastructures supporting industrial entrepreneurship in the Arab sector in Israel. The structures of industrial entrepreneurship may be complex. Thus, we chose to focus on a limited number of structures and selected those most relevant to depicting the features of the primary infrastructures that support entrepreneurship. We defined first the level of entrepreneurship and then the indicators of the infrastructure.

The most appropriate indicator for characterizing a factory's entrepreneurship level are volume and total investments in the plant in the five year period of 1987 to 1991. Indeed, a direct relation has been found between the level of sophistication and modernization of a factory and the total investments in it in recent years. Moreover, the greater the financial investments in a plant, the higher the volume of its economic activity. The correlation between these two factors is extremely high (R = .92 for Pearson correlation coefficient). This means that both indicators equally express a factory's economic strength and growth potential. Thus, one feature alone—total investments in the plant over the past five years—may be employed to represent both the plant's economic strength and its growth potential.

In the Arab sector, most factories, both new and old, invested in development over the past five years, although actual amounts were relatively low. Sixty-one percent invested less than NIS150,000. Some 20 percent invested between NIS150,000 and 500,000. The percent of those investing between NIS500,000 and 1,000,000 was 13, and another 6 percent invested over one million shekels. Accordingly, we divided the plants into four levels of development. A question then arises about the degree to which the total investment in an enterprise and its annual volume are dependent on the adoption of infrastructures on hierarchically higher levels on the scale of entrepreneurship.

Analysis of the statistical correlations between features of the infrastructure supporting industrial entrepreneurship, on the one hand, and the variable of investments, on the other, revealed that the adoption of these infrastructures is indeed essential for a factory's development and growth. We chose to focus on seven features of the infrastructure: management; organization; labor and employment; technology; capital; physical infrastructure; and markets (see Table 6.1). Each feature of the infrastructure was examined by means of several indicators. Only weak statistical correlations were found between each of the infrastructure indicators and total investments over the past five years. This indicates that none of the industrial infrastructure features on its own can directly explain total investments. Furthermore, there are no linear relations between the infrastructure features and total investments. Had there been so, it would mean that greater access to a given infrastructure feature would enable an entrepreneur to increase his investments accordingly. Nevertheless, the Pearson correlation coefficient between the total of the scores assigned the plants for all infrastructure features, on the one hand, and total investments over the past five years, on the other, reveals a relatively strong connection (R = 0.72), indicating that the infrastructures chosen do in fact represent various aspects of industrial entrepreneurship. In addition, the combination of infrastructure features seems to explain about one half of total investments in the plant. The more a factory adopts higher levels of entrepreneurship in the different infrastructures listed in Table 6.1, the greater the chance that its profits will grow and its owners will be willing to increase their investments in further development, thereby making it possible to introduce more modernization.

The fact that no significant statistical correlations were found between total investments and any of the indicators individually suggests two things. First, none of the infrastructure variables on its own is a critical factor in encouraging economic growth but must work in conjunction with other features of the infrastructure. Second, different sets of infrastructure features may together constitute a structural threshold without which potential entrepreneurs may have

Table 6.1
Infrastructure Features Supporting Industrial Entrepreneurship

Infrastructure Feature	Indicator	Abbreviated Term
1. Managerial	1) Separation of management & ownership	Management
	2) Professional management	Manager
2. Organizational	3) Private ownership or public company	Ownership
	4) Division into departments	Departments
3. Employment	5) No. of employees	Employees
	6) % of employees from *hamula*	*Hamula*
	7) Presence of university graduates, engineers & technicians	Professionals
4. Technological	8) New or used machinery	Machinery
	9) Use of computers	Computers
	10) Existence of quality control	Quality
5. Financial	11) Reliance on bank financing	Bank

Table 6.1, continued

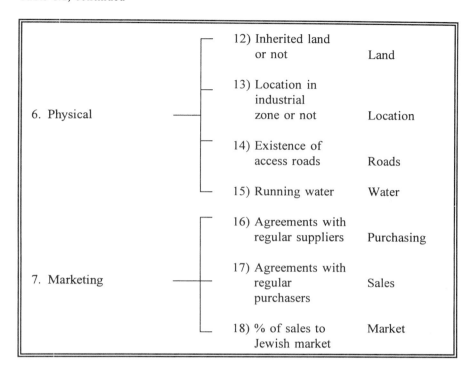

6. Physical	12) Inherited land or not	Land
	13) Location in industrial zone or not	Location
	14) Existence of access roads	Roads
	15) Running water	Water
7. Marketing	16) Agreements with regular suppliers	Purchasing
	17) Agreements with regular purchasers	Sales
	18) % of sales to Jewish market	Market

little chance of achieving higher levels of entrepreneurship. Several indicators might become a major or necessary condition for the advancement of a factory from a given entrepreneurship level to a higher one, while additional features of the infrastructure might prove more important for progress to the next higher level. Such a relationship between infrastructure features and total investments derives from our perception of factory growth as associated not only with increased capital investments but also with qualitative changes in both the plants themselves and in the structural features of the entrepreneurial environment. Our analysis examines the infrastructure indicators facilitating the transitions between the various entrepreneurship levels, from that of limited investments and infrastructures to the highest level of sophistication to be found in the Arab economy—where modern methods are implemented in diverse aspects of industrial activity. This analysis makes it possible to identify the features needed for plants to move to a higher level as well as those impeding such growth.

The infrastructure features that might facilitate entrepreneurial processes were defined on the basis of a preliminary analysis of all the sample variables. The distribution of the indicator and that of the simple correlations between it and other indicators were examined. Each of the indicators describing the 514 plants in the sample was defined as dichotomous, distinguishing between a higher and lower level of entrepreneurship. The indicators relate to the seven major areas of activity as defined in this study (see Table 6.1).

The way in which a factory is run is a major aspect of the entrepreneurial process. Most plants in the Arab economy lack an established management, and in many cases the owner performs the functions of manager, production worker, salesman, and comptroller. The institution of management exists, in fact, in only 17 percent of the plants, and in only 11 percent is it in the hands of a professional manager. The existence of a separate management level manned by at least one professional would seem to be a necessary condition for ensuring the efficient and controlled running of factories on higher entrepreneurship levels. Accordingly, the lack of professional management and the performance of functions of different sorts by the plant head would seem to be an impeding factor for advancement to higher levels.

The organizational structure of most of the factories suggests a low level of complexity. The plant is not divided into departments; nor are the various stages of production carried out by different specialist divisions. The degree of expertise and professionalism is also low. Furthermore, in most cases the factory is not defined as an economic unit in itself, separate from the owner's other activities. Our study suggests that registration of the plant as a separate economic entity—an incorporated or public company—and the adoption of proper bookkeeping and management practices are necessary for the smooth operation of factories at higher levels of entrepreneurship. In fact, only 13 percent of the plants are defined as economic entities distinct from their owners' households, and in only one third was the division of labor anchored in the existence of separate departments.

A factory's ability to mobilize a trained work force, without relying on family connections, is a major factor in creating a high potential for the adoption of modern innovations and economic growth. When workers are hired from within the family or *hamula* (clan), the primary motivations are often not economic considerations, which place the good of the factory first. Giving preference to technicians, practical engineers, and university graduates who have received the proper training may encourage entrepreneurship on a higher level than can be found in plants where the work force consists of people with little formal education and who learn their trade primarily on the job. Of the 514 factories sampled, some 35 percent employed more than six workers. These include five factories with over 80 employees. Here the majority of the work force is recruited from sources outside the *hamula*. In contrast, plants employing less than 6 workers, and sewing shops employing up to 10 women, show a tendency to hire from within the *hamula*. In fact, in half of all the factories, over half of the workers are members of the owner's *hamula*. The tendency to hire from other *hamula* is strongest where a very low level of skill is required. Since most of the factories are of this sort, even when the majority of the work force comes from outside the *hamula*, most of the workers lack formal professional training. In only 12 percent of the plants is at least the manager, or one of his staff, a university graduate, practical engineer, or technician. Indeed, Arab workers in Arab industry have significantly less formal education than the total population of Arab workers. The lack of a professional work force is thus another feature liable to impede the development of industrial entrepreneurship in the Arab economy. What we might be seeing is a vicious circle: The low level of development of Arab industry thwarts its attempts to attract skilled professionals, while the lack of these professionals hinders the establishment of modern enterprises. It is no surprise, then, that Arab professionals prefer to seek work in Jewish industry, where they can use their professional skills and receive higher wages and better social benefits (Yiftachel, 1991).

As in other traditional economies in the first stages of integration in a modern market economy, the capital for Arab industry comes primarily from the personal savings of the entrepreneur and financial assistance from members of his extended family. The use of this source for capital naturally gives higher priority to family interests than to economic considerations. As a result, the entrepreneur's obligation to the extended family as his prime unit of solidarity affects his decisions in a variety of realms. Moreover, the amount of capital available from family savings, particularly in the case of a family of laborers, is limited. The figures reveal that only 15 percent of the plant owners relied on bank loans to set up their factories. Most of the households that did not seek significant bank financing mainly did so for a number of reasons: a high interest rate that might jeopardize the plant's future; inability to provide the financial collateral needed for a loan; uncertainty about the future success of the business and the concurrent ability to return the loan; and lack of faith in banks as a mechanism for raising capital.

The level of technology in Arab industry is, to a large extent, dependent on the capital investment and constitutes a major factor in the emergence of industrial entrepreneurship. Three main aspects were examined in this regard: the quality of machinery purchased; the existence of a system of quality control; and the use of computers. Despite their limited access to capital, many plants succeeded in acquiring new machinery on a level of sophistication equivalent to that in Jewish enterprises of similar size. Only about one quarter of the factories purchased secondhand or renovated machinery. Quality control represents a necessary condition for breaking into markets beyond the Arab settlement. Public institutions and private companies in the Jewish sector are reluctant to purchase products that do not bear the seal of the Standards Institute. With the exception of only 9 percent, the Arab industrialists either did not fully appreciate the importance of this approval (reflecting the existence of quality control) or complained that the costs involved in obtaining it put it beyond their reach. The use of computers reflects a desire to organize plant management and/or production in a systematic and controlled manner. Here, too, only about 11 percent of the factories introduced computers into their management of production and/or labor. Thus, the lack of quality control and computerization may constitute a major obstacle to the emergence of higher levels of entrepreneurship.

The first condition for industrial development on higher investment levels is the existence of industrial zones allocated in outline plans (statutory town plan). Small, simple plants can exist in residential areas.   However, more advanced factories require an appropriate industrial infrastructure and the security that their investment in permanent facilities will be protected by the outline plan, which has the force of legal statute.   The present level of development of the physical infrastructure is extremely low for all the enterprises in the sample, with some 25 percent having no paved access road or regular water supply.   Only just over 10 percent of the factories in Arab settlements are located in regulated industrial zones that offer access to industrial land.   The problem of access to land for industry generates the need for a real estate market that enables a large number of potential entrepreneurs who do not own appropriate land to purchase or rent it. Around two thirds of the plants in Arab settlements were built on land inherited by their owners, and only one third of land that was purchased or leased.   The relatively low number of land purchases and rentals is an indicator of the limited proportions of the real estate market and the low availability of land for potential entrepreneurs.

The structure of the plants' business relations was found to be more highly developed than anticipated from the accepted model of traditional economies being integrated into a market economy.   The majority of factories maintain regular contact with most of their suppliers and customers, although these relationships are seldom guaranteed in long-term contracts.   Only some 20 percent of the plants stated that their purchases and sales were made as opportunities presented themselves.   Sales of the industrial products of traditional plants are restricted to the local markets of *hamula* and settlement.   Entrance into new markets requires larger scale production, marketing mechanisms, and a reputation.   The challenge facing Arab manufacturers is to break into the regional markets in neighboring Arab settlements, the regional markets of neighboring Jewish settlements in peripheral areas of the country' markets in the major urban centers of Israel, and international markets.   Except for a few cases, Arab industry has yet to reach international markets.   Entrance into regional markets and Jewish towns, however, is expanding steadily, and therefore the percentage of sales to the Jewish market was chosen as a representative indicator.   About one half of the factories sell over three quarters of their output to local markets, while the other half sell over one quarter to Jewish markets.

Identification of the infrastructures supporting the different levels of entrepreneurship was performed by means of the qualitative analysis method known as Q analysis.   This method makes it possible to identify the internal organization of complex structures without any prior assumptions and on an unlimited number of dimensions.   The infrastructure variables are arranged so that on each level of entrepreneurship, the necessary conditions for supporting that level are revealed.   In addition, it is also possible to examine the degree to which the infrastructure indicators constitute a combined set in a single structure or split up into substructures, differentially supporting the variable of total investments

(Atkin, 1974; Gaspar & Gould, 1981). Each analysis highlights the order in which the infrastructures appear at the various stages in the rise in total investments and the identification of those infrastructures found to have considerable weight in a plant's advance to a higher level of entrepreneurship.

STRUCTURAL CHARACTERISTICS

This section focuses on analysis of the hierarchical structure of Arab entrepreneurship. The infrastructures required for industrial entrepreneurship to rise to higher levels of investment are presented in a Q analysis with 15 entrepreneurial dimensions (see Table 6.2). These are divided into four steps, which also represent the different levels of total investment in the plant, from low to high. The various infrastructure indicators are listed opposite the dimension in which their existence becomes a major condition for the implementation of entrepreneurship on higher levels.

The entrepreneurship structure indicates that while no single infrastructure feature alone constitutes a necessary condition for plant growth, its existence increases the probability that a plant will succeed in rising to a higher level. Such success is measured by means of the centrality coefficient. Values approximating 1 signify that the given infrastructure indicator is a necessary condition for plant growth, while values approximating 0 signify that the indicator may increase the probability of success but is not a necessary condition for it. Statistical analysis revealed the centrality coefficients to be relatively weak, although several infrastructure indicators (sales, purchases, divisions, and water) had a greater effect than others on the plant's chances of growing beyond the level of entrepreneurship possible without their existence (centrality coefficients of 0.3 and 0.4). Furthermore, the structure of the entrepreneurship scale did not indicate division into sub-structures related to a rise on the scale. The existence of sub-structures might have suggested that certain groups of plants advance by following alternative channels of industrial growth. We can therefore conclude that the sets of infrastructures presented in Table 6.2 affect the chances for growth of all plants in a similar fashion. In each of the four groups of plants, which represent different levels of investment, several infrastructures actualized at this level emerged together. The more infrastructures in each group to which a plant has access, the better its chances of rising to a higher level of entrepreneurship.

As shown in Table 6.2, about two thirds of the plants display a low entrepreneurship level, and only 2 percent achieved the highest level. The latter are large modern factories fully integrated into the national economy. The remainder divide more or less equally between the two moderate groups.

Dimensions 14 and 15 indicate a lack of minimal infrastructure conditions, except connection to the electricity grid and the purchase of simple machinery. The continued existence of plants on these dimensions suggests that there are still cottage industries in Arab settlements. These are characteristically located on the

Table 6.2
Industrial Entrepreneurship Scale

Dimension	Level of Investments	Infrastructure Indicators	Percent of plants
15 14 13 12 11 10 9 8	Low	Purchasing Roads, Water, Machinery, Sales	67
7 6 5 4 3	Moderate Low	*Hamula* Markets Computers, Employees, Departments, Land	15
2 1	Moderate High	Management, Professionals, Ownership, Location	16
0	High	Bank, Quality, Manager	2
Total			100

ground floor of a residence or in an old building within the residential area. Working methods are simple, and the enterprise relies primarily on the family for its work force, markets, financing, and management. In addition, production technologies are old-fashioned and there is no regulated quality control, production divisions, or professional management. Furthermore, the plants lack basic infrastructures, such as a paved access road and running water. To rise to the moderate-low level of entrepreneurship, the plant must introduce three types of infrastructures. The first are fundamental physical infrastructures such as running water and access roads, which enable the steady receipt and unloading of raw materials and the marketing of finished products. The second consists of reliable and efficient machinery. The third requires basing both supply of raw materials and marketing on contractual relations.

The most prominent indicator in terms of the strength of its effect on a plant's chances for growth at this stage is the volume of sales deriving from contractual agreements (centrality coefficient 0.4). Casual business relations are possible for small enterprises in metropolitan centers where demands are large. However, in Arab settlements the *hamula*'s purchasing power is limited, and itinerant buyers do not often appear. Since these plants are located in outlying areas where the population's purchasing power is extremely limited and can not ensure a minimal economic base, contractual business relations are even more vital.

Hence, the entrepreneurship scale has four ranks, and the move from one to the next requires the entrepreneur to introduce a number of infrastructure indicators. The move up to the level of moderate-low demands changes in patterns of production. First, if a plant's work force is to grow (particularly if the workers are unskilled laborers employed at low wages), workers must be recruited from outside the *hamula*. The increase in the size of the work force is reflected in a reduction in the percent of *hamula* members (Dimension 7) and a rise in the total number of workers to more than six (Dimension 5). The increase in the work force to this level requires that the entrepreneur break into broader markets, both regional Arab and Jewish, and that he divide the labor in the plant into departments, with different employees specializing in the different stages of production and marketing. Entrepreneurs seeking to rise on the scale must also deal with the problem of lack of land. It is often difficult to continue to work on the ground floor of a residence, which does not allow room to expand or sufficient space for vehicles loading and unloading raw materials and finished products. The lack of land for industry offered by the meager real estate market in the Arab sector represents a critical obstacle for entrepreneurs who do not own appropriate land and wish to develop their plants to a moderate-high or high level on the entrepreneurship scale.

The transition to the moderate-high level of entrepreneurship generally requires the introduction of four additional infrastructure conditions. First is the obvious need for the plant to relocate in an approved industrial zone anchored in a legal outline plan. Physical infrastructures naturally include the buildings needed for industrial activity on the moderate-high level. The noise, pollution, and other disturbances generated by such a plant make it impossible for its owners to continue to operate efficiently in a residential area. Even in improvised areas at the edges of a settlement, there is always the risk that the authorities will force the factory to cease operations because of local bylaws. Second, enterprises on the moderate-high level generally demand that the entrepreneur protect himself financially by registering the factory as an incorporated or public company. Third, executives must be appointed. Finally, at this level it is important to hire professional workers who have been trained as managers or skilled laborers at appropriate institutions.

The transition to the high level of entrepreneurship—reflecting full integration into the Israeli economy—entails the implementation of four necessary conditions. First, the factory's operations have now expanded to such an extent that family savings together with profits are no longer sufficient to finance the investments needed for plant growth. Therefore, bank credit must now become the major source of financing operations and development. Second, professional management, even if it means hiring executives from outside the family, is essential in dealing with the complexities of running a modern industrial plant. Third, advanced methods of quality control must be introduced. The ability to maintain high-level quality control is related both to the nature of management and to issues of financing. Our interviews with entrepreneurs revealed that the seal of the Standards Institute on their products was a prerequisite for their entrance into new markets, where personal acquaintance and trust between the manufacturer and the consumer no longer apply. Nevertheless, for many entrepreneurs the further development of their plants was blocked by the lack of quality control mechanisms, unawareness of the importance of this subject, or reluctance to raise the capital needed to introduce a modern system of quality control.

CHANGES IN THE STRUCTURE OF ENTREPRENEURSHIP

Since the early 1950s, there have been considerable changes in the nature of Arab factories and the features of the entrepreneurial environment in which they operate. Thus, for example, today one can expect the family unit to be more open to the changes required for its factory to adapt to the competitive conditions of a free market. Similarly, one can expect to see greater use of modern technology, including computers, with the emergence of a new generation of entrepreneurs. We would therefore anticipate that a division of the past 45 years into subperiods would reveal that the transition from one entrepreneurship level to the next would demand a different set of infrastructures in each period.

Differences were found between the growth potentials of factories according to the period of their establishment. Those founded in the early 1970s, during the first wave of rapid industrialization, have developed to the highest levels of entrepreneurship in Arab industry. In contrast, plants founded before 1965 are prominent on the lowest level of entrepreneurship. Only a few enterprises in this group showed sufficient growth potential to enable them to adopt innovations and rise to the highest level (see Table 6.3). The factories established in the past five years also display relatively low levels of entrepreneurship, with only two defined as belonging to the highest level.

These differences raise the question of why factories founded in the past five years do not display higher levels of entrepreneurship, since they could be expected to enjoy a relatively high level of sophistication. Moreover, why have most of the older plants founded before 1965 failed to modernize themselves and improve their entrepreneurship level? We suggest that the key to understanding the dynamics of the development of industrial initiatives in the Arab economy is allied to its nature as a family enterprise and the typical raising of capital from family sources. Plants founded before 1965 display a tendency to maintain traditional patterns of activity. Beyond the infrastructures which appear at the

Table 6.3
Level of Entrepreneurship by Year of Factory Foundation (percentage)

Year Founded	Before 1965	1971-1975	1988-1992
Entrepreneurship Level			
Low	69	52	73
Moderate-Low	25	20	8
Moderate-High	3	26	18
High	3	2	1
Total	100	100	100
Total—absolute numbers	32	51	119

lowest level of entrepreneurship—physical infrastructure, contractual business relations, and machinery—these plants show no inclination to advance to Dimension 4, where total investments already reach the moderate-high level. The transition from low to moderate-low investments appears to derive from an increase in the work force and the introduction of new machines in the production line, yet traditional work patterns are still maintained. These patterns were preserved in some 94 percent of the factories founded before 1965, in which more modern methods of management, organization, and financing were not adopted.

Our analysis reveals that for plants founded before 1965, the most striking obstacles to advancement to the moderate-high level are their inability to free themselves from the obligation to hire workers from within the *hamula* and the difficulty of breaking into markets outside the settlement, particularly the Jewish market (Table 6.4, Dimension 4). These two variables represent the primary conditions that must be realized in order for a factory to rise to the moderate-high level. The plants which did not develop are those which continued to recruit the bulk of their workers from the extended family and *hamula*, even when the total number of employees was more than six. The family character of the plant stifled any incentive to hire professional workers or introduce modern methods of management, organization, and control. These enterprises are characteristically located in residential areas on land inherited by the entrepreneur, who in most cases is unable to transfer his plant to a site outside the residential area or to an approved industrial zone. The family, which had initially been the primary factor

Table 6.4
Changes in the Structure of the Entrepreneurship Scale by Periods

Dim.	Entreprene-urship Level	Infrastructure Indicators		
		Before 1960	1971-1975	1988-1992
15 14			Roads 0.2 Purchasing 0.2	
13 12	Low	Roads, Water, Purchasing 0.3		Purchasing 0.3
11			Machinery, Sales, Water	
10		Sales		Machinery, Water, Sales 0.4
9 8		Employees 0.2 Machinery		Roads 0.2 Land
7			*Hamula*	*Hamula*
6			Computers	Markets
5	Moderate Low		Employees, Markets	Computers Departments Employees 0.3

Table 6.4, continued

4		*Hamula*, Markets	Departments	
3	Moderate High	Departments, Computers	Management, Land, Professionals,	Manager, Management, Ownership, Location
2		Management,	Ownership,	
1		Manager, Quality	Quality, Location	
0	High	Ownership, Professionals, Land, Bank	Manager, Bank	Bank 0.3 Quality
Not App-lied		Location		Professionals

Dim. = Dimension

Note: The figures in the table represent the centrality coefficient of the given infrastructure. When no figure is given, the value of the centrality coefficient is 0.1.

encouraging the industrial venture, now seems to become a factor impeding its rise to the moderate-high level of entrepreneurship.

The factories established in the past five years show the opposite trend. Even those characterized by low total investments have adopted relatively advanced infrastructures, such as the hiring of workers from other *hamula*; entrance into markets outside the settlement, including those in the Jewish sector; and the use of computers in management. When total investments reached the moderate-high level, the work force increased to more than six laborers per plant and the plant was divided into departments. For this group, the major obstacle to continued development is the lack of the following infrastructures: location in an industrial zone anchored in an outline plan; modern professional management; quality control procedures; and, most particularly, bank financing. The data suggest that these factories have a high potential for rapid growth since they have introduced most of the necessary infrastructures.

Our interviews indicate that for the majority of plants established since the 1970s, one of the primary impediments to advancement to the higher levels of entrepreneurship concerns the patterns of raising capital. To this day, most of the seed capital, even for enterprises owned by the generation born after 1948 into the realities of the Israeli economy, comes from personal savings and the extended family. The extent of such capital is inherently limited and only allows for the establishment of plants on a relatively low level of entrepreneurship. Over the years, many entrepreneurs display a strong tendency to invest in the development and modernization of their factories by means of capital deriving from profits. It therefore follows that those enterprises established in recent years, unlike those founded in the early 1970s, have not yet managed to set aside sufficient funds to invest in the development of new initiatives or to establish activities on higher levels.

Despite this situation, plants founded in the early 1970s display a strong tendency to develop to the moderate-high level (see Table 6.3). These factories grew at a time when the basic infrastructure already existed in most Arab settlements and a new generation of industrial entrepreneurs had emerged. These entrepreneurs were high school graduates familiar with the patterns of activity in the larger Israeli economy. The fact that they have been operating for quite some time has enabled them to set aside funds from their profits and invest them in expansion. As their enterprises grew, these entrepreneurs incorporated innovations in various realms of plant activity and learned to exploit the potential of existing infrastructures more efficiently. As a result, the transition to moderate-low investments occurred at Dimension 8 rather than at Dimension 6, as it did in the other two periods.

Between the different periods, major changes in the availability or scarcity of several infrastructures occurred. The most extreme change took place with regard to the entrepreneur's ability to make use of land he had not inherited. In the 1960s, only one factory was located on land belonging to the Israel Lands Administration, while virtually all the others were erected on land the entrepreneur had inherited from his parents. Ninety-five percent of these were located on the ground floor of a residence. These factories continued to follow traditional patterns of activity, and their limited capital did not allow for the purchase of land or the development of the infrastructures needed to establish them on a sound footing. The indicator of land therefore appears as Dimension 0 for the years before 1965. In contrast, for recent years, land appears as Dimension 8. In other words, the ability to purchase land becomes a necessary condition for development of entrepreneurship on the moderate level and above. Furthermore, the development of a plant on the moderate level or above is impossible, or at least encounters severe difficulties, in densely populated residential areas. The fact that about one quarter of the factories managed to develop to such levels during this period indicates the emergence of a real estate market in Arab settlements. In recent years, the proportion of factories erected on land acquired in this market has grown, and in several cases land has even been leased from its owners. We may thus assume that the further availability of land in industrial zones, for sale or long-term lease, is a major condition likely to encourage industrial initiatives in Arab settlements.

Appreciable changes also took place in the variables of *hamula* and markets. The plants established before 1965 relied to a large extent on the resources of the *hamula*, which provided the entrepreneur with both workers and guaranteed markets. In most cases, the factory's employees were the entrepreneur's brothers or cousins, and the bulk of its output was sold to members of the *hamula* and related *hamula*. Supporting this claim is the fact that entrance into broader markets and the hiring of workers from outside the *hamula* occurred only in plants where the entrepreneurship level is moderate-high, or on Dimension 4. On the other hand, over the past five years even small plants on a low level of investments (Dimension 7) have entered markets outside the settlement and begun to hire workers from outside the *hamula*. This trend can be interpreted as a breaking out of traditional industrial patterns and adaptation to modern forms of activity.

To conclude, the set of indicators impeding the incorporation of modern methods and therefore the rise to higher levels of entrepreneurship is concentrated in three primary areas. First is the difficulty of raising enough capital from the banks at favorable terms. Second is the lack of approved industrial zones which offer a modern infrastructure at reasonable financing terms. This is particularly important in the initial stage of erecting the factory, when it is not yet earning profits and the entrepreneur does not have the funds for expensive infrastructures. This problem was solved in development towns by the participation of government-owned companies in the financing of the infrastructure and construction of industrial buildings for rent to entrepreneurs. No such activity exists in Arab settlements, where the local authorities, lacking development capital, are unable to develop a minimal infrastructure in industrial zones. The third area displaying impeding factors is the structure of management and its implications for production quality. In the absence of professional managers, there is no awareness in the factory of the importance of advanced manufacturing characteristics, such as registration as an incorporated company, professional regulated bookkeeping, or quality control procedures and the seal of the Standards Institute as a prerequisite for entrance into the ordered and established Israeli and international economies.

DIFFERENCES BETWEEN INDUSTRIAL BRANCHES AND ETHNIC GROUPS

The model of entrepreneurship displays a uniform structure according to which the entrepreneurship scale presented earlier is valid for most factories. Nonetheless, it may be assumed that (1) some industrial branches displayed faster processes of growth and introduction of modern production methods; and (2) the order in which new thresholds are actualized in the various infrastructures is not

Table 6.5
Level of Entrepreneurship by Economic Branch

Percent of plants in Branch	Entrepreneurship Level					
	Low	Moderate Low	Moderate High	High	Total	Total Absolute number
Food	27	54	18	1	100	119
Textiles	0	20	65	15	100	71
Wood	21	61	16	2	100	102
Constr. materials	31	32	29	6	100	147
Metals	19	68	9	4	100	44
Printing	0	75	21	4	100	28
Rubber & Plastics	14	61	22	3	100	36
Other	0	72	9	19	100	11

identical for all branches due to their differing characteristics. Analysis of these differences makes it possible to asses the contribution of the various branches to the introduction of innovations in the different areas of industrial entrepreneurship as well as to discover the infrastructure needs particular to each branch. Our analysis revealed that the branches of food, wood, and metal were more prominent on the lowest entrepreneurship level than other branches. Over 80 percent of the plants in these fields achieved only a low or moderate-low level of incorporation of industrial infrastructures. In contrast, the construction branch displays a striking split, with enterprises on the lowest level as well as about one third of the plants developing to the highest level (see Table 6.5).

In the textile and clothing industry, some two thirds of the factories achieved the moderate-high level, with 15 percent attaining the highest level. This means that although the textile and clothing industry is dependent on Jewish-owned parent companies and pays its workers a relatively low wage, it provides an opportunity for Arab industry to establish higher levels of entrepreneurship. Under the influence of their Jewish parent companies, textile and clothing plants stand out particularly for adopting modern methods of management, labor, and quality control, thereby aiding the proliferation of these methods throughout Arab industry. It follows that the textile plants may play a major role in encouraging patterns of industrial growth in the Arab sector if their entrepreneurs can cast off the chains of the parent company and if entrepreneurs in other branches adopt the methods they have introduced. The category "Other" also includes two electronics and diamond factories on the highest entrepreneurship level.

There are marked differences in the order in which the different branches introduce and adopt entrepreneurial infrastructures. Prominent in the interbranch variability are five features of the entrepreneurial infrastructure, the most outstanding of which are the number of workers and the percent of workers hired from outside the *hamula*. The textile and clothing, and food branches employ a large number of workers even at the lower entrepreneurship levels. These are labor-intensive branches which make relatively little use of outside capital. They rely on virtually guaranteed markets, whether as subcontractors for Jewish corporations (textiles and clothing) or as suppliers to the local market (food). The low wages paid the workers makes these branches less attractive employers than the textile factories in neighboring development towns, so they are reserved primarily for women unwilling to work outside their settlement, even if these women belong to a different *hamula* than the entrepreneur. The relatively large size of the textile and clothing plant and the need to maintain strict quality standards regularly checked by the parent company compel such a factory to adopt the accepted management and quality control practices of industries in the Jewish sector. The food plants, which rely primarily on Arab markets, sell 82 percent of their output to this market, some two thirds of which goes to Arab settlements outside the region of the plant. Their contribution to marketing to the Jewish sector is extremely small in comparison to the other branches.

The construction branch is distinguished by the hiring of *hamula* members in relatively small enterprises. The total capital invested in the plant is on the high side, although it is lower in proportion to plant size than in the food industry. Building materials factories require a physical infrastructure of roads and water (an integral part of their production process) and a relatively large area in which concrete blocks or floor tiles can be dried and stored. Moreover, these plants represent an environmental nuisance. In view of these features and pressure brought to bear by the authorities and the residents, these plants tend to be located on the edges of a settlement rather than in a residential area.

The ethnic affiliation of the entrepreneur is a major factor in determining the growth potential of an Arab factory. The Christian Arabs and Druze have certain advantages when competing for the opportunity for industrial start-ups and the incorporation of modern methods. The characteristics of the Christian community—a higher level of education and smaller families—afford them better

Table 6.6
Distribution of Industrial Plants by Total Investments and Ethnic Group

Ethnic Group	Total Investments, 1988-1992				Total	Mean Score
	Low	Moderate Low	Moderate High	High		
Muslim	60	21	16	3	100	1.62
Christian	61	17	20	2	100	1.63
Druze	70	9	17	4	100	1.55

Table 6.7
Distribution of Industrial Plants by Level of Entrepreneurship and Ethnic Group

Ethnic Group	Entrepreneurship Index				Total	Mean Score
	Low	Moderate Low	Moderate High	High		
Muslim	57	22	16	5	100	1.69
Christian	60	8	26	6	100	1.78
Druze	54	17	20	9	100	1.84

chances of saving money for investment along with the training needed to establish factories on the higher levels of entrepreneurship (see Table 6.6).

Members of the Druze community are closer to the Moslems in terms of demographic behavior and education. However, they have a certain preferential status regarding government aid. The Israeli government has recognized the Druze villages as development settlements and has begun assisting in laying physical infrastructures for industry. Support for these claims can be found in the distribution of factories by ethnic group and entrepreneurship level (Table 6.7).

The index of the average entrepreneurship scale for Muslims lags somewhat behind the index for Christians and Druze. Table 6.7 shows that the Druze constructed entrepreneurial infrastructures with a higher growth potential than the other two groups, with the growth potential for the Christians only slightly behind them. It must be stated, however, that intergroup variability is relatively small and is explained primarily by the fact that a few plants on the higher entrepreneurship levels are located in Druze and Christian settlements.

These trends change if we compare the actual total investments of the three ethnic groups between 1988 and 1992. For this period, the difference between the groups is not at all significant. This is true despite the fact that total investments for Druze were comparatively somewhat low, although the infrastructures in Druze factories indicate a slight advantage in terms of potential. This phenomenon is difficult to explain except in terms of the geographical factor of proximity to metropolitan centers. The factories located in Western Galilee show the highest entrepreneurship levels in the Arab sector, while those in smaller and more remote settlements in Upper and Central Galilee are characterized by the lowest levels in the sector. A more detailed examination would be needed, however, to confirm this hypothesis.

The major advantages for industries in Druze villages stem from the availability of land and industrial zones for potential entrepreneurs. As a result of government support, even entrepreneurs operating on relatively low entrepreneurship levels typically purchased land for their plants in industrial zones, as shown in Table 6.8. Moreover, Table 6.8 reveals the Druze to be less reliant than the other groups on workers from their own *hamula*. On the other hand, Druze villages suffer more severely from the problem of access to water. The difficulty of ensuring a regular water supply to many of the factories probably derives from their location in peripheral mountainous regions.

In comparison to the Druze factories, the Christian-owned plants are characterized by an advanced system of organization and management reflected in a separate management, division into departments, and contractual agreements for sales and purchasing. It would thus seem that the Christian Arabs are distinguished by better organizational and managerial skills in the entrepreneurial process. This finding is in line with the claims in the literature that formal training in the field in which the entrepreneur operates, or even in a different field, contributes considerably to success because of greater familiarity with the various aspects of entrepreneurship (Cooper & Dunkelberg, 1986).

Only a small number of plants have thus far been founded in Bedouin settlements. Of these, only four were included in our sample, and they are characterized by a low entrepreneurship level. The Bedouins, who are undergoing a sedentarization process, indeed lag behind the other Arab groups with regard to industrial development. Most of the Bedouin townships are fairly new and have had a physical infrastructure (such as electricity) for just a few years. Furthermore, the Bedouins' level of education and professional training is lower than that of the other Arab sectors. Industrialization of the Bedouin townships, with their high rate of unemployment and lack of internal sources of employment, thus poses one of the greatest challenges to the industrialization of Arab settlements.

Table 6.8
Scale of Entrepreneurial Infrastructures by Ethnic Group

Dimension	Infrastructure Indicators by Ethnic Group		
	Muslim	Christian	Druze
9	–	Purchasing	–
8	Water, Purchasing	Employees, Machinery, Water, Sales	*Hamula*
7	Employees, Machinery	Markets	Machinery, Purchasing
6	*Hamula*, Roads, Markets	Roads	Land, Roads
5	Computers, Sales	*Hamula*, Computers	Employees, Computers, Water, Markets, Sales
4	–	Departments, Management	Location
3	Departments	Ownership	Professionals, Ownership
2	Professionals, Land, Bank	–	Departments, Manager, Management, Quality
1	Ownership, Management, Quality	Manager, Professionals, Quality, Location, Land, Bank	Capital
0	Manager, Location	–	–

CONCLUSIONS

Small factory entrepreneurship is generally prey to a wide range of constraints and restrictions (Felsenstein & Schwartz, 1993; OECD, 1990). This is particularly true in the case of an ethnic minority. Risk-reducing institutions in the economy are not usually sensitive enough to the needs of small plants. This problem comes to the fore especially with regard to the activities of financing institutions (Binks, 1979), the difficulty of obtaining access to infrastructures suited to the particular needs of small industries (Department of the Environment, 1988), the lack of sufficient managerial skills (Townroe & Mallalieu, 1990), and the lack of contacts with and information from external bodies (Rothwell & Dodgson, 1991). Different sorts of problems are typically encountered at the various stages of entrepreneurial development. In the initial stages, the factories find it difficult to obtain collateral for loans, so capital is raised from family resources (Markusen & Teitz, 1983). In addition, the need for information and communication lines to centers of information and assessment, while essential, is beyond the reach of most small entrepreneurs (Lawton Smith, Dickson, & Lloyd Smith, 1991). At this stage, the plants also suffer from the difficulty of establishing themselves in industrial zones, both because these zones lack the flexibility necessary to adapt to the needs of small plants and because of the high cost of the services they provide (Nabarro et al., 1986). The larger the enterprise grows, the greater the importance of professional and knowledgeable management, especially in the advanced stages, when the plant enters wider markets and must compete with large corporations in the economy (A.C.O.S.T., 1990). At this point, a knowledge of marketing, cost accounting, quality control, and warehousing techniques becomes a necessary condition for ensuring the factory's ability to compete, and indeed for its survival.

Applying this theoretical discussion to the findings presented in this chapter leads to several important conclusions. First, parallel to the progression of small factories in general, qualitatively different stages can be found in the development of Arab industry, with each stage demanding structural modifications in both the functioning of the entrepreneur and the patterns of activity in the entrepreneurial environment. In fact, the past 40 years provide little evidence that Arab industry has developed according to Vernon's (1966) deterministic model. At the same time, Nanjundan's (1987) model seems not to be sensitive enough to the four stages of restructuring identified in our model. Most plants have remained small in size. Only the few most progressive do compete with large corporations, while the rest complement these corporations by their activities. Therefore, we made use of an analysis that starts with a statistical examination of a wide range of industrial activities without any preconceived notions and without forcing it to adhere to assumptions derived from general models. This enabled us to discover basic processes in Arab entrepreneurship, even if it should turn out that on the whole it complies with the general model. Second, the difficulties confronting Arab entrepreneurs due to the size of their plants and their position on the fringe of the Israeli economy are similar to the general model of difficulties facing small-scale initiatives. The major difference is that Arab entrepreneurs belong to an ethnic minority, a fact which makes it even harder for them to deal with these difficulties. On the other hand, however, their minority status encourages them to call on traditional institutions, such as the extended family, for help in founding a business and even in running and expanding industrial enterprises. The analysis also reveals that when alternative institutions in the modern economy are offered them, Arab entrepreneurs are soon able to adapt to them.

Arab industry has developed primarily by means of entrepreneurial investments from family capital raised from personal savings, the assistance of the extended family, and profits. As a result, growth is slow and gradual, and entrepreneurs take care to reduce the risk they are willing to bear for purposes of expansion. Entrepreneurship itself has developed in four main stages. At each stage, characterized by increasing levels of investment, the entrepreneur makes use of a different set of infrastructures. Success in incorporating these infrastructures ensures the conditions required to rise to the next highest level, while failure to apply even some of these necessary infrastructures reduces the probability of rise.

At the first stage after establishment of a factory, the primary challenge facing the entrepreneur is the struggle to survive while being willing to make do with low earnings. The regular supply of raw materials must first be ensured. The location of the plants in peripheral areas and their ownership by members of an ethnic minority distance them from the sources of raw materials. Thus, even at the initial stages, supply must be guaranteed by means of long-term agreements. Furthermore, the existence of an infrastructure of electricity, water, and roads, along with guaranteed customers (even if the volume of their purchases is small), is a prerequisite for the survival of a factory in the Arab periphery. At the founding stage, the entrepreneur is financially dependent largely on his relations for capital, workers, and market. In addition, the problem of the physical infrastructure is solved by locating the plant on the ground floor of a residence belonging to the extended family, which allocates the area to one of its members for his business.

The second stage is characterized by moving outside the boundaries of the family system, at least in part, although the family continues to play a major role both in lending support to the entrepreneur and in affecting his decision making. Plant growth is now reflected primarily in the hiring of additional workers (most from outside the *hamula*), a more formal organization of the labor into departments, and the use of computers for management and bookkeeping. Most importantly, at this stage the factory enters new markets outside the settlement.

At the third stage, the plant is placed on a firm footing and defined as a financial entity separate from its owners. As a result, an official management is appointed, and there is a need to hire skilled workers with a broader formal education, at least in the fields of management and marketing. There is increasing pressure to move the factory to an approved industrial zone, in which the investment in permanent facilities can be guaranteed for the long term and the plant can enjoy sufficient infrastructure and land.

At the final stage, the highest level, the factory begins to compete for national Jewish and Arab markets. Professional management, access to sources of information, a system of quality control, and bank financing are essential for handling the greater demand.

In historical terms, only a few plants founded before 1970 have managed to rise to the higher levels of entrepreneurship. The owners of most of these factories lacked the formal education and skills needed to expand into markets outside their settlements and to meet the organizational challenge. Alternatively, they lacked the capital required to take the necessary steps to move up to higher levels. Similarly, a considerable number of factories founded in the past five years have not had sufficient time to accumulate enough capital to rise on the entrepreneurship scale. This is true despite the fact that their owners have acquired the infrastructures needed to rise and many have the personal qualifications for facing this challenge. For them, it is the difficulty of raising capital that impedes advancement. Those plants that have risen to the highest levels have done so because they adopted modern methods of management and quality control procedures and hired a large work force. Most of the enterprises in this category are textile and clothing plants and sewing shops, although the category also includes a number of factories in construction and other branches. In the textile and clothing industry, the help of the parent company became a facilitating factor for growth, although this came at the cost of the factory's independence.

Further development of Arab industry through the incorporation of the features of higher entrepreneurship levels has been blocked by four major factors from among the seven entrepreneurial aspects examined. The most prominent of these are a lack of approved industrial zones offering a physical infrastructure and available land; limited access to investment capital; and lack of professional management with good access to information networks that provide an assessment of the state of the economy and decision making on the national level. In addition, difficulties in breaking into Jewish and international markets represent another factor impeding the rise of industrial enterprises to higher levels.

The remaining factors had a marginal effect on the development of Arab industry. Entrepreneurs displayed an ability to incorporate the technologies needed for their plants to produce at the volume they are capable of and to organize production to deal with the appropriate level of complexity and volume. Similarly, although the work force lacks sufficient training and formal education, this is due to the plants' inability to offer wages high enough to attract skilled workers rather than the scarcity of such workers in the Arab sector.

Chapter 7

Capital and Human Resources

This chapter examines the effects of the major variables of capital and human resources on the development of Arab industrialization and entrepreneurship. Our discussion focuses on the central variables of industrial activity, such as the raising of capital, the organization and management of production, the recruitment of labor, and the use of technology. Each of these factors may present Arab entrepreneurs with obstacles that inhibit their mobility on the entrepreneurship scale (as shown in Chapter 6).

Our model of entrepreneurship shows that the difficulty of raising investment capital is a major impediment to entrepreneurial growth. While on the three lowest levels of the scale entrepreneurs need only draw on their personal savings and plant profits for capital, the rise to the fourth level is impossible without substantial bank loans. Thus, although lack of capital may slow plant growth on the first three levels, it will entirely preclude the rise to the fourth.

Similarly, professional management based on extensive know-how and information becomes a prerequisite only on the fourth level of entrepreneurial development. Until this level, the plant may be managed by a skilled laborer also involved in production, assisted by a bookkeeper. However, the third level of entrepreneurship requires that the plant be defined as a financial entity separate from its owners, that work be divided into departments and the appropriate employees hired, and that production be streamlined.

CAPITAL AND INVESTMENTS

To a large extent, the availability of capital determines the volume of a factory's business, its ability to incorporate new methods into the various aspects of its activities, and the nature of the resources it can employ in its production process. On the whole, in the initial stages of development, industrial firms suffer from a lack of capital (and thus also of technology), on the one hand, and benefit from a relatively large supply of labor, on the other. The willingness of financial institutions to aid the entrepreneur is dependent on how well he can cope with numerous difficulties. The large banks are reluctant to provide assistance to small businesses in general (Felsenstein & Schwartz, 1993; Haidar, 1993) and are even less likely to do so in the case of plants located in Arab settlements. In view of this lack of financial support and risk-reducing institutions, examination of the amount and sources of capital invested in Arab factories is of particular significance. The essential question here is whether a scale has been developed within Arab industry that is based on the degree of capital accumulation and the ability to invest in plant development.

The annual monetary value of a plant's sales volume is an indication of the extent of its activities, its size, and its financial strength. It is this annual volume, determined in the present study by our interviews with the entrepreneurs, with which our discussion is concerned. Although we may assume that these estimates are skewed downward to a certain degree, they enable us to draw general conclusions about the volume of the plant's activities and the differences between branches with respect to the use of capital as a production factor. The findings, presented in Table 7.1, indicate that the annual sales volume of some 35 percent of the factories is below NIS100,000, and that of around 80 percent is below half a million shekels. The volume of only some 6 percent of the enterprises exceeds one million Israeli shekels.

The figures in Table 7.1 enable division of the various industrial branches into three groups according to the monetary value of sales volume. The printing and food branches stand out for the large proportion of factories with a low annual volume. The sales of over one half of the plants in these branches are under NIS100,000 (at the time of the survey, US$1 = NIS2.5, approximately), while the annual volume of less than 10 percent in this group reached over NIS700,000. The second group consists of the branches of woodworking, rubber and plastics, and, to a certain degree, metals. In this group, about one half of the plants show a volume between NIS100,000 and 500,000, while the percent of factories with a volume over NIS500,000 is similar to that in the first group. The third group contains the construction and textile and clothing industries, with more than one third of the factories having an annual volume of over NIS700,000. The total number of plants with a volume exceeding NIS700,000, thereby defining them as large enterprises in the Arab sector, is only 30. Of these, over 40 percent are in construction and about 23 percent are in the textile and clothing industry. These figures underscore the fact that Arab industry is still characterized by a large number of small enterprises, some of which have maintained their size since the 1970s, while others have grown over the years as a result of a rise on the entrepreneurship scale. Most of the large and more advanced factories were founded in the 1970s and 1980s, and their steady growth derived primarily from repeated investment in development.

Table 7.1
Sales Volume in NIS by Industrial Branch, 1992 (percentages)

Sales Volume NIS	Branch									Total
	Printing	Food	Metals	Wood	Rubber & plastics	Textiles	Cons. materials	Others		
To 100,000	57	50	42	35	37	23	16	42		35
101,000 - 300,000	18	25	22	35	28	23	22	33		26
301,000 - 500,000	21	17	25	15	26	17	27	8		20
501,000 - 1,500,000	4	4	9	13	3	26	22	0		13
Over 1,500,000	0	4	2	2	6	11	13	17		6
Total	100	100	100	100	100	100	100	100		100
No. of plants	28	115	45	100	35	65	99	12		499

Capital investment in Arab industrial firms was assessed on the basis of owners' reports.   The most significant finding here is that some 90 percent of the entrepreneurs did invest in modernizing and expanding industrial activity over the past five years, between 1987 and 1992.   About 80 percent invested less than NIS150,000 in their plants, while some 12 percent invested between NIS150,000 and 500,000, and another 4 percent invested about one million shekels.   This means than many entrepreneurs actually doubled their investment in the course of the past five years.   These investments undoubtedly made it possible for a considerable proportion of the factories to introduce new methods into various aspects of their activities, in addition to remodeling or replacing old equipment. This trend is a sign of the prevailing optimistic entrepreneurial climate and the determination of these entrepreneurs to invest in the development and modernization of their plants. Their determination is particularly striking in view of the lack of capital and financial institutions willing to aid Arab entrepreneurs. In response to questions aimed at defining attitudes, the majority of entrepreneurs referred to a distinct difficulty in obtaining bank loans or credit at terms they could afford. In the personal interviews, over one half of the entrepreneurs stated that they would invest more in plant development if they could raise the necessary capital.   They expressed faith in their ability to market the potential increase in output and thus ensure a return on their investment if the costs of financing and collateral were lower.

Examination of the sources of capital supports the claim of a lack of capital for plant development.   Table 7.2 presents the different sources of initial capital and the proportion of entrepreneurs who sought capital from each source. Clearly, a given entrepreneur could (and in fact nearly all did) turn to more than one source to raise capital.   Table 7.2 indicates that in the case of 86 percent of the entrepreneurs, one of the sources for the initial capital needed to establish the plant was personal savings. In addition, 21 percent obtained capital from their father and brothers. Banks, the primary source of capital for modern economic enterprises, provided loans for only some 14 percent of the Arab entrepreneurs. The *hamula*–beyond the extended family–showed even less of a willingness to lend financial support to its members.

If we consider the proportion of each source of capital in the total initial investment, we find that in 70 percent and 45 percent of the cases, respectively, personal savings and savings from other extended family members constituted virtually the only source (91 to 100 percent of the investment). In one half of the cases in which brothers aided in establishing the enterprise, their personal savings represented almost the exclusive source of capital. This solution is especially common when the plant is owned in partnership by several brothers. The place of capital raised in the Jewish sector is of particular interest. For about 60 percent of the few plants financed in part by Jewish entrepreneurs, Jewish capital predominated. This occurred most frequently in textile and clothing factories, with the majority of the financing for sewing machines in the Arab enterprise

(percentages)**

Sources of Capital	% of Enterprises Employing Source	% of Capital from Source			
		91-100	51-90	1-50	Total
Personal savings	86	69	13	18	100
Father	7	18	9	79	100
Brothers	14	49	5	46	100
Other *hamula* members	2	45	0	55	100
Private individuals	3	4	20	76	100
Banks	14	23	17	60	100
Private individuals in Jewish sector	2	60	0	40	100

coming from the parent company. The limited contribution of the father, the banks, and private investors is also reflected in the fact that even when these sources were tapped, they generally accounted for less than 50 percent of the total initial capital investment. These figures bear out the claim that the banks do not serve as the primary source of capital for initial investments.

Reliance on personal savings and those of other members of the extended family for investment capital is typical of an economy in the early stages of development as well as of ethnic minorities. Developmental aspects can be understood in light of the fact that Arab society is composed primarily of salaried workers, so that the amount of capital that can be raised by the family is extremely limited. Since all the plants rely to a certain degree on kinship relations for financing, the possibility of raising more capital than can be provided by whatever several families are capable of saving is an obstacle for the development of large-scale industrial enterprises.

Table 7.3
Sources of Capital for Further Development (percentages)

Sources of Capital	% of Enterprises Employing Source	% of Capital From Source			
		91-100	51-90	1-50	Total
Personal savings	52	20	8	72	100
Plant profits	75	48	5	47	100
Father	1	25	25	50	100
Brothers	4	42	16	42	100
Other *Hamula* members	1	50	0	50	100
Private individuals	2	8	13	79	100
Banks	6	6	13	81	100
Private individuals in Jewish sector	2	75	0	25	100

Analysis of the sources of capital investment for the further development of existing plants, presented in Table 7.3, reveals that here, too, the proportion of financing obtained from banks and private financial sources is small. The figures in Table 7.3 reveal that banks participated in the financing of some 6 percent of the enterprises, and in about 81 percent of these their contribution represented less than 50 percent of the total investment. This finding bolsters our contention that most entrepreneurs refrain from the use of bank loans for industrial development, deterred by the risks involved, even when they can provide the required guarantee. Nonetheless, for the majority of factories, profits and personal savings remain the primary sources of investment capital for replacing equipment and for expansion. The modernization of some three quarters of the plants was financed by profits.

For one half of these, profits constituted virtually the only source of capital, while for the other half they were of marginal weight. Personal savings were used to finance the modernization of half of the firms but were only a marginal source of capital in most of these cases. Other factors played an even smaller part in financing plant development.

Our analysis indicates signs of a hierarchy emerging in Arab industry, with factories whose annual sales volume is over one million Israeli shekels at the top and those whose volume does not exceed several tens of thousands at the bottom. Nearly all the entrepreneurs expressed a strong commitment to invest in development, upgrading of equipment, and modernization. Indeed, the ratio between sales volume and investments demonstrates that many factories at least doubled the monetary value of their sales volume over the past five years, an indication both of dynamic growth and of the entrepreneurial climate in Arab industry. In view of this finding, it is particularly striking that most entrepreneurs are compelled to raise capital from personal and family sources and refrain from seeking the aid of financial institutions. The minimal exploitation of these sources, due to the relatively limited opportunities they offer, naturally affects the capacity for plant expansion and the consequent rise on the entrepreneurship scale.

LEVEL OF TECHNOLOGY

The term *level of technology* refers to the technology intrinsic to the product itself, to the human resources involved in its production, and to the production process (Bar-El, 1993). The first two aspects of this concept have been addressed in previous chapters. It is the third—the production process—in terms of intrinsic capital and technological sophistication that will be considered here.

Our survey revealed Arab industrial products to be either relatively simple standard items serving as intermediary products for the construction materials and textile industries or finished products in the branches of food, woodworking, and printing.   Factories producing items of high sophistication are virtually nonexistent.   Accordingly, Arab industrial enterprises have no research and development divisions and are not involved with hi-tech commodities such as computer components or electronic equipment. The Kadmani factories in Yirka, turning out metal products that require sophisticated welding, represent the most advanced level of Arab industry.

To examine the plants' level of sophistication, two measures were chosen: the use of computers and the existence of a system of quality control. In addition, factory owners were asked to rate the sophistication of their machinery in relation to plants of similar size in the same branch in the Jewish sector. Our analysis revealed that 67 percent of the Arab enterprises employed no computers whatsoever. In 23 percent, personal computers were used for management tasks, in most cases for bookkeeping and payroll, and infrequently for marketing as well. Only in 10 percent of the cases were computers employed in production, most often for management purposes. In only a very small number of plants did computers constitute a vital link in the production process itself.

Reliable quality control, ensuring the quality of the product and the maintenance of official standards, is a prerequisite for entrance into markets outside the settlement, especially those in the Jewish sector. In respect to this measure, Arab industry can be divided into three groups. The first, consisting of 23 percent of the plants, has no system of quality control at all. The second, 69 percent, is characterized by owners' claims of internal quality control. This means that the managers informally supervise the quality of their products, a system whose reliability is questionable. The third, and conspicuously smallest, groups report the existence of a separate department for quality control. The textile and clothing factories represent an exceptional category, with most maintaining quality control departments and quality assurance mechanisms. Since most of these enterprises work for Jewish customers and may even export some of their output, there is greater awareness of the importance of quality control in this industry, where it is, in fact, an integral part of the production process. Many entrepreneurs displayed difficulty in comprehending the crucial nature of quality control for breaking into markets outside the settlement. Others stated that they could not afford the cost involved in applying to the Standards Institute of Israel or establishing a reliable quality control department. The more sophisticated entrepreneurs, however, did recognize the importance of such a department as a condition for entrance into broader markets beyond the settlement.

Table 7.4 presents the plant owners' assessments of the level of their machinery as compared to that of similar factories in the Jewish sector. The results of the entrepreneurs' subjective assessments, as shown in Table 7.4, indicate that just over one half rated the level of sophistication of their machinery to be similar to that of their counterparts in the Jewish sector. Of the other half, two thirds believed the sophistication of their machinery to be lower than in similar Jewish enterprises, with only one third rating it higher. The assessment of a relatively higher level of technology is particularly apparent in the branches of food and woodworking, while the assessment of a lower level is most prominent in the metals industry. The owners of factories in the textiles, rubber, and plastics industries, on the other hand, rated the level of sophistication of their plants as similar to that of parallel enterprises in the Jewish sector with the greatest frequency.

Support for the claim that the level of technology in a considerable proportion of Arab factories does not fall below that of similar plants in the Jewish sector can be found in the fact that three quarters of the owners had purchased new machinery from among the best on the market. This trend is especially apparent in the construction materials industry, where owners stated that they had purchased the standard equipment for enterprises of their size. Another conspicuous trend in this branch was that during the past five years, many plants had replaced their old equipment with new machinery of a greater productive capacity, thereby reducing their work force. In contrast, in the textile and clothing industry there

Table 7.4
Assessment of Level of Technology as Compared to Similar Plants in the Jewish Sector, by Industrial Branch (percentages)

Branch	Level of Technology			
	Lower	Same	Higher	Total
Food	34	41	25	100
Textiles & Clothing	22	65	13	100
Wood	31	54	15	100
Construction Materials	29	60	11	100
Metals	47	44	9	100
Printing	33	52	15	100
Rubber & Plastics	31	63	6	100
Others	50	8	42	100
Total	16	52	16	100

is a clear preference to acquire relatively simple sewing machines that perform a small number of functions. In most cases, it was found that it is the parent companies which maintain the sophisticated machines that are capable of performing a wider range of sewing tasks.

In sum, our analysis reveals that although the level of sophistication of Arab factories is not the highest, in recent years Arab entrepreneurs have been making an effort to close the technological gap between them and the Jewish sector.

MANAGERIAL AND ORGANIZATIONAL STRUCTURE

The complexity of the managerial and organizational structure of a factory is a clear indication of its entrepreneurial level. Larger plants, characterized by a substantial capital investment and the manufacture of more sophisticated products, require a more complex organization and the employment of personnel specializing in management. Quality of management directly affects the ability

Table 7.5
Distribution of Factories by Type of Ownership and Industrial Branch (percentages)

Branch	Ownership			
	Private	Partnership	Corp.	Public Co.
Food and beverages	96	3	1	0
Textiles & clothing	62	10	26	2
Woodworking & wood products	92	2	6	0
Printing & publishing	96	4	0	0
Rubber & plastics	84	3	11	2
Construction materials	67	4	29	0
Basic metals	89	7	4	0
Others	83	0	9	8
Total	83	4	12	1

of the enterprise to survive in changing competitive conditions. In regard to Arab industry, the three major distinguishing features between plants with simple or complex structures are the nature of factory ownership; the degree of separation between management and other functions; and the degree of division into specialized departments.

Table 7.5 presents the results of the survey regarding plant ownership. According to these figures, 83 percent of the factories in Arab settlements are privately owned by a single entrepreneur, while another 4 percent are owned in partnership (usually two or three partners), most often by members of the same extended family. The distribution of ownership indicates that only 12 percent of the firms are registered as corporations (although privately owned), and less than 1 percent are public companies (e.g. Bolus Brothers and Kadmani Brothers). Thus, only a small number factories—under 100—are incorporated or public companies registered as separate entities from their owners. If we compare the industrial branches, we find that the percentage of private companies is relatively lower in the textile and construction materials industries (concrete blocks, stone, and cement). These branches contain a number of comparatively large factories, which demand a legally established separation between management and ownership.

A unit defined as a managerial division exists in only 17 percent of the firms. In the others, the plant owner is involved in management, marketing, and often even in production. When a plant is owned in partnership, management generally falls to one of the partners. Since the partners are invariably members of one extended family, management is usually in the hands of the father or eldest brother. Thus, in 97 percent of the factories, the owners are also managers. Nevertheless, there is a certain variance among the different branches. In the food and woodworking industries, the same person is both manager and owner in 90 percent of the plants. In contrast, in the textile and clothing industry, the manager of 15 percent of the factories is the owner, while in 7 percent he is a salaried employee. Similarly, there is a variance regarding the nature of management with respect to company registration. A distinct managerial level exists only in incorporated or public companies, although even in two thirds of these enterprises the sole owner of the plant is also its manager. In 20 percent of the firms registered as corporations or public companies, shareholders in the factory also participate in its management, while in another 9 percent the factory is managed by a hired professional.

Analysis of the connection between the nature of plant ownership and year of foundation, shown in Table 7.6, demonstrates certain progress in the attitude toward management. The figures reveal that nearly all the plants established before 1961 are characterized by private ownership and the lack of any distinction between owner, management, and labor. The owner is not only the manager but also part of the work force. Only in plants that are not privately owned does a separate management level exist. In factories established between the 1960s and 1980s, the proportion of private ownership and lack of separate management falls to about 85 percent, with a parallel rise in the percent of enterprises defined as partnerships or companies maintaining a separate managerial level. On the whole, this trend continued into the 1990s, when the rate at which new factories with a separate managerial level were established was stepped up. During this latter period, some 30 percent of the new firms included an institutionalized form of management.

Analysis of the organizational structure of the factories indicates that nearly one third are divided into departments. In the overwhelming majority of these there are only two departments, with a small number maintaining three. Most departmentalized plants are in the construction materials and textile and clothing industries. Moreover, the nature of the division changes according to the specific needs of the branch. The construction materials and food industries show a division into two departments, production and marketing, with only 4 percent organized into more than two. These plants market the bulk of their products to the Arab sector and face severe competition with their Jewish counterparts for the Jewish market. In most cases, their edge in the marketplace is related to their

Table 7.6
Distribution of Plants by Years of Establishment and Type of Ownership
(percentages)

Year Established	Ownership			
	Private	Partnership	Corpo.	Public Co.
To 1960	96	0	4	0
1961-1970	85	4	11	0
1971-1980	82	2	8	8
1981-1985	86	4	9	1
1986-1990	84	4	12	0
1991-	70	14	14	2
Total	83	4	12	1

ability to supply goods with greater flexibility and more sensitivity to the particular needs of the customer. These advantages assist them in coping with the monopolistic pressures of large Jewish corporations.

The most common division in textile and clothing plants is into sewing and packing departments. Here the question of marketing is less complex, since the majority of factories work as subcontractors for Jewish parent companies. Fourteen percent of the textile and clothing factories are divided into three departments—most commonly either cutting, sewing, and packing or sewing, packing, and quality control. This division indicates the degree of dependency on the Jewish parent companies. Only a small proportion of the factories maintain systems of quality control; in most cases, it is performed by the parent company. These Jewish corporations direct the work in such a way that it is difficult for potential Arab entrepreneurs to gain experience in the more prestigious stages of production, such as design and cutting. Rather, they are assigned the sewing tasks, which are considered the simpler stage of production in the fashion industry.

There is also a correlation between the size of the plant and its managerial and organizational structure. The larger factories are organized as economic entities requiring formal patterns of management and division into departments. Departmentalization and managerial structure also display a clear effect of industrial branch, whereby the textile and clothing industry is conspicuous for its advanced features.   In this industry, managerial methods, organization, work procedures, and quality control systems are passed down to the factories from the Jewish-owned concerns with which they are so closely linked. The textile industry is, in fact, the vanguard of Arab industry for the incorporation of modern methods of management and organization.   As a rule, the other branches are still having difficulty freeing themselves from their informal, family-based managerial and organizational structure.

FEATURES OF THE WORK FORCE

Given the lack of capital and informal managerial practices, Arab industrial production can be expected to be labor intensive. We would also anticipate a minimal use of technology due to the scarcity of, and lack of access to, capital. In ethnic terms, we would expect a preference for a kindred work force recruited from the extended family, or *hamula*. According to the theory that the support of the ethnic group encourages the employment of members of the group in economic ventures in the ethnic sector (Waldinger, Aldrich, & Ward, 1990), Arab workers should prefer jobs in Arab industry over commuting to factories in the Jewish sector. In Israeli reality, however, the Jewish economy offers a wide range of jobs on various levels of skill, and Arab industrial enterprises seem to encounter difficulty in competing for professional workers in the Arab labor market (Bar-el, 1993; Yiftachel, 1991).

Arab factories are characterized by the production of standard products, which requires workers with a relatively low level of professional training.   These patterns of production, along with the small size of many plants, dictate the nature of the work force. The functions within this work force can be divided into four groups, as shown in Table 7.7. The largest group of employees in Arab industry consists of production workers, which account for over 80 percent of the total work force. The second largest group, 12 percent of the work force, is that of the managers (in most cases the entrepreneurs themselves). The relative weight of this group stems from the small size of most plants, so that the entrepreneur not only serves as manager but is also involved in production and perhaps even marketing.   The third and fourth groups consist of clerical and marketing personnel, who together account for only 6 percent of all employees.   These groups represent an intermediate level responsible for day-to-day management and marketing. The small proportion of this category indicates the difficulty of Arab industry to employ workers not directly involved in production, despite their critical importance if the firm is to break into markets in the broader Israeli economy.

Generally, the level of professional training of the production workers in Arab industry is low. Close to 90 percent are defined as skilled laborers, although they acquired their training on the production line and not in professional schools. Another 9 percent, defined as unskilled laborers, are employed in general tasks

Table 7.7
Distribution of Work Force by Job and Professional Training (percentages)

Distribution of Workers by Job	Professional Training				
	Academics	Technicians & Engineers	Skilled Workers	Unskilled Workers	Total
Manager 12.2	5.9	6.1	83.8	4.2	100
Clerk 2.6	3.6	4.4	73.9	18.1	100
Production 81.8	0	0.1	92.4	7.5	100
Marketing 3.4	1.0	0.5	56.0	42.5	100
Total 100.0	0.9	0.9	89.6	8.6	100

supporting the production process—as porters, cleaners, and so on. Evidence for the low level of professional training of the Arab work force can be found in the fact that only some 2 percent of the employees have a technical or academic education on the level of technician or above (Table 7.7). These constraints affect their ability to learn new methods and function well in modern industry. The same low level of training also typifies the intermediate level responsible for marketing and the day-to-day management of the plant. Nearly half of the marketing personnel and about 20 percent of the clerical workers received no professional training for their positions, and the percent of technicians, practical engineers, and academics among them is marginal. The fact that the work force is characterized by a low level of training and lacks the skills needed to cope with modern industrial methods and a competitive market hampers the attempts of Arab enterprises to break into Jewish markets. Moreover, it reflects the tendency of skilled Arab workers to prefer more highly professional jobs in Jewish-owned factories over employment in Arab plants. The jobs offered in the Jewish sector represent a professional challenge unmatched in Arab communities.

The level of training of the managers is not much better than that of the other groups. Only some 12 percent have minimal formal training, on the level of technician or above, in their own field or indeed in any advanced subject. This problem is particularly salient in view of the entrepreneurial research literature, which indicates that formal education in any field is a major condition for the success of small entrepreneurs. The challenges facing an entrepreneur—the acquisition of information on market conditions, adjustment to changing situations under conditions of uncertainty, organization of the entrepreneurial process, and so on—are so complex that anyone lacking some sort of formal education will find it practically impossible to cope with them (Felsenstein & Schwartz, 1993).

The degree to which entrepreneurs rely on a variety of labor markets is an indication of their sophistication regarding the recruitment of workers. In traditional societies, most employees are found within the kinship group, with a preference for the extended family, followed by the clan and fellow religionists. On the other hand, in modern society it is assumed that individual affiliations have no real effect on the labor market. Table 7.8 presents the features of work force recruitment in Arab industry by settlement, kinship, and ethnic group. The figures reveal that over 70 percent of the employees in Arab industry come from the settlement itself and from the same religious group. Another one quarter of the workers are hired from among the members of other religions in the same settlement or from nearby settlements. Only a very small proportion come from more remote geographical or ethnic groups. This finding demonstrates the fact that Arab industry relies on a local work force, and it indicates a certain preference for workers from the same settlement and religious affiliation.

As for the hiring of workers from the kinship group, there is a clear preference for reserving the more privileged positions in management and clerical functions for family members. The percentage of employees from the extended family in managerial posts is extremely high. Only rarely are professionals brought in who do not come from the extended family (the *hamula*) or the settlement. Similarly, over one third of the clerical workers are *hamula* members, as compared to only 15 percent of the production workers. This pattern of work force recruitment stems from the fact that the wages and social benefits of production workers in Arab industry are inferior to those in the Jewish sector. As a result, the status of production worker in an Arab factory is low, and there is consequently no economic advantage in reserving these positions for members of the *hamula*.

With regard to the gender composition of the work force, there is a striking difference between the textile and clothing industry and all other branches. In textile factories, which provide jobs for about two thirds of the total Arab work force, some 86 percent of the employees are women. Women account for 98 percent of the production workers and only 25 percent of the managerial staff in this industry. With very few exceptions, women can attain the post of supervisor over a group of female workers, but the management of the plant itself and its major departments remains in the hands of men. In the other industrial branches, men represent around 95 percent of the work force, with women accounting for

Table 7.8
Distribution of Employees by Job and Origin (percentages)

Origin	Job				Total
	Manager	Clerk	Production	Market	
Extended family	84.3	10.2	4.6	2.9	14.5
Hamula	2.4	28.7	10.1	6.3	9.6
Others, same settlement, same religion	3.7	27.5	52.2	45.1	45.3
Nearby settlement, same religion	1.4	8.4	12.9	16.0	11.5
Arabs, different religion, same or nearby settlement	1.0	6.0	14.4	22.9	12.8
Distant Arab settlement	4.4	10.2	2.6	5.7	3.2
Jews	2.7	4.2	0.03	1.1	0.71
West Bank & Gaza	0.0	4.8	2.8	0.0	2.4
Total	100	100	100	100	100

94 percent of the clerical workers. These figures indicate the existence of a nearly absolute distinction between feminine and masculine jobs in Arab industry. A woman's chances of rising to a key post, even in the textile and clothing industry, are practically nil. She must be content to work either in a clerical job or in textile production for decidedly low wages, or, rarely, in a low-level managerial position.

Workers' benefits in Arab industry may reveal something of the degree to which this work force is integrated into an organized, unionized labor market as well as the degree of the employers' commitment to their workers. These benefits are also a good indication of an entrepreneur's belief in his ability to remain in business for any length of time and his faith in the skill of his staff to ensure the factory's survival. Lamentably, we find that the majority of workers do not enjoy the social benefits typical of an organized labor market. Only 8.8 percent are members of pension funds to which the employer contributes, and other social and wage benefits are similarly rare. In many cases, the employer does not make even the most minimal contribution to ensure his workers' pension rights. These conditions bring the entrepreneur's production costs below those of other sectors or factories in which workers' committees or labor unions guarantee that indirect payments are made for the benefit of the personnel. The obvious conclusion is that only in very few instances in the Arab sector do workers' committees function on behalf of the employees; employers pay wages alone, saving themselves the peripheral costs intended for worker welfare. The workers agree to these conditions because they see themselves as helping out their family or community, whereas if they sought better conditions they would be promoting development of the Jewish sector. The entrepreneur may thus exploit his employees' desire to work in the ethnic Arab sector and the conviction of those with whom he has a kinship relation that the entire extended family will profit from the factory.

Our survey also reveals a relative stability in employment, with most people employed in tenured posts (except for the seasonal workers, who account for only 7.1 percent of the total work force). This stability is promoted, *inter alia*, by the system of internal and community relations and by the perception that excellence at one's job plays a role in determining one's status in the community.

Do these conditions prevail in all industrial branches? To answer this question, the branches were divided into two groups: the textile and clothing industry, employing primarily women; and the other branches, employing mainly men, from whom a higher level of professional skill is demanded than from women. In the textile and clothing industry, 14.1 percent of the employers pay into pension funds in addition to Social Security, as compared to 4.6 percent in the other branches. The percent of tenured workers not included in a pension fund is 74 in the textile and clothing industry and 91.1 in the other branches. It would thus appear that owners do not afford their workers full social benefits even where a high level of skill is required. The strict provision of social benefits in some of the textile and clothing plants is a result of the involvement of Jewish partners and the presence of a number of fully Jewish-owned factories in Arab villages. Here, conditions are better than in Arab-owned firms.

Seasonal and temporary workers account for about 20 percent of the work force in the textile and clothing industry and around 4 percent in the other branches. Labor turnover is high in the textile industry, primarily because many women consider their jobs to be "temporary"; they tend to stop working immediately after their marriage or the birth of their first child. Furthermore, production volumes in this industry are affected more by seasonal fluctuations than in other branches.

Breakdown of employees by years on the job reveals that 21.5 percent have held their positions for one year or less. Another 21.4 percent have worked for five to six years, 5.8 percent for seven to eight years, and 14.3 percent for nine years or more. Although new factories have been erected over the past two years, only a small number of additional workers have entered Arab industry, an indication of the high rate of labor turnover. This conclusion is supported by the fact that only 43 percent of the industrial workers in Arab settlements have been in the work force for two years or less. The percent of workers employed by the same factory for less than two years is 46 in the textile and clothing industry and 40 in the other branches. Since the textile and clothing industry employs close to 65 percent of the total work force in Arab industry, with all the other branches employing the remaining 35 percent, it may be held that the other branches are more stable with regard to labor turnover. Indeed, in the other branches 25.5 percent of the employees have held their jobs for more than seven years, while 17.7 percent have been with the same firm for at least nine years. In the textile industry, these figures are 15.8 percent and 10.2 percent respectively. We may thus conclude that the male industrial branches are more stable and suffer less from the effects of market and seasonal fluctuations than the textile and clothing industry.

Our analysis thus far indicates that Arab industry has absorbed the less skilled members of the Arab work force. Skilled workers prefer the employment opportunities offered by Jewish industry, where wages are higher and they enjoy the social benefits generally lacking in Arab enterprises. Employment practices in Arab plants are determined by the entrepreneurs and managers, most of whom lack any formal professional education or training. Rather, they have gained their professional skills through their own experience as employees and employers. Given this fact, it is easy to understand why these factories find it difficult to introduce advanced and sophisticated technologies into either their production processes or their managerial and organizational structure.

CONCLUSIONS

The data and analysis presented in this chapter indicate that Arab entrepreneurs have an interest in investing in their plants, within the constraints deriving from the limited available capital and small size of most enterprises. This investment is reflected primarily in the expansion of the factory and the acquisition of the equipment needed to promote production. The relatively low level of skill and professional training of the work force stands out in sharp contrast to the investment in technology. Arab industry hires mostly women and workers who have acquired their training on the job; these people are employed under conditions that are often contrary to Israeli labor law. In deciding where to invest their capital, entrepreneurs opt more for technology than for labor. In fact, Arab industry has largely failed to recruit the more skilled, professional and highly trained workers from among the Arab work force and has relied for a long time on cheap, unskilled labor. Even the managers and entrepreneurs themselves lack appropriate professional training. This state of affairs has repercussions for the complexity of plant organization and managerial conduct, which make little use of the formal and more advanced practices common in the Jewish sector.

These assertions do not contradict the claim that Arab entrepreneurs display a strong motivation to invest in and develop their factories. Although the total investment may be comparatively small, it is often high in relation to the size of the enterprise and the availability of capital. The desire to invest in and expand their ventures requires entrepreneurs to alter their perception of industrial activity. They must fulfill a number of conditions in order to progress, grow, and maintain efficient production in a competitive market. This set of conditions is at the heart of plant growth and the steady rise to higher levels of entrepreneurship.

Chapter 8

Industrial Linkages

INTRODUCTION

The diversification of the sales and purchasing networks of Arab plants constitutes a measure of the degree to which Arab industry is integrated into the Israeli economy as well as a measure of the entrepreneurial level of the individual factory owner and manager. The more a plant sells to markets outside its own settlement—to nearby or distant Arab markets, Jewish settlements, and markets overseas—the greater the degree of its integration into the Israeli economy. Diversification of sales may indicate both that ethnic barriers have been overcome and that the entrepreneur has broken into markets with high quality demands, with which he is not required to deal within the local settlement market. Diversification of purchasing—expanding the volume of inputs purchased from Arab plants, thereby reducing dependency on inputs acquired directly from Jewish sources—may indicate the extent and level of development of interlinkages in the Arab economy. The broadening of these two types of diversification can lead to a rise in the added value created internally by Arab industrial activity, therefore making it possible to increase the capital accumulation that enables industrial development and growth.

This chapter examines the degree of penetration into markets outside a plant's own settlement, a process that presents particular difficulties for the Arab entrepreneur. Because of their location in the national periphery, plants in Arab settlements typically suffer the effects of being remote from large markets, remote from the complementary economic activities which offer the economies of scale that enhance profitability, and remote from information about market conditions and potential at any given time (Pred, 1977; van Geenhuizen & Nijkamp, 1993). As members of an ethnic-national minority, Arab entrepreneurs may find it hard to insinuate themselves into an economy controlled by the majority, for two principal reasons. First are the differences in business culture, and second are the preference of the minority to rely on internal, albeit limited, sources of labor, capital, or managerial reserves. As a result, any attempt to establish business relations between the ethnic groups on both sides of the divide will have to overcome even more hurdles than only those deriving from the location of Arab plants in peripheral areas (Camagni, 1991; Ratti, 1992). Minority entrepreneurs may respond to the communications gap between the entrepreneurial cultures by adopting a strategy of risk reduction. This happens when the risk involved in ventures that rely on interethnic resources and markets is considered too great to employ a strategy aimed at maximizing profit. Ethnic markets therefore become the firm base on which the continued operation of the business is founded. Expansion within this market creates opportunities for the entrepreneur to take calculated risks at a later stage in an attempt to enter wider markets (Waldinger, 1986).

In a society undergoing transformation processes from a semisubsistence economy to a modern one integrated into a developed market economy, the absence of risk-reducing institutions generally deters potential entrepreneurs from incurring the risks entailed in entrepreneurial activity (Czamanski & Taylor, 1986). In addition to encouraging mimicking behavior on the part of new plants, this factor also strengthens the tendency of Arab entrepreneurs to rely on the assured markets of the *hamula* and local community. Nevertheless, less-developed economies and ethnic minorities do show a trend for slow and cautious entrance into interethnic markets, even in the absence of risk-reducing institutions (Geertz, 1963; Roberts, 1978).

In Israel, the development of Arab industrial entrepreneurship began when capital accumulation in the Israeli market was controlled by large national corporations. Under such circumstances, industrial activity in the national periphery tends to be organized around large plants—owned by these concerns—specializing in standardized production and maintaining relations primarily with the economic core of the country, both for purchases and for sales. Alongside these enterprises, small plants operating in the regional markets of the periphery are established. Both types of ventures have developed in Arab industry. Sewing shops in the textile and clothing industry market their goods to parent companies under conditions of total dependency. Most of the other plants are small-scale enterprises that began to break into markets outside their own and nearby settlements only in the 1980s.

SALES DESTINATIONS

The destinations of the goods produced by Arab plants were derived from owners' reports. Each destination mentioned by a factory owner indicates the existence of business relations between two settlements: that of the plant and that of the customer. The spatial pattern of sales was determined by means of cluster analysis, in which settlements selling to similar localities were grouped together.

Our analysis yielded eight groups (regions) of settlements, each showing a similar intragroup spatial pattern of sales which is different from that of the other groups. The groups are composed of neighboring settlements, identical to the settlement complexes mentioned in Chapter 5. The one exception is the village of Maghar, which is linked with the markets of the Nazareth region rather than those of Sakhnin Valley, in which it is located. The reason for this is that Maghar industries purchase relatively more raw materials from Nazareth and therefore prefer to sell to Nazareth as well.

Table 8.1 shows the distribution of sales of the industrial plants by region. As the table indicates, the volume of sales to settlements within the region of the plant represent, on the average, about half of all sales, with around one half of these sold within the settlement of the plant itself and the rest to other settlements in the region. For our purposes, the remaining sales destinations can be divided into two groups: other Arab regions and Jewish markets.

The spatial distribution of sales is shown in Figure 8.1. Spatial analysis revealed that in most regions, 30 to 40 percent of sales go to Jewish markets, primarily those in the large urban centers. This is especially striking with regard to the Arab settlements in the vicinity of Tel Aviv and Haifa. In the region of the Little Triangle, over 50 percent of the output of Arab industry is sold in the metropolitan area of Tel Aviv, and some 40 percent of the output of Lower Western Galilee goes to the area of Haifa. In contrast to the relatively high degree of integration of the Little Triangle into the Jewish urban economy, Arab industries in the national periphery tend to establish fewer links to Jewish settlements. As a result of the effect of distance and the existence of intervening opportunities, only about 15 percent of the output of industries in Beit Kerem Valley and Sakhnin Valley is sold to Jewish markets. Sales of Arab industrial products to the regions of the West Bank and Gaza Strip and to markets abroad are nil.

The volume of sales to the Jewish sector varies according to industrial branch, as shown in Table 8.2, which reveals that, as expected, the major branch marketing its products outside the Arab sector is the textile and clothing industry, most of whose output is sold to Jewish-owned parent companies in Tel Aviv, Haifa, and the new development towns neighboring on Arab settlements. The frequency of sales to new towns near the Arab settlement in which the plant is located is particularly high. It appears that many textile and clothing companies employ a three-part division of labor. Management is located in Tel Aviv, while mass production is located in the development towns, especially in the north. Here production is mechanized, and the workers enjoy the wages and social benefits that are typical of the organized work force. A considerable number of the female workers in these plants come from nearby Arab villages. The third division of labor is the production performed by Arab subcontractors. These people typically close off the ground level space under their residences and employ women, either from their own *hamula* or from the village, on a temporary basis and under poor working conditions. The less entrepreneurial subcontractor

Table 8.1
Distribution of Factory Sales by Primary Destinations (percentages)

Sales to Region of plant	Own settlement*	Own region	Other Arab regions	Jewish settlements**	West Bank & Gaza	Abroad	Total
Upper Central Galilee	25	47	19	33	–	1	100
Upper Western Galilee	29	58	8	32	–	2	100
Beit Kerem Valley	27	55	29	16	–	–	100
Sakhnin Valley	23	40	45	14	–	1	100
Lower Western Galilee	27	45	16	37	1	1	100
Nazareth region	28	53	8	37	1	1	100
Ara Valley	25	43	21	35	1	–	100
Little Triangle	18	25	26	48	1	–	100
Total Arab industry	25	48	16	34	1	1	100

** Sales within own settlement are also included in sales to own region.
** About one half of the sales to the Jewish sector are to the metropolitan areas of Tel-Aviv and Haifa; the other half are to Jewish towns in the vicinity of the plant.

Figure 8.1
The Spatial Distribution of Sales by Three Major Destinations

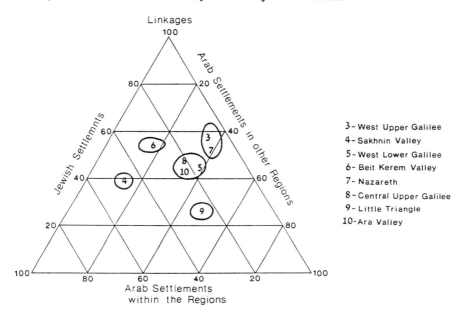

3 – West Upper Galilee
4 – Sakhnin Valley
5 – West Lower Galilee
6 – Beit Kerem Valley
7 – Nazareth
8 – Central Upper Galilee
9 – Little Triangle
10 – Ara Valley

purchases relatively basic sewing machines, at times with the assistance of the parent company, and performs the simplest sewing jobs for the parent company. The company thereby saves on labor costs for the comparatively simple tasks which require little professional know-how. It may also use the subcontractor to meet seasonal demands, without having to guarantee the workers year-round employment.

Factories in the construction materials industry—nonmetallic minerals and woodworking and metalworking plants serving the construction branch—also appear to be selling over one third of their production output to the Jewish sector today. A considerable number of Arab manufacturers in the woodworking branch have managed to make a name for themselves in the Jewish market, offering the major advantage of bypassing intermediaries and thus selling at low prices. In the metals industry, the Kadmani factory is a prime example of a plant that has earned a reputation for the quality of its products and its performance and, as a result, has broken through the ethnic barrier, marketing its products throughout the construction and metals industries. Similarly, the Bolus factories in the building materials branch, as well as a number of concrete block and premixed concrete plants in Galilee and the Little Triangle, market their products to the Jewish sector. Some of these enterprises have opened marketing offices in central Jewish towns to facilitate contact with their customers. In contrast, the volume of sales to the Jewish market is severely limited in the food and printing industries, which

Table 8.2
Percent of Production Sold to the Jewish Sector by Industrial Branch

Branch	Products sold to Jewish sector (%)	First Region		Second Region	
		Region I	Mean SD	Region II	Mean SD
Food	18	Triangle	1.7	–	–
Printing	21	Triangle	2.0	Nazareth	1.3
Construction materials	34	Lower Western Galilee	1.4	Nazareth	1.3
Metals and metalworking	35	Lower Western Galilee	1.7	Triangle	1.4
Woodworking	41	Triangle	1.6	Nazareth	1.2
Textiles	80	–	–	–	–

SD = standard deviation

sell primarily to Arab markets. Among the reasons for this is the specificity of their products, which are suited to the taste and traditions of the ethnic market.

A more detailed description of the patterns of sales is demonstrated by the analytical maps in Figure 8.2. In this set of maps, based on the computer program Arcad used for the analysis of Geographic Information System, the sales linkages of five industrial branches are analyzed from origin to destination for two regions. The maps present the Little Triangle as an example of an Arab region well integrated with Jewish markets, and the Sakhnin Valley region as far less integrated. They show that almost all branches in the Little Triangle are well integrated in the markets of Jewish towns at different levels of the Jewish core, such as Hadera, Netanya, Kefar Saba, and Petach Tiqwa. In the more developed branches of construction materials and textiles, the region even has sales linkages

Figure 8.2
Industrial Sales Linkages by Branch in Two Selected Regions

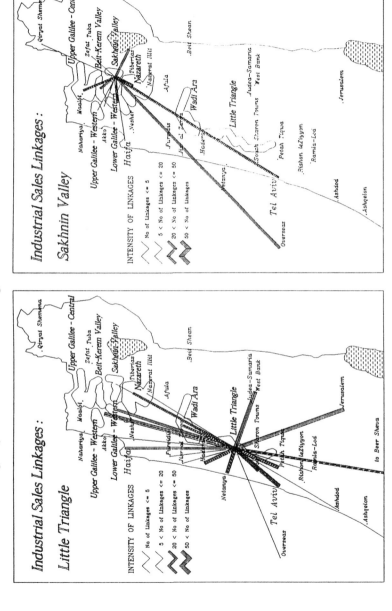

Figure 8.2, continued

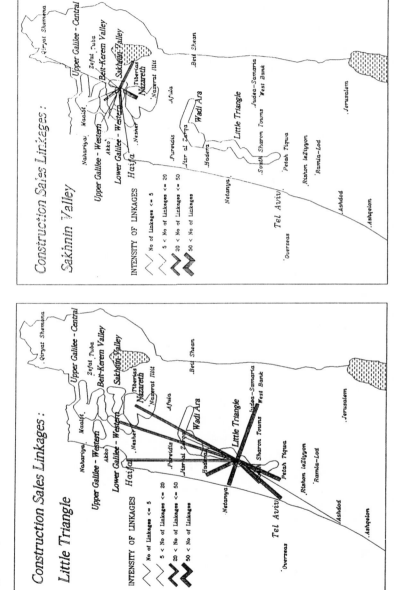

118

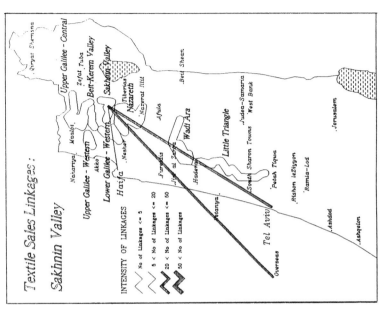

Textile Sales Linkages : Sakhnin Valley

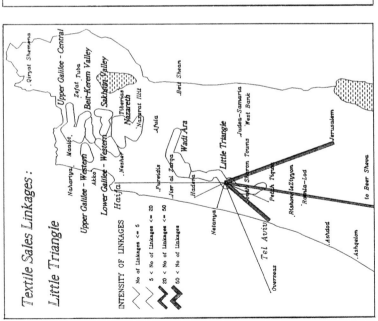

Textile Sales Linkages : Little Triangle

119

Figure 8.2, continued

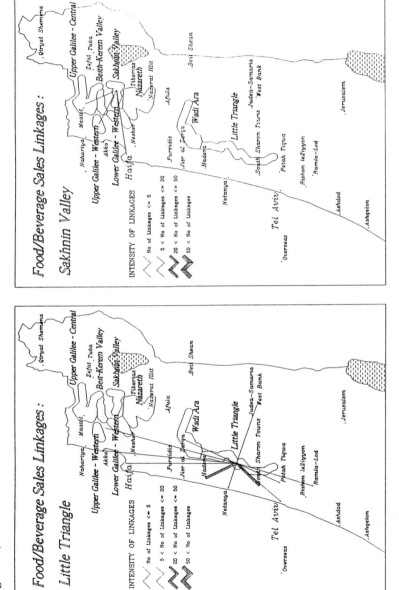

with the core city of Tel Aviv. These maps highlight the intensity of the linkages between the Little Triangle and the Jewish economy. In contrast, the Sakhnin Valley is much more integrated with other neighboring Arab regions, such as Nazareth, Lower Western Galilee, and Upper Central Galilee. The major Jewish centers that interact with industries in the Sakhnin Valley are the smaller towns of Tiberias, Zefat, Ma'alot, and Qiryat Shemona. Only the textile and clothing factories of the Sakhnin Valley are more intensively linked with the Jewish core.

Our analysis indicates that Arab industry has broken into regional and Jewish markets, a phenomenon that virtually began in the 1980s. Entrance into regional markets—referring only to other Arab settlements—is more conspicuous in some branches than in others. Nearby Jewish towns do not represent a natural market. Limiting operations only to the regional ethnic market is in line with the general tendency of ethnic groups that lack risk-reducing institutions to restrict themselves to such markets. Entrance into the Jewish market was spearheaded by the textile and clothing industry but later spread to additional branches as well. As we have seen, sales to the Jewish sector are an indication of the degree of a plant's integration in the national economy.

PURCHASING SOURCES

No less interesting than the pattern of sales is the spatial pattern of input purchases, primarily that of raw materials. The distribution of purchases by industrial branch is displayed in Figure 8.3, in which purchasing regions are divided into three groups: the region of the plant, other Arab regions, and Jewish towns. Except for the food industry, whose purchases are divided similarly among all three regional groups, the other industrial branches all purchase their inputs primarily from Jewish sources, with percentages ranging from around 60 (woodworking, construction materials) to about 90 (textiles and clothing). The proportion of purchases from Arab settlements either within or without the region of the plant is relatively low.

Table 8.3 shows the spatial distribution of the areas from which inputs originate. As the table indicates, most inputs are purchased in the large metropolitan areas of Haifa and Tel Aviv. There are two reasons why Haifa is the source of a larger volume of purchases. First, Haifa, which is highly industrialized and serves as the country's major port, is closer to the Galilee settlements, which are home to about one half of the Arab population in Israel. Second, the Nesher factory outside Haifa is virtually the only source of cement in the north for the construction materials industry. The Tel Aviv area is a major source of inputs for the textile industry, joined by the nearby regions of Rishon Le-Zion and Ashdod, which supply most of the sand and gravel to the construction materials industry.

Linkages are beginning to develop among the Arab settlements themselves, representing around one third of the total volume of input purchases for Arab

Figure 8.3
The Spatial Distribution of Purchasing by Three Major Origins

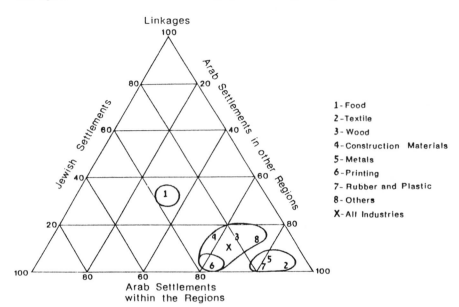

industry. Arab factories, particularly in the Nazareth and Umm al Fahm regions, have become major production sites for Arab industrial inputs in a variety of branches. These two regions together produce about one half of the total inputs purchased from Arab settlements and intended for Arab industry. As a result, Nazareth and, to a certain extent Umm el Fahm, have established their status in the Arab economy as the core of growth, where industrial consolidation and expansion begin.

The most conspicuous branch whose inputs are supplied by the Arab market is the food industry. Some two thirds of all inputs to this branch are purchased from Arab farmers, around one half of these in the region of the plant and the rest from Arab settlements in neighboring regions (see Figure 8.3). Arab farmers sell a variety of products to industrial plants, including olives, milk, humus, sesame seeds, and so on. In the construction materials industry (concrete blocks, floor tiles, concrete, etc.) as well, about 43 percent of purchases are made in the Arab sector. Prominent among these inputs are the products of quarries, some of which are Jewish-owned although they are adjacent to Arab settlements. Three branches stand out for their large volume of purchases from the Jewish sector: textiles and clothing, basic metals, and rubber and plastics. In the remaining branches, between 65 and 75 percent of purchases have their source in the Jewish sector.

In conclusion, purchasing patterns reveal the marked dependency of Arab industry on inputs purchased in the Jewish sector. Only the food industry employs

Table 8.3
Origins of Arab Industrial Inputs

Source	% of Total Purchases
Haifa metropolitan area	31
Tel Aviv metropolitan area	26
Other Jewish towns	8
Jewish sources—total	65
Nazareth	9
Umm al Fahm	6
Other Arab settlements	18
Arab sources—total	33
Abroad	1
West Bank & Gaza Strip	1

inputs whose source is largely in Arab farm units. The fact that some two thirds of Arab industrial output is sold within the Arab market and a good part of the remainder is sold under conditions of dependency to Jewish parent companies paints a picture of the structure of relations between the two economies. These findings underline the degree of Arab industry's dependency on the Jewish economy. Such dependency fits the notion of internal colonialism put forward by Zureik (1979).

Nevertheless, Arab industry has begun to develop marketing networks that have broken out of settlement borders and ethnic frameworks. In the 1980s, some of the factories grew, modernized themselves, and expanded their markets beyond the settlement. The 1980s also saw the development of regional industrial complexes, in which complementary functional relations evolved among a large number of neighboring Arab settlements. In these regions, there is a clear distinction, along ethnic lines, between the markets of Arab industrial zones and those of Jewish industrial zones. No Jewish settlement adjacent to Arab villages has become part of the network of business relations among Arab factories. However, Arab industry exports a considerable volume of goods to Jewish markets, particularly in the branches of textiles and clothing and construction materials. Arab entrepreneurs have found niches that have enabled them to penetrate Jewish markets and even to compete for these markets against Jewish-owned factories. As soon as Arab plants improved the quality of their products, adapted them to the demands of the Standards Institute, and introduced procedural quality control, they began to compete successfully for Jewish markets. The Kadmani brothers' concrete factories and the Bolus marble factory are outstanding examples of this success. Moreover, the construction boom of the late 1980s, occasioned by mass immigration from the former Soviet Union, opened the doors of large contractors to concrete block factories, floor tile manufacturers, and stone masonries in the Arab sector.

Entrance into the Jewish market is a significant indication of a rise in entrepreneurship level and of the willingness to cope with new market conditions. Indeed, Arab plants striving to rise to a higher level of entrepreneurship cannot restrict themselves to the relatively small Arab market. To advance, they must accept the challenge of entrance into markets in the Jewish sector.

Chapter 9

Land and Infrastructure

THE IMPORTANCE OF INDUSTRIAL ZONES AND INFRASTRUCTURE

The model of Arab industrial entrepreneurship highlights the key role of land and infrastructure in facilitating mobility along the entrepreneurial scale (Chapter 6). The existence of basic infrastructure, such as electricity, water, and roads, is a necessary condition for the establishment of enterprises even in the lower stages of the scale. Further development based on the incorporation of higher entrepreneurship levels has been blocked by four major factors. Most prominent among these factors are the availability of land for industry and the lack of approved industrial zones offering appropriate modern infrastructure. In fact, it is only in the third stage in the model, when the need for further growth and expansion arises and when entrepreneurs have access to enough resources, that the absence of industrial zones may hamper industrial development.

Industrial zones (especially their advanced form of industrial parks) and their physical infrastructure can be perceived as mechanisms which reduce the objective and subjective sense of risk for entrepreneurs. Various case studies indicate that potential entrepreneurs are more willing to start a venture when economic mechanisms and institutions are more developed because these can reduce the risk level (Czamanski & Taylor, 1986). The importance of these mechanisms is especially significant in peripheral areas, where potential entrepreneurs face relatively high risks. The case of the Cornwall district in England (Shaw & Williams, 1985), for example, illustrates the advantages of building industrial parks as part of the restructuring policy of a peripheral, mostly rural area. Here the number of enterprises situated in industrial parks, and subsequently the number of people employed in industry, increased steadily between 1971 and 1983. About 45 percent of all plants erected in industrial parks were transferred to the parks from other areas in Cornwall. This relocation took place at different points in time, and it may be that some plants were forced to move in order to survive.

When compared with the economy in the district at the time, and especially with other plants, the factories located in industrial parks demonstrated greater survival capabilities during the recession period.

In Israel, the availability of industrial zones becomes a key factor in the further industrialization of Arab settlements in Israel. For this sector, a number of factors work against internally initiated industrial entrepreneurship. These include the lack of industrial zones; split ownership of land; the absence of a land market; the lack of public programs for the development of industrial infrastructure; and the fact that national legislation aimed at encouraging capital investments has not been applied to Arab settlements. All reduce the ability of the Arab periphery to attract industrial enterprises. This pattern is especially noticeable in light of the obvious advantages enjoyed by new towns in the Jewish periphery. These towns, in many cases located in the vicinity of Arab settlements, benefit from relatively developed industrial areas and infrastructures as well as from financial advantages stemming largely from legislation that encourages capital investments.

THE NATURE OF LAND OWNERSHIP

In the traditional village, extended families lived in well-defined homogeneous areas, with their agricultural units usually concentrated near the residential quarter. As a result of inheritance procedures, the land was divided into small plots with different owners. An increase in the number of heirs and the principle of equal distribution of land among all sons in the family led to additional subdivisions of plots into even smaller units. By the 1940s, over two thirds of the plots were smaller than one hectare (Shmueli, Schnell, & Soffer, 1985), and since then they have continued to be subdivided. Therefore, in the 1990s, most families have only small plots of land for their various needs, of which residency is the most important. Thus, the land allotted for industrial purposes is often in the form of small plots divided among a number of extended family members.

Land supply in Arab settlements is also affected by the absence of land market. Due to an increasing shortage of land (resulting from delays in approving outline plans as well as other factors) and the linkage of households to their kinship, there is a growing tendency in Arab settlements to hold land reserves for future generations (Schnell, 1994b). For this reason, in addition to short-term economic considerations, there is a reluctance to sell land. If a situation arises which necessitates that land be sold, there is still a clear preference to sell to one's own family or clan members (Shmueli, Schnell, & Soffer, 1985).

Analysis of data concerning the distribution of enterprises according to the nature of ownership shows that only a small percentage (8 percent) are located on land purchased from former owners. This pattern confirms that the sale of land in Arab settlements is extremely limited, often forcing landless potential entrepreneurs to abandon their plans for industrial initiatives. With the increasing shortage of available land for industry, there is a growing tendency to rent premises. This can be seen in Table 9.1. At least 28 percent of all plants located in residential areas operate from rented buildings. This percentage rises if we include plants on the outskirts of settlements and in industrial zones. Of all plants shown in Table 9.1, only three were erected on land external to the village, leased from the Israel Land Authority.

In some cases, however, the extended family and *hamula* members may serve as a social institution supporting processes of development and may be willing to rent out appropriate plots on favorable terms. Renting under these terms, however, entails a degree of uncertainty, since the needs of the household owning the land are usually given preference. Such needs may arise at any time (Shmueli, Schnell, & Soffer, 1985), thus increasing the level of risk for the entrepreneur. Indeed, plant formation usually requires a large investment in premises and considerable time to organize the positioning of machinery and matching of assembly lines. For this reason, if an entrepreneur locates in a rented building, he will prefer to remain on site and to reduce the likelihood of relocating.

An analysis of the correlation between the number of plants built on land inherited by the entrepreneur and the total number of plants in a settlement indicates a negative correlation coefficient of -0.44. This means that the smaller the percentage of plants located on inherited land, the higher the chances of developing enterprises in the settlement. The answer for this lies in the absence of a commercial land market. The development of such a market in Arab settlements and the availability of buildings for rental enable potential entrepreneurs to implement industrial initiatives. Support for this claim can be seen in a number of settlements in the Little Triangle and in Galilee.

AVAILABILITY OF LAND FOR INDUSTRY

Enterprises located in the residential areas of Arab settlements find it difficult to function efficiently and lack the room to expand. With regard to land allocated to industry, the 51 Arab settlements for which data were collected can be divided into four groups. In the first, comprising 30 percent of the settlements, zones were allocated for industry in the outline plan and plants were erected in these zones. In the second group (which again comprised 30 percent), though land was allocated for industrial zones in an outline plan which was either approved or deposited for public hearing, industrial plants were not erected there but remained in residential areas. In half the settlements in this group, the absence of factories in the industrial zones can be attributed to the fact that the outline plan was deposited in 1990 or thereafter. In the third group, comprising 19 percent of the settlements, an approved or deposited outline plan existed but did not include an industrial zone. The fourth group, consisting of 21 percent of the settlements, had no outline plan at all. Thus it can be seen that in 40 percent of the settlements, including some with over 10,000 inhabitants, no land is allocated for industry in the outline plan, whether already approved or deposited for public hearing. The

Table 9.1
Distribution of Plant Locations by Branch (absolute numbers and percentages)

Branch / Location	Food	Textiles & Clothing	Wood	Construction materials	Metals	Printing	Rubber & Plastics	Others	Total
Family dwelling	70 / 58.8	40 / 58.0	70 / 68.0	24 / 24.0	29 / 63.0	9 / 32.1	25 / 67.6	3 / 25.0	270 / 52.5
Rented dwelling	25 / 21.0	18 / 26.1	11 / 10.7	11 / 11.0	2 / 4.3	9 / 32.1	3 / 8.1	6 / 50.0	85 / 16.5
Rented in residential area	18 / 15.1	7 / 10.1	12 / 11.7	7 / 7.0	3 / 6.5	9 / 32.1	3 / 8.1	— / —	59 / 11.5
Settlement outskirts	5 / 4.2	— / —	5 / 4.9	29 / 29.0	2 / 4.3	1 / 3.6	4 / 10.8	— / —	46 / 8.9
Industrial zone	1 / 0.8	4 / 5.8	5 / 4.9	29 / 29.0	10 / 21.7	— / —	2 / 5.4	3 / 25.0	5 / 10.5
Total Percent	119 / 23.2	69 / 13.4	103 / 20.0	100 / 19.5	46 / 8.9	28 / 5.4	37 / 7.2	12 / 2.3	51 / 100.0

Note: Top figures relate to absolute numbers, bottom figures relate to percentage of total plants in the specific branch.

nonexistence of industrial zones in 70 percent of the settlements clearly hinders the expansion of existing plants and has a negative influence on entrepreneurial potential aimed at industrial development.

In general, industrial zones in Arab settlements cover small areas, and the average is 150,000 square meters. In contrast, the average area of industrial zones in comparable Jewish development towns in northern Israel is 600,000 square meters (State of Israel, 1989). In one third of the Arab settlements with industrial zones, the area was found to be smaller than 50,000 square meters; and in two thirds of the settlements, the zone was smaller than 170,000 square meters. Only in 20 percent of the settlements did the industrial zone range from 300,000 to 500,000 square meters. To demonstrate the significance of these figures, it may be noted that the area required for an average concrete-block factory is no less than 3,000 square meters, not including the public areas needed for infrastructure. Thus, the industrial zones in most Arab settlements are capable of absorbing local enterprises currently situated in residential areas. However, they will be extremely limited in their ability to offer land for new local industrial initiatives or to entrepreneurs from outside the settlement.

It appears that despite the limited land available for industry, a significant number of these industrial zones are not utilized, and many plants remain in residential areas. The distribution of location of plants by branches is shown in Table 9.1. Most plants are located in residential areas; 9 percent are outside built-up areas on land not recognized as industrial zones in the outline plan; and only 11 percent are in approved industrial zones. In two thirds of the settlements with empty plots in their industrial zones, no more than 20 percent of the plants in the settlement are situated in the industrial zone. Only in two settlements are most plants located in industrial zones. Thus, the allocation of an industrial zone in an outline plan is not sufficient to encourage industrialization.

According to Table 9.1, over one half of all enterprises are situated in the building that houses the entrepreneur's family. Typically, the workshop or plant is on the ground or first floor. This is relevant for all branches, with two exceptions: building materials and printing. Building materials plants need a fair amount of space since they produce a high level of pollution. Therefore, many have been forced to move to the outskirts of settlements, either within or outside industrial zones. Many printing firms, which use movable machinery, are located in rented buildings in residential areas, but not necessarily within their owners' dwellings.

CONDITIONS OF INFRASTRUCTURE

The survey, carried by the authors among local Arab councils, indicates that infrastructure for industry is only partially developed in Arab settlements. In fact, 70 percent of the industrial zones have a very limited infrastructure, and only 30 percent are connected to the electricity grid and water system and include access roads. Only 22 percent of these areas are connected to telephone lines, and only in one industrial zone does the infrastructure include sewage and industrial buildings in addition to electricity, water, and telephones. As can be seen in Table 9.2, it was only in 1970 that Arab industrial zones began to be connected to the necessary infrastructures. This delay and the defects in the existing infrastructure in the Arab industrial zones are the subjects of owners' complaints.

In mountainous areas, the site of many Arab settlements, the cost of preparing land for industry is extremely high. According to the above mentioned survey, carried in May of 1992, prices reached as high as NIS125,000 to 180,000 (US$50,000 to 70,000) per 1,000 square meters. The severe budget constraints under which the Arab local authorities operate also contribute to the relatively low priority given to developing industrial zones.

As a result of these problems, the plants survey reveals that industrial zones do not afford potential entrepreneurs significant advantages. In most cases, location in an industrial zone leads to increased costs for development of the deficient infrastructure. Furthermore, the level of infrastructure services is often lower than the accepted level in residential areas in the same settlements. Therefore, it is not surprising that entrepreneurs are in no rush to move to industrial zones and that the present level of development in these zones does not encourage industrialization in Arab settlements. Moreover, in neighboring Jewish development towns, the level of the industrial infrastructure is relatively high and industrial buildings can be rented at reasonable prices, thus placing the Arab entrepreneur at a distinct competitive disadvantage.

THE DIFFERENCE BETWEEN PLANTS LOCATED INSIDE AND OUTSIDE INDUSTRIAL ZONES

The allocation of land for industrial zones began in Arab settlements in the 1970s. Nevertheless, only a few enterprises were established in or moved to these zones. In the 1960s, about 7 percent of all new firms were built in industrial zones, and in the 1970s this figure rose to 12 percent. It is only in the early 1990s that significant change is visible, with about 20 percent of all new enterprises located in industrial zones. For the past 30 years, however, the majority of plants have continued to operate from residential areas. As stated earlier, this trend prevails in most settlements, where industrial zones were established several years ago. Plants not situated in residential areas or industrial zones are located on the outskirts of the settlements. Thus, the claim that the establishment of industrial zones is not an adequate condition for the encouragement of industrialization is further confirmed.

The affinity between location and plant size is presented in Table 9.3. Here the observed and expected numbers of plants, by location, are divided into three groups by number of workers. The significant level of the X^2 (chi square) test of these figures is below 0.001. This confirms that plants employing a small number

Table 9.2
Year of First Connection of Any Industrial Zone to Infrastructure

Type of Infrastructure	Year of First Connection
Electricity	1970
Water	1970
Access roads	1972
Telephone	1982
Industrial buildings	1985
Sewage	1990

Table 9.3
Observed and Expected Distribution of Plants by Location and Number of Workers

Number of Workers		Industrial zone	Settlement outskirts	Residential area	Total
1-5	observed	14	15	257	285
	expected	30	25	230	(55%)
6-69	observed	35	31	156	224
	expected	24	20	180	(44%)
70+	observed	5	0	1	5
	expected	0.5	0.4	4	(1%)
Total		54	46	414	514
		(10%)	(9%)	(81%)	(100%)

of workers tend to be located in residential areas, while larger plants are more likely to be situated in industrial zones.

Plants located in industrial zones tend to be relatively large, their ownership structure is more complex, and they specialize in branches where investment in equipment and capital is higher than that required of industries in residential areas.

Table 9.4
Distribution of Plants by Location and Annual Sales Volume for 1991

Sales Volume (NIS)	Industrial zone (%)	Residential area (%)	Settlement outskirts (%)
<149	44	66	46
150-499	19	19	26
500-999	17	11	20
>1000	20	4	8
Total	100	100	100

Table 9.5
Distribution of Plants by Location and Total Investments, 1987-1991

Investment (NIS)	Industrial zone (%)	Residential zone (%)	Settlement outskirts (%)
<149	62	85	75
150-499	19	10	9
500-999	8	3	9
>1000	11	2	7
Total	100	100	100

Table 9.4 indicates that two thirds of the plants in residential areas have an annual turnover of less than NIS150,000 (in mid-1992, there were approximately NIS2.5 to US$1), and only 15 percent of these plants have an annual turnover greater than NIS500,000. In contrast, 37 percent of the plants in industrial zones have an annual turnover of over NIS500,000. Enterprises located on the outskirts of settlements are characterized by an annual turnover that is higher than for plants in residential areas but lower than for those in industrial zones.

The distribution of investments in enterprises over the past five years (Table 9.5) indicates an even greater discrepancy between plants located in industrial zones and those outside them. Almost one fifth of the owners of plants in industrial zones invested over half a million Israeli Shekels in their factories over the last five years, and nearly 40 percent invested over NIS150,000 during the same period. Plants on the outskirts of settlements, and especially those located in residential areas, significantly lag behind as far as investments are concerned.

Over half (56 percent) of all plants located in industrial zones are registered as partnerships and limited liabilities companies (Sofer, Schnell, & Drori, 1993). In comparison, 88 percent of all plants in residential areas are privately owned by one entrepreneur. It appears that only in a few cases can a private investor raise more than NIS150,000 to invest in industrial development, as most capital comes from personal savings and family members. The overall proportion of investment capital acquired from banks or other sources is small and does not exceed 30 percent of all investment (Schnell, 1994b; Sofer, Schnell, & Drori, 1993). In this context, a problem related to the entrepreneurial culture of most investors arises: Partnerships exist mostly between brothers, wherein mutual trust is based on blood-linked solidarity and not on management or organizational norms. With such a limited source of capital, it is difficult to raise enough for industrial development. The shortage of capital delays the adoption of sophisticated technology, which is more common in plants located in industrial zones. Moreover, it discourages the move of plants into these areas, even for those settlements in which relatively well-established industrial zones are available.

More than two thirds of all plants in industrial zones belong to two branches: (1) building materials (mostly concrete, concrete blocks, and floor tiles), and (2) basic metals (mostly metalworking shops; see Table 9.1). In comparison, only 18 percent of the enterprises in residential areas specialize in these branches, which are characterized by a demand for large production and storage space as well as sufficient room for loading and unloading. They are also among the most environmentally polluting plants, so that the pressure to move them away from built-up areas is greater than for other plants that are not as bothersome. About two thirds of the plants on the outskirts of settlements also belong to these two branches. This results from the desire to force them away from the residential areas in settlements that lack industrial zones.

It appears that the location of plants in industrial zones necessitates a higher entrepreneurship level than does locating them in residential areas. Investment in the required infrastructure as well as higher compulsory taxes are especially worthwhile for large enterprises, for which the initial investment is high but the flexibility needed to relocate after the plant has been erected is low. Moreover, entrepreneurs willing to invest in large plants seek to avoid incurring the high risk which might arise as a result of changes in future outline plans. Such enterprises will thus tend to be established in an industrial zone, despite the relatively high initial costs. In contrast, entrepreneurs with little initial capital and high fixed costs will tend to remain in the residential areas where they have established their enterprises, relying on the infrastructure in that area, however inadequate.

DISCUSSION

Figure 9.1 offers a model in which three complementary aspects concerning land, industrial zones, and infrastructure are the basic factors of the settlement level which inhibit industrial entrepreneurship in Arab settlements. Two aspects, the availability of industrial zones and the level of infrastructure, were invoked by the entrepreneurs themselves; the third aspect is the structure of land ownership.

The availability of an industrial zone in a settlement, as shown in the model, is linked to the total amount of land owned by the inhabitants, the status of the land according to the prevailing outline plan, and the alternative demand for land. The structure of land ownership (most of which is privately owned) is dictated by two main factors: inheritance procedures that breed split ownership of small, nonadjacent plots of land; and the fact that land is not regarded as a tradeable commodity. In addition, the nature of the infrastructure—electricity, water, sewage, industrial buildings, roads and land preparation—is influenced by both the level of investment in infrastructure and the degree of development of the industrial zone.

Factors of the sector and national level also influence the availability of industrial zones. Theses are related to the traditional patterns of economic, social, and demographic activities which characterize the Arab population in Israel as well as to the marginal status of Arab industry in the Israeli economic sphere. The traditional cultural patterns predetermine the entrepreneurial culture and the availability of investment and production capital. For example, entrepreneurship is hampered by an overcautious and suspicious attitude toward bank loans, which limits reliance on banks as a means of raising capital (Sofer, Schnell, & Drori, 1993). In addition, the ability of Arab entrepreneurs to raise capital is already limited by their unwillingness to enter into partnerships or economic companies with members of different clans. The reluctance to take out bank loans makes it difficult for entrepreneurs to invest in land preparation, the development of industrial zones, or infrastructure improvement.

The natural population increase in Arab settlements and the concurrent growing demand for land resources heightens the competition for land for housing purposes and industrial and commercial uses. The traditional attitudes toward land give lower priority to the short-term economic interests of the nuclear family. This approach prevents the emergence of a sophisticated land market and limits the extent of trade in land, thus curtailing the potential land reserves available for industrial use. The division of land ownership as a result of inheritance laws, which dictate that land be split equally among inheriting brothers, leaves the household with relatively small, noncontiguous plots unsuitable for the establishment of modern industrial plants. In addition, in the present absence of outline plans, the one factor which could encourage the unification of land units or lead to change in the traditional attitude toward land is lacking.

On the national level, the government's nonincentive policy works to the disadvantage of the Arab entrepreneur. The ability of Arab entrepreneurs to absorb technological innovations quickly and easily was proven in agriculture

Figure 9.1
Linkages between the Factors Influencing the Development of Industrial Zones

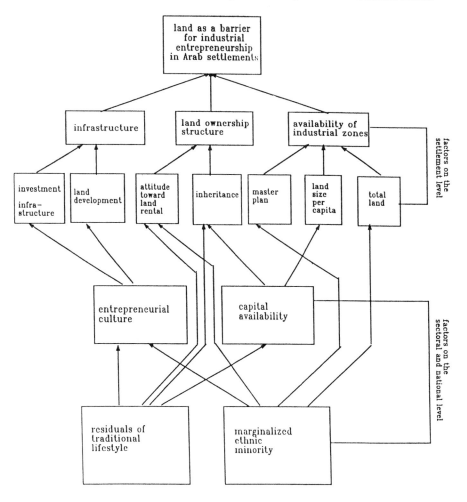

(Schnell, 1986), especially when the state developed mechanisms to reduce risk, such as crop insurance and agricultural training.   The lack of risk-reducing mechanisms in industry discourages Arab entrepreneurs from modifying traditional norms of investment and accumulation of capital.   In addition, the lack of government incentives (i.e., encouraging capital investments and building an appropriate industrial infrastructure, especially in the form of industrial zones) contributes to the minimized investments in industry.

The model suggests that the marginalization processes influence entrepreneurial culture, which in turn affects industrialization processes.   Hence, there is no specific procedure in Arab society for the allocation of land for industrial zones, and thus no opportunity for the allocation of industrial zones to encourage potential entrepreneurs to invest in industry. This specific failure of Arab society is striking when compared with the success of the Arab economy in consolidating land for agricultural development in the hands of a few members of the extended family and enabling them to enjoy government assistance and easy access to Jewish markets (Shmueli, Schnell, & Soffer, 1985).

The discussion so far has emphasized that the form of incorporation of the industrial production factor of land is linked to the status of Arab industry within the Israeli economy.   The explanation of the past and present form of Arab industrial development and integration demands a wider critical perspective. To link the data collected at the plant level into a coherent meaning and to explain the underlying mechanisms of industrial development in Israel, a discussion of the role of Arab entrepreneurial culture is required. Moreover, a critical scrutiny of the mechanisms concerning peripheralization and ethnicity within a polarized structure is necessary to comprehend better those forces which operate at the sectoral and national level and tend to maintain the structure. This is the focus of the following part of this book.

PART IV

ENTREPRENEURIAL MILIEU

Chapter 10

The Arab Entrepreneurial Milieu

INTRODUCTION

On the whole, entrepreneurship in the Arab sector may be considered typical of that of any ethnic minority. For a minority in an economically marginal position, industrial entrepreneurship can become a major mechanism for socio-economic mobility. Insofar as it reflects the entrepreneur's ability to take risks, recruit human resources, raise capital, and organize and manage production processes on various levels of complexity, such an initiative also involves the entrepreneur in relationships of a different order. In the more advanced stages, contacts are sought outside the settlement, outside the borders of the social and economic spheres that have influenced the entrepreneur for so long, as he looks to new labor markets and previously unknown financial realms.

The nature of entrepreneurial development is affected, among other factors, by the culture and social structure of the society in which the entrepreneur operates. The conceptualization that evolved following the work of Max Weber on the role of the Protestant ethic in the development of capitalism views entrepreneurship as a source of socio-economic progress. The entrepreneur is seen as a person of high motivation, values, and attitudes without which it would be impossible to take risks and undertake entrepreneurial ventures (Geertz, 1963; McClelland, 1961). As for ethnic minorities, various studies have shown how such groups take advantage of cultural traits in order to create a foundation for entrepreneurship. These traits include community solidarity, well-defined family relations based on seniority, a tradition of professional associations, institutions for raising capital (such as credit unions), patterns of saving, the use of family members as a source of manpower, a work ethic, and partnerships (Benedict, 1979; Boissevain et al., 1990; Light, 1972; Wong, 1977). Here the meaning of *entrepreneurial culture* must be clarified. *Culture* refers to the way in which entrepreneurs give expression to normative patterns of traditions and behavior in establishing industrial ventures. Indeed, it may be assumed that cultural identity supplies the primary mechanism for entrepreneurial behavior regarding issues such as decision making, assessing market potential, developing commercial strategy, calculating risks versus opportunities, and implementing methods for procuring resources.

However, focusing on the group culture as the primary factor underlying entrepreneurship does not give sufficient weight to socio-economic changes and structural conditions which influence the entrepreneur's desire for financial gains (Aldrich & Waldinger, 1990). In our view, the entrepreneurial environment in which the entrepreneur operates is of considerable importance. Similarly of significance is his status as a member of a minority group and the manner in which the group manipulates resources to formulate strategy and entrepreneurial culture. Thus, in addition to the effect of cultural traits, the entrepreneur operates in a social system dictating the structure of opportunities, the capability of competing in the market, and the accessibility of resources. With this in mind, this chapter considers the nature of the Arab industrial entrepreneurial environment, the patterns of resource procurement, and the style, motivation, and attitudes of the entrepreneur.

The molding and consolidation of the entrepreneurial culture of the Arab entrepreneur can be seen as the result of three factors: (1) the Arab and Jewish entrepreneurial environment in which he operates; (2) the manner in which he procures personal, family, and community resources; and (3) the Arab society's system of values and norms in general, and business behaviors in particular (see Figure 10.1).

Figure 10.1
A Model of Entrepreneurial Culture

Resources   Environment
•Family support   •Geographical location
•Family & *hamula* status   •Industrial branch
•Political connections ——▶ **Entrepreneurial** ◀—— •Markets
•Capital & ability to   **Culture**   •Physical infrastructure
 raise capital   ▲   •Entrepreneur's contacts
•Technology | with suppliers and
•Labor   customers

                    Values and Norms
                    •Family values
                    •Distrust of establishment
                    •Willingness to take risks
                    •Industriousness, integrity
                     & independence
                    •Professional & managerial know-how

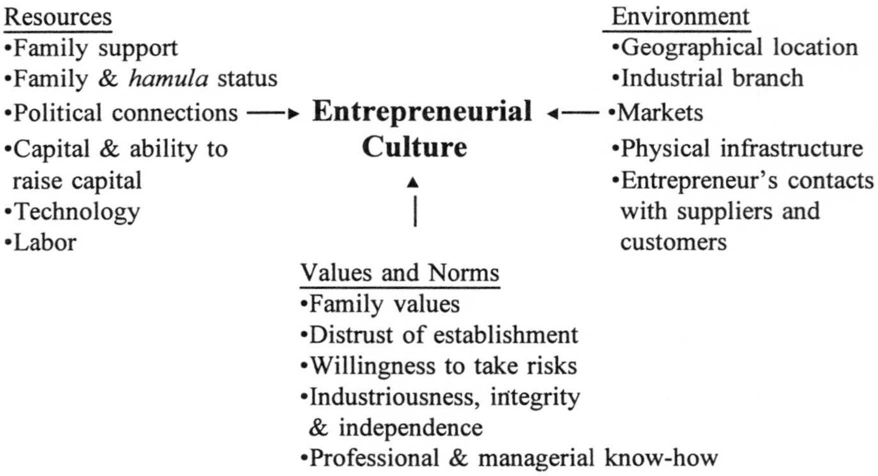

Our basic assumption is similar to that of Aldrich and Waldinger (1990), which sees a system of environmental, social, and personal conditions, anchored in behavioral and normative attitudes, as the basis for entrepreneurship and the motives impelling it. It is important to note that the entrepreneur's commercial and economic conduct is not rigid but rather responds to business opportunities. The entrepreneur assesses the potential of the commercial activity in view of the resources at his disposal and his ability to operate in the given economic environment, while his economic behavior reflects his status as an Arab industrial entrepreneur.

In addition to the survey, the data on which this chapter is based were collected for the most part from interviews conducted with some 70 industrial entrepreneurs from various Arab settlements. This is not, therefore, essentially quantitative data but is presented in an attempt to document the experiences and attitudes of these entrepreneurs.

THE ENTREPRENEUR'S ATTITUDES TOWARD HIS ENTREPRENEURIAL ENVIRONMENT

Operating from their peripheral position, Arab entrepreneurs may face a set of difficulties: (1) a convoluted bureaucracy whose workings and complexities are unfamiliar to the Arab entrepreneur; (2) unfair division of resources resulting from a lack of information regarding sources of financing, marketing methods, and incentives; (3) lack of access to the core of decision making and unfamiliarity with the mechanisms by which the government and other public bodies promote industrialization; and (4) problems concerning the daily running of a business, such as marketing opportunities, maintenance, and managerial and technological know-how.

The position of Israeli Arabs on the socio-spatial periphery of the national economy affects the range of opportunities open to them as industrial entrepreneurs. In the survey conducted among the 514 industrialists, entrepreneurs expressed their views regarding their needs and the factors impeding industrial development. The impeding factors can be divided into four groups, as shown in Table 10.1. They relate to the inadequacy of the physical infrastructure, the lack of capital, the lack of government aid, and insufficient professional training. Three specific factors, one in each of the first three groups, were cited by more than two thirds of the entrepreneurs interviewed as central elements hindering their operations: the unavailability of physical infrastructures (electricity, water, sewerage, roads, and communication lines); a scarcity of investment capital; and the fact that their settlements do not receive the entitlement of development areas, which would render them eligible for government aid.

Prominent in the first group of factors—regardless of plant location, size, or entrepreneurship level—are the problems faced by nearly all entrepreneurs in view of the lack of the basic infrastructures required for industrial development. This

Table 10.1
Factors Impeding Industrial Development by Location of Plant (percentages)

General Factors	Specific Factors	Percent of Responses by Location of Plant		
		Residential Area	Settlement outskirts	Industrial Zone
Physical Infrastructure	•Land	6	5	5
	•Developed industrial zone	37	63	20
	•Electricity, water, roads, sewerage, etc.	92	95	90
	•Industrial buildings	2	5	0
Financing	•General financing	35	30	25
	•Investment capital	63	64	46
	•Operating capital	2	0	0
	•Nonpayment	22	21	38
	•Problems of bank financing	13	15	16
Government Assistance	•Aid to entrepreneurs	2	2	2
	•Authorized development area	78	96	46
	•Taxes	3	3	3
Training *	•Entrepreneurs •Managers •Workers			

* The percentage noting these factors ranged between 5% and 10%, but it was impossible to divide the responses by location of plant.

coincides with the finding that the existence of physical infrastructures is one of the first prerequisites for a plant to rise on the entrepreneurship scale. It is interesting to note that only a small percentage of the entrepreneurs were able to purchase land on which to erect their factories. For this reason, potential entrepreneurs may not have managed to gain access to land and thus never became actual entrepreneurs. Although the first signs of the purchase and lease of property for industry have appeared over the past two years, there is no guarantee that the problem of land will be less critical in the future. In fact, the major problem today is the nonallocation, or very limited allocation, of legally recognized industrial zones and the lack of industrial zone infrastructures. The relatively small proportion of entrepreneurs noting problems associated with the absence of industrial zones, as compared with those complaining of the lack of basic infrastructures, derives from the fact that industrial zones become a necessary condition for growth only at the moderate-high level of entrepreneurship (Chapter 9). Moreover, in recent years, even entrepreneurs on the moderate-low level have managed to acquire land on which to erect their plants. In fact, the need for institutionalized support (particularly the establishment of industrial zones) is perceived as extremely important by the entrepreneurs. They fully understand that industrial zones represent a considerable improvement in the range of opportunities open to them, especially regarding infrastructure and capital.

Financing difficulties are expressed by the entrepreneurs primarily in regard to investment capital. Some 60 percent stated that they lacked capital for investment. This finding is even more significant in view of the fact that more than two thirds of the entrepreneurs invested considerable amounts in the development of their plants over the preceding five years. This trend suggests the emergence of a relatively optimistic climate in the Arab business environment, reflected in the entrepreneurs' willingness to expand their enterprises, improve work methods, and compete in new markets. Despite the numerous complaints of lack of capital, as we have seen in previous chapters, only 15 percent of the entrepreneurs actually sought bank financing. This suggests that the majority do not view the bank as a major source of investment capital. The entrepreneurship model indicates that bank financing only becomes a necessary condition on the higher entrepreneurship levels. It follows that most of the entrepreneurs still prefer to rely on capital raised from personal savings, family sources, or profits. Our interviews revealed that although the bank is indeed an available source of capital, the interest and collateral required to obtain a loan put it beyond the reach of a large number of Arab industrialists.

In the third group of impeding factors, the majority of entrepreneurs complained of the lack of development area entitlement. They feel that this situation places them at a disadvantage in their attempt to compete with Jewish entrepreneurs located in development towns and rural settlements in outlying regions, which enjoy the status of development areas. In the opinion of the entrepreneurs, granting their settlements the privileges of development areas would make it possible to construct modern industrial zones and thereby eliminate a major hardship for the settlement and its entrepreneurs. Only 2 to 3 percent of the interviewees expressed a desire for individual economic aid or tax exemptions. Most hoped that government aid would enable them to rent space in an industrial zone and receive financing assistance at favorable terms for investment in the development of their factories.

In the fourth group of factors, only a small number of entrepreneurs complained of a lack of training for managers and workers. This can be explained by the fact that most of the plants on the lower levels of entrepreneurship have not yet reached the stage at which professional management becomes a central factor in the success of the enterprise. Furthermore, their staff is typically employed in unskilled or semiskilled labor. Only at the highest entrepreneurship level, which only a small number of plants have attained, does the problem of management become critical. At that point, the factory requires personnel specializing in management, production control, quality control, computerization, and marketing.

A comparison of plants located in residential areas, on the periphery of settlements, and in industrial zones may shed more light on the difficulties encountered by Arab entrepreneurs as they perceive them. The factories located in residential areas are involved primarily in the branches of wood, printing, and food or are workshops or small textile plants. Those located outside built-up areas are mostly in the building materials and metals industries or are larger operations in the other branches. In general, factories in industrial zones suffer most severely from the lack of physical infrastructures. The lack of capital and government aid, which represent major impeding factors for the development of entrepreneurship, was the subject of complaints by less than one half of the entrepreneurs in industrial zones. Plants on the outskirts of settlements generally suffer the greatest difficulties. These enterprises need large space but do not have any appropriate infrastructures. As a result, the demand for government aid and the construction of industrial zones is expressed most strongly by entrepreneurs whose plants are located on the outskirts of their settlements.

The absence of an industrial zone precludes expansion, since zoning laws often limit activities in the residential area or on the outskirts of a settlement. Owners may define their business to meet the conditions of these laws (as a bake shop rather than a bakery, for example) they are while actually involved in decidedly industrial production. Moreover, the Arab industrialist's need for an industrial zone goes beyond the question of expansion and growth. As long as there is doubt about his ability to compete with and sell to markets in the Jewish sector, it is important for him not to be far from the assured local markets he can always fall back on. In an industrial zone outside his own settlement, the entrepreneur may feel something like a guest who can never know when he will have outstayed his welcome. There is always the fear that when his lease is up, he will be offered less favorable terms for renewal or will be forced to cease operations at the site. Meanwhile, the space he vacated in his own settlement may have been occupied by another entrepreneur. In the words of a bakery owner from Dabburiya:

I considered relocating in the industrial zone of Kefar Tavor (a nearby Jewish settlement), even though no Arab had ever gotten in there. But on second thought I gave up the idea. I was afraid that when the lease was up they'd throw me out, and if I leave here, someone else will open a bakery in the village and take my market away.

The Arab entrepreneur is well aware that he is a member of a disadvantaged minority. He therefore prefers to rely on secure local markets and, through them, to break out into broader markets. This is the model of behavior typically shown by entrepreneurs from ethnic minorities, for whom it is fairly easy to gain the support of their own group in terms of material and social resources such as capital, self-help, social contacts, markets, and labor (Light, 1984; Wilter, 1979).

Generally, a marginal economic and political status, along with professional and educational frustration, have been noted as factors encouraging business entrepreneurship by minority groups (Ronstadt, 1984; Waldinger, Aldrich, & Ward, 1990). Our interviewees, despite the obstacles they confronted, also saw industrial entrepreneurship as a means of getting around the even tougher obstacles, such as inferiority and discrimination, which they faced as laborers in the wider economy. Entrepreneurship represents a way to tackle a challenge from an inferior position and to prove that, in spite of it all, they can make a go of it. According to one interviewee (the owner of a factory from Umm al Fahm),

There is discrimination in the Jewish market, but you can break into it. You have to prove to them that you're a little better than a Jew, that you keep your promises and your products are better and cheaper. We don't have any choice. If you want to make it without taking favors from anyone, you have to start your own business. What good did it do me that I went to university? I didn't want to be a teacher, so the only option was to be self-employed, and thank the Lord my customers are happy and come here even from Tel Aviv.

These comments touch on three significant points. First, as an educated man, the entrepreneur feels that alternative employment opportunities are largely closed to him as a member of a minority. Hence entrepreneurship is virtually his only avenue for socio-economic mobility. Second, as an individual seeking professional challenges along with ethnic pride, there is a particular determination to prove to himself and his fellow Arabs that despite their inferiority in markets controlled by the Jewish majority, a minority member can succeed just as well as, and perhaps even better than, a member of the majority. Third, as a representative of Arab entrepreneurs, this factory owner expresses his belief that the ethnic-based obstacles in the economy are not insurmountable if the entrepreneur is willing to invest in building a reputation for himself. Later, we consider several aspects of the entrepreneurial culture, as revealed in our interviews with Arab entrepreneurs.

ENTREPRENEURIAL MOTIVES

To analyze the motives underlying entrepreneurship, we divided them into two major categories: motives for choosing entrepreneurship as a professional career path, and motives concerning the determination to persevere and succeed as entrepreneurs.

The first category may be divided into dominant groups of motives impelling the majority of entrepreneurs to choose this avenue of activity. The first group involves the desire to achieve professional success bearing high rewards in terms of both income and interest, along with a willingness to take risks. Individuals responding to this motive generally tend to prepare themselves for entrepreneurship over a prolonged period of time. They create the basis for their undertaking in stages, often taking advantage of skills and contacts they have acquired as salaried workers in their former jobs. At the initial stage of developing their own business, the entrepreneurs exploit existing contacts by attracting customers away from their former place of work or entering into agreements with the parent company. The owners of one of the larger metalworking plants in the Arab sector began as wage earners in Israeli industry. When they left the factory in which they were employed, they received job lots from it as subcontractors. This agreement enabled them to create a foundation for their own factory from which they could gradually develop additional markets. In most cases, the source of know-how is a Jewish-owned plant, and at times the Arab entrepreneur even enjoys the active support of a Jewish partner. As one sewing shop owner from Rihaniya explained,

> I worked as a foreman at Tefron [a textile plant]. My boss, a Jew, decided to leave. He's from Karmiel. We talked it over, and I took the space under the house, closed it off, installed machines, got some girls, and we started to work. He has the contacts and gets the jobs and deals with the planning, and I manage the production. We're equal partners.

The owner of an aluminum plant from Baqa al Gharbiya stressed the assistance he had received from his former employer, a Jewish factory owner. This contact helped him both to create a market for himself in a new branch, unprecedented in the Arab sector, and to compete in the Jewish market against his previous employers by taking advantage of connections he had made during his job in the Jewish factory.

> I produce different types of aluminum and copper dies. I set up the factory, the only one of its kind in the Arab sector, with the help of my family. At first there were problems of financing and operations, but I got professional help from friends and the owner of a Jewish workshop in South Tel Aviv that I had worked for. As the business grew, my contacts helped me to move to the industrial zone and buy the land on which I built the factory. The plant has regular customers both in the Arab

sector and in the Tel Aviv metropolitan area, mostly small workshops and factories producing food machines.

The remaining two groups of motives are particularly prominent among minority populations in an economically marginal position, for whom entrepreneurship is virtually the only means of socio-economic mobility in a society controlled by a majority population. The second group of motives relates to the difficulty of finding a place in the Jewish labor market. The problems take different forms. Many workers suffered through prolonged periods of unemployment, always the first to be laid off. Indeed, the unemployment rate for Arabs is significantly higher than for Jews (Schnell, forthcoming). This was especially apparent during the recession in the mid-1960s, when most of the Arab labor force worked as "migrant workers" and so received no Social Security benefits. The owner of a furniture factory from Nazareth specifically stated that "because unemployment in our sector is high, everyone tries to start his own business, but the only ones who make it are those who have patience, perseverance, a knowledge of money management, and good relations with people." The owner of a metalworking shop from Arara expressed a similar idea in the clearest of terms:

> I was laid off by Solel Boneh (construction company) at the age of 51 after 18 years on the job because of my age and my health. I couldn't find a job so I decided to find something else. At first I tried agriculture but it didn't go well. Someone rented space for a metalworking shop from me and went bankrupt. I bought the equipment from him and started to work in the business. First I worked for him and learned the profession from him and then I worked for myself.

Another significant factor in this group, in addition to unemployment, is the mistrust of Arab workers for Jewish employers. These workers fear that at Jewish-owned plants they will be the first to be laid off, regardless of their qualifications or how many years they have been with the company. This concern was validated, to a certain extent, in a survey of Jewish employers, who claimed that they felt a greater obligation to ensure their Jewish workers' income (Schnell, 1994b). Other Arab entrepreneurs noted that they were tired of long commutes for relatively low wages. Compelled to spend most of the day away from home, the men felt cut off from the life of their village and at the same time suffered from a sense of alienation and disadvantage in the work place (Schnell, 1994a). It is thus understandable that many Arabs seek employment opportunities within the borders of their settlement. The owner of a furniture factory in Upper Galilee stated that he had been willing to work as a laborer in Haifa for wages that barely covered his travel and other work-related expenses in order to train himself professionally in a field in which he could open his own business.

In the words of the owner of a concrete block factory from Dabburiya,

> I used to work long hours in construction in different parts of the center of the country. I left for work at 5:00 in the morning and got home after dark. I had no family life, I didn't see my children, and it was hard for me to keep up my social contacts. It's customary for us to visit relatives in the afternoon and evening. I got tired of it and decided to save to set up a concrete block factory. I'd rather earn less and work in the village.

The third group of motives underlying entrepreneurship as a career relates to education. Arabs with an academic or vocational education who discover that, as members of a minority, their chances of finding work in their profession or of professional advancement are limited turn instead to industrial entrepreneurship. Many feel it is beneath their dignity to hire themselves out as blue-collar workers, while as independent businessmen they enjoy a higher status and better income. As the owner of a concrete block factory in Nazareth put it, "I studied accounting and worked in an office in Haifa. But my salary was low and I saw that my chances of promotion were not so good, so I decided to open a concrete block business with my brothers."

The vicious circle in which the educated Arab finds himself is clear from the words of the owner of a metalworking shop from Nazareth:

> My brothers helped me to get through school. I graduated as a practical engineer in electronics, but there's no work for Arabs in that field. At the age of 26 I started the business, also to help my brothers, who have no profession, and my other brother, who didn't pass the Israeli tests for a doctor's license after he graduated from medical school in Romania.

As a practical engineer in electronics, this entrepreneur had no chance of finding work in the labor market controlled by the more privileged work force in Jewish society. Finding the doors of advanced hi-tech plants in Israeli industry closed to him, the potential entrepreneur returned to his extended family, to whom he owed his education. His brothers had saved money to pay for his studies, and now he had to help them solve their economic problems while taking advantage of his higher skills, acquired with their assistance. The only solution available to him was entrepreneurship, even in a field other than that in which he was trained. The interviewee acted in a manner typical of Arabs and many other educated minority members whose actual employment does not correspond with their level of education or training (Czamanski, Jubran, & Khamaisi, 1986; Haidar, 1993; Lewin-Epstein, 1990; Lewin-Epstein & Semyonov, 1993).

The second category of motives is concerned with the determination to succeed. One feature runs like a thread through our interviews with entrepreneurs: their determination to succeed by relying on family resources, and immediately and flexibly exploiting any opportunity that offers the chance to enter markets or gain access to sources of information and communication systems in the Jewish economy. Moreover, the interviews reveal that the entrepreneurs believe firmly that economic success must inevitably come to those who display values such as industriousness, willingness to work hard, dedication, and general and professional education. They also believe that financial success holds out a promise of economic mobility. This challenge affords high social prestige to professions that in other contexts would be seen as blue-collar jobs. As an entrepreneur in the metals industry in a Galilee village stated, "We in the Arab sector have to succeed, and in order to do that we invest not only money, but also our soul. My willingness to accept failure is less than in the Jewish sector, so I give myself, body and soul, to the business."

The Arab entrepreneur sees his Jewish counterpart as someone willing to invest in a business only if the returns he gets from it are particularly high. In contrast, the Arab entrepreneur, for whom available alternatives are extremely limited, is compelled to exhibit immense determination even in the most unfavorable circumstances. The story of a furniture factory owner from Nazareth aptly demonstrates the complex of issues involved:

> First I sold newspapers and cakes, in 1954. Then I persuaded my father to let me study a trade, and he finally agreed to let me work for a Jewish carpenter in Haifa. My wages were less than the fare back and forth to Haifa. Later I specialized in furniture polishing and took whatever jobs came along in private homes. As the eldest brother in a large family (three brothers and eight sisters), my wages went to support the family. It was like that until 1968, the year I got married. After the wedding, I found myself with no house or land, paying a high rent, and I had a large loan to repay. I started a business and worked under terrible conditions in a shelter without electricity (using flashlights). Then I rented a small building with electricity. In 1973 I set up a polishing workshop. I worked hard, days and nights on end, not wasting any time or money, and in that way I grew and opened a furniture store too. In 1983 I bought my first car, a 1973 model. In our sector you have to work very hard to succeed. Because unemployment is high in our sector, everyone tries to start a business. The ones who make it are those that have patience, perseverance, a knowledge of money management, and good relations with people.

This story illustrates the long-term program through which the entrepreneur, displaying a willingness to work hard and live in poor conditions, trained himself professionally as a carpenter and furniture polisher. Throughout the course of his career, the family was his only supporting element on his way to becoming a successful entrepreneur.

COMMUNITY AND FAMILY

The family unit, with its particular features, is an extremely important element in understanding the entrepreneurial culture. Among the prominent changes that have taken place in Arab society in Israel is the splitting up of the household into nuclear families displaying increasing degrees of independence (Avitzur, 1986; Ginat, 1983; Habash, 1973). Nevertheless, kinship continues to play a major role in encouraging modernization and economic growth (Schnell, 1980, 1994b). The status deriving from membership in a certain family remains a primary factor in determining an individual's standing in society, and, as a result, each person bears responsibility for the entire family. In addition, the family provides social and economic security and is the source of a variety of resources required to run a factory (which, in most cases, is under family management). In turn, the business is also exploited for the benefit and welfare of all members of the extended family, particularly those who participated in providing the resources for its development.

The majority of entrepreneurs interviewed stressed the importance of the family's involvement in founding the plant. The most common pattern is the acquisition of capital and managers from the immediate family as well as family intervention in numerous aspects of the plant's activities. Often, the family's involvement is so deep that it is impossible to distinguish between the interests of the factory and those of the extended family. The owner of a sewing shop from Kafr Yasif revealed the extent of the involvement of members of his extended family in his business:

> I'm the eldest. Two other brothers work with me and two sisters sew. One brother manages production and the other keeps the books. I'm the general manager, but I work mainly with customers. Each of us also knows the jobs of the others, so when I'm not here my brothers fill in for me and I have nothing to worry about.

In this case, having brothers on the staff allows for operational flexibility along with a high level of mutual trust with regard to running the plant. The entrepreneur's status as eldest brother grants him authority with respect to organization and division of responsibilities and labor in the factory. In this manner, the family hierarchy is carried over into the business and aids in organizing labor and management.

In most cases, when a factory is family owned, it is the eldest brother who garners family resources to start an industrial enterprise. Of the 70 entrepreneurs interviewed, 85 percent were first-born sons. This is not a coincidence but derives from two primary factors. The first is allied with the status of the eldest brother, for whom it is easier to lead the younger children because of the authority he has in traditional society as deputy father. The second relates to the patterns by which the family adjusts to the rapid changes that Arab society in Israel is undergoing. The entire extended family is mobilized to solve the economic problems of its children, such as the need to build a home and acquire an education. The family often divides responsibilities so that some of the children are sent to study while others are sent to work in order to earn enough to support the whole family. In such a situation, the function of starting a business is frequently assigned to the eldest brother, with the support and encouragement of all other members of the family, and the ultimate aim is to serve family needs. It follows that the entrepreneur's obligations to his family are great, as can be seen in this excerpt from the interview with the owner of a print shop in Maghar:

Q: How come you were the one who started a business?

A: I'm the first born and I studied literature and Middle Eastern studies at the university, but when I decided to start a business, it was obvious that the family would help. My brothers gave me money, and so did my two sisters, who work for Delta [a sewing firm].

Q: And what will happen if the business doesn't go well?

A: That can't happen. My two brothers also work [in it] and there are plenty of orders. I sent my wife to learn to use the Macintosh [computer]. My success is the success of the whole family.

Assistance is not restricted to the supply of labor, managers, and initial capital but also includes the allocation of land. Generally, the ground floor under the residence of the extended family is earmarked, by the entire family in a joint decision, for the planned enterprise. This is explained by the owner of a sewing shop from Bir al Sikka:

In order to set up the plant, I took the ground floor under the house, closed it off, installed machines, got some girls, and started to work. I got permission to use the ground floor from my father, who lives on the first floor, with the agreement of two brothers who live in the house with us.

Family assistance is not only of instrumental importance but is also of major value in terms of morale. The support of the family creates a sense of security, a feeling that one can more readily succeed in business. Success is seen as that of the entire family, and the eldest brother—the entrepreneur—owes this to them. The response of one entrepreneur to a question concerning the factors hindering his ability to expand his plant—given with no evidence of complaint or bitterness—is telling: "I'm having trouble raising the capital for further development because a large part of the profit goes to building a house for my two younger brothers. I have to help them like they helped me because that's the way things are with us."

Strong family solidarity affords the entrepreneur advantages stemming from the immense trust of members of the extended family for each other regarding management of the factory. In the absence of well-developed formal patterns of management, this trust is the foundation of entrepreneurial managerial activity. Incomplete bookkeeping, deals closed for cash and not formally recorded, the location of the plant in a residential area without the proper license, and so on are all common practices in Arab industry. In such a situation, the gaps are filled by kinship relations. As the owner of a sewing shop from Kafr Yasif stated, "If the manager isn't from the family, there's always the danger he'll steal from you."

Another entrepreneur claimed that "it's even hard to trust your brothers, and there are plenty of problems with them, so how could you trust a manager from another family?" According to a third entrepreneur, "That's how it is with us, you don't trust people from other families, only your own family." Reliance on the extended family for management is typical not only of plants on the lower entrepreneurial levels but also of prominently successful factories, such as the Bulus Brothers (marble) and Kadmani Brothers (metals). Here and in other factories, control and management of the operation is based on the involvement of family members in all aspects of the business, from production management and labor to marketing.

We might ask whether reliance on the family continues to be a positive factor for development as the factory rises to higher levels of entrepreneurship. Several responses reveal that while the contribution of the extended family to the foundation and establishment of the plant is critical, at a certain stage it becomes a factor impeding further development. The foreman of a relatively large factory, who asked to remain anonymous, related the following:

> I work as a foreman in a factory that belongs to someone from another *hamula*. There are too many managers in the plant who give orders and drive you crazy, and since they belong to the family you can't talk back to them. They get a salary without contributing anything to the plant, and I can't get promoted or have any influence.

These might appear to be merely the comments of a foreman frustrated by his lack of advancement. However, several entrepreneurs operating factories on higher entrepreneurship levels noted similar problems. The owner of a concrete block factory, for example, complained about his two brothers who work in the plant:

> It's bad because I can't give instructions to brothers freely. I have to consult with them and accept all their crazy ideas. I also can't fire a brother or reprimand him. It's a serious problem for the work in the factory. I'd rather work with managers from outside the family. I could demand from them what I think should be done and could fire them if they weren't good.

Such situations reveal the conflict between a system meant to operate according to economic and managerial principles and hierarchical-bureaucratic rules, on the one hand, and family interests that give priority to collegiality and social obligations and needs, on the other. As the owner of a textile factory explained, "My brother gave me money to set up the factory. I owe him, so I can't undermine his status and I have to consider his needs and opinions. . . . Brothers often permit themselves to act in a way that's not good for the company, and you can't do anything about it."

In addition to the mutual support and interdependence between the extended family as supplier of production factors and the entrepreneur as supplier of employment, there is also a major role played by the *hamula* in encouraging entrepreneurship. The *hamula*, once the primary political unit in traditional Arab society, now limits its political activity to the realm of the municipality (Rekhess, 1986). In economic terms, this means that belonging to a large and influential *hamula* may provide greater access to decision makers at the local level. A consequence of this access is the ability to realize potential entrepreneurship. The owner of a sewing shop situated within the built-up area of a village in Western Galilee noted his bloodline and local political connections with more than a little pride:

> Our family is the largest in the village. We've also controlled the local council for two terms.
>
> Q: What does this mean for the sewing shop?
> A: A lot. Why do you think all the girls are cousins? That's good, because there's no carrying on here and they all work hard. You don't feel right making trouble; the whole family would know. . . .
>
> Q: And what about politics?
> A: It's good. . . . Our family favors developing the village, and you saw the road and the sewers they're building. Local taxes aren't too bad either, and there's no problem getting a building license. Just this year I expanded by another 200 square meters and nobody said a word about it. [The sewing shop is located in an area designated as a residential zone.]

This interview underlines several aspects of the community support afforded the entrepreneur by virtue of his *hamula* membership. First and foremost, the personal status accorded the plant workers becomes a major tool in raising their motivation. It is not only their prestige as workers that is determined by their place of work but also their overall prestige in the community. Furthermore, *hamula* control of the local authority enables the entrepreneur to obtain a license to set up his plant in a residential area, to receive a license at a reduced tax rate, and sometimes even to get around the bylaws, which makes it easier to establish and operate the factory.

The community and *hamula* also support the entrepreneur by affording his achievements a particularly high socio-economic value. Alongside determination of an individual's status by kinship—belonging to a distinguished family and *hamula*—is an achievement-based status system whereby successful economic entrepreneurship is highly prestigious. This prestige derives from several factors: (1) appreciation of the supreme effort required from an Arab entrepreneur, inherently at a disadvantage in competing for Jewish markets; (2) the freedom achieved for himself by an entrepreneur who is no longer dependent on labor markets that are remote from his settlement and controlled by economic norms anchored in the Jewish economy; and (3) the financial influence of an entrepreneur within the family and community in which he lives.

It can also be held that an individual's success is not a source of envy in Arab society. Improvement of one's state in life and a rise in one's standard of living are seen as fitting rewards for the hard work invested in building a business. As a whole, Arab society encourages and admires success, and the entrepreneur is considered a role model. Entrepreneurs are not seen to have succeeded at the expense of others. As the owner of a concrete block factory in Yafia said,

> Take me, for example. I began as a floor layer and today I have a concrete block factory. I'm even considering buying a drying machine to shorten the time the blocks have to sit outside and not have to worry about the winter. Everyone is rooting for me. Having your own business is good. If I want to, I fly to Turkey to the casino. Nobody tells me what to do. Everyone says, "Way to go! I hope I can do the same some day."

Economic success thus seems to enable the entrepreneur to adopt aspects of a modern lifestyle, periodically stepping out of the constricting traditional social order. The traditional forces in the society have, however, certain expectations of the successful entrepreneur. These generally concern his contribution to the community and participation in charity, social and other public activities, as well as political involvement. On the personal level, entrepreneurs take on themselves the function of "watchdogs" of accepted behavioral norms and values, particularly as regards the family. According to an industrialist in the construction branch from Yafia, "A person who succeeds has to help the others too. Not that I wouldn't take care of my family. Their standard of living and conditions have to be improved, but it's also important that businessmen be involved in public affairs."

Elders of the Islamic movement, who represent traditional norms, take advantage of this attitude and preach for contributions to the community, basing their demand on the commandments of Islam. Moneys collected in part from industrialists, to a large extent the agents of modernization, are used to establish educational and cultural institutions aimed at preserving the traditional way of life and entrenching it in the contemporary reality.

THE ENTREPRENEUR AND THE MARKET

The entrepreneurial environment of the Arab industrialist distinguishes between markets in the Arab and the Jewish economies, which do not operate according to the same economic norms. Entrance into the Jewish market is perceived by many entrepreneurs to be possible but extremely difficult. Thus, the Arab entrepreneur who succeeds in breaking into Jewish markets is generally seen as being on a relatively high entrepreneurial level and gains great prestige in his village. Many entrepreneurs view this as a major challenge to be confronted, since local markets are too small and consumption is limited. In fact, however, only a few plants in the branches of construction, metals, wood, and textiles and clothing have managed to break into Jewish markets, and these did so after overcoming considerable obstacles, as explained earlier.

Some Arab entrepreneurs perceived of the Jewish markets as closed to them. As the owner of a concrete block factory in a small Galilean village complained,

> Jews refuse to buy concrete blocks from an Arab factory because of discrimination against the Arabs. They want to give their business to Jews, not Arabs. I sell a block for 20 agorot [an agora is one hundredth of an Israeli shekel] less than the price in Jewish plants and my blocks are of higher quality, but I don't get Jewish customers.

When asked if he had made any attempt to reach Jewish markets, this entrepreneur responded that he had not and that there was no point in doing so because the Jews would not buy from him in any case. When we asked if his products bore the seal of the Israel Standards Institute, he stated that he needed no proof of the quality of his blocks because they were good. Our attempt to persuade him that the seal of the Standards Institute might encourage potential Jewish buyers was a dismal failure. He felt that in view of the high cost involved, it was not worthwhile to invest in external quality control. This entrepreneur, from the generation of older industrialists with limited formal education, is representative of many plant owners on the lower levels of the entrepreneurship scale that find it difficult to break into markets outside their own community. They fail to develop the awareness and tools that might prepare them to compete in modern markets outside their immediate community.

Younger entrepreneurs, most with a high level of formal education, apply various strategies in any attempt to break into the Jewish market. The owner of a concrete block factory from Taiyibe related how a kinsman of his who worked as a self-employed contractor in the Jewish construction industry had purchased blocks from him for homes he was building in Sharon region towns. In this manner, the Arab contractor in the family served as a spearhead for entrance into Jewish markets. Another contractor from Sakhnin explained that the programs that enabled people to build their own homes in the new Jewish towns and communal settlements in Galilee had presented him with new opportunities. Families erecting their own homes preferred to purchase building materials from nearby Arab factories at a price lower than that demanded by the large Jewish-owned companies. In some of these cases, an Arab contractor served as a go-between, while in others the Jewish buyers themselves dealt directly with the factory. Entrance into Jewish markets is vital for increasing a factory's income and enabling it to rise on the entrepreneurship scale. Although the plant may be able to survive by continuing to rely on the more guaranteed markets in the Arab sector, the entrepreneurial challenge to expand one's markets is tempting. According to the owner of a carpentry shop in Yafia,

> It's not that it's impossible to survive on the market in Nazareth and Yafia, but when people hear about you they come on Saturdays from Migdal Ha'Emeq and Afula and even Haifa. They know that here furniture is cheaper and better, and I show my customers respect, so they recommend us to others.

The owner of a food products factory from Tamra remarked that he sold to several Jewish customers in the center of the country. In answer to our question of why he sold to a few distant Jewish settlements and not to the ones in the vicinity, he replied that when he goes to his suppliers in the center of the country to purchase raw materials, he takes advantage of that opportunity and sells to a few stores in their area. This example similarly demonstrates the attempt to expand into those Jewish markets that happen to become available, without regularly competing for this market against large concerns.

At more advanced levels of entrepreneurship, the industrialist may even be willing to adapt his marketing methods especially for the Jewish market. The owner of a carpentry shop from Jaljulya hired a Jewish secretary and employs the services of a Jewish designer. This entrepreneur understood that improving the Jewish customer's ability to conduct the kind of clear and simple negotiations he was used to was a necessary condition for a significant entrance into Jewish markets. What this means is that an Arab entrepreneur competing in the Jewish market must adapt himself to the demands of the customer and meet the accepted quality requirements of this market.

In the textile and clothing industry, which relies largely on the Jewish parent company for its market, the expansion into wider markets necessary for rising on the entrepreneurship scale takes a different course. Here plants seek to develop their own independent markets in addition to carrying out sewing jobs for the parent company. Within the confines of their relations with the parent company, their chances of growth are slight. The Jewish-owned companies prefer not to enable them to develop the know-how to perform other tasks besides sewing. Moreover, the parent companies deliberately divide the job lots among different subsidiaries and block their access to parent companies' markets. Under these circumstances, the advancement of a sewing shop is dependent on the creation of independent markets. In the initial stage, the plant sells surplus goods to the Arab market in its own and neighboring settlements. Only at a later stage does the entrepreneur attempt to make his own break into Jewish markets or even to export his goods abroad. At the most advanced stage, the plant may attempt to free itself from dependency on the parent company. Thus far, however, we have not found a single textile factory that managed to maintain its independent status for any length of time. The dynamics by which textile and clothing plants develop new markets becomes apparent from the comments of a sewing shop owner from Kafr Manda:

> When I started, I worked for several offices and purchasing agents in Tel Aviv. Whatever I sewed, I made certain of its quality. Orders came in. I increased the number of seamstresses and opened another sewing shop in Bu'eina that my younger brother runs.

Q: In other words, the idea for setting up the business came from the company in Tel Aviv?

A: Not exactly. First I worked as a driver and I brought the girls to the Delta sewing shops. Later I opened a sewing shop in the village, and today I work for everyone, for stores in the villages and Nazareth (mainly surplus goods), for offices in Tel Aviv, and I even started to export. When you're good and people know you, there's a lot of work, and we do it better and cheaper.

The most difficult phase of integration in the Jewish market is that at which the Arab entrepreneur must compete against large corporations. Under such circumstances, the large company often brings pressure to bear against the small factory. Resourcefulness, perseverance, taking clever advantage of relative advantages, and skill in the art of negotiations all served the owner of a pita bread bakery from Dabburiya when he was forced to compete with the Oranim Bakery in Kefar HaHoresh:

> It was hard to compete with Oranim because the bakery forced its customers to buy its pita if they wanted to buy its bread. Since our pita is better, we had to buy bread in Haifa and supply our customers with both pita and bread in order to fight Oranim's monopoly. Then Oranim proposed an agreement: They would supply the bread and we would supply the pita. There's still competition and some hitting below the belt. Oranim gets tax exemptions and subsidies, so they can give the buyers discounts. Here we don't get subsidies; it's not a development area. I managed to compete because of my personal approach to the customers and because my product is better than the others. I supply on time, in the amount required, and on credit.

Another strategy for breaking into Jewish markets springs from traditional values. The owners of food plants customarily produce products according to traditional methods, thereby answering the demands of the market for natural and authentic ethnic foods. As the owner of a cheese factory from Tamra related,

> My father had a herd of goats and my mother made cheese from their milk. When we started the factory, I took my mother's recipes for cheese and began producing them on a large scale. At first we only sold in the village. In time we bought more sophisticated equipment and increased our production by purchasing milk from other herds, and today we sell to all the villages in the area and even to a few Jewish markets. Our cheese is made from whole milk, without any milk powder, according to a special secret formula. There's no other plant in the market like this one.

Most of the factories producing olives and olive oil, humus, sesame, and other foods sell a small proportion of their output to the health and natural food market or to gourmet shops. They find it difficult to compete on a large scale for Jewish markets, since these are supplied by large concerns that are well known in Jewish industry. Moreover, the consumer's faith in the quality of the product is extremely important in the food industry, and Arab industrialists have not managed to gain that trust; one reason for this is the tension between the two groups stemming from concerns of nationality and security.

ACCESS TO INFORMATION

Another major factor impeding industrial development in the Arab sector relates to access to information, particularly concerning consulting services, marketing and commercial matters, and the laws, regulations, and procedures of the governmental bodies charged with promoting industry. There is a feeling that the lack of business information is a major obstacle that prevents the entrepreneur from taking advantage of opportunities. The entrepreneurs we interviewed claimed that they severely lacked official information on aspects relating to governmental bodies. Most of their business information was collected informally, primarily through their network of customers and suppliers. Information is also acquired at social occasions, such as weddings and parties or political meetings. Such information is fundamental because it enables an entrepreneur to locate sources of labor, raw materials, and customers. Sources of relevant business information are Jewish professionals with specific skills which the Arab entrepreneur does not have, such as economists or accountants. In many cases, these professionals make it possible to rise a step on the entrepreneurship scale, as the owner of a concrete block factory explained:

> Take the Sa'ida family from Peqi'in. They were small-scale producers of concrete blocks and building materials. When they started grow, they hired a Jewish economist. He helped them, and today they deal in the millions. All the settlements in the area work with them, even the Jewish ones. You have no choice. If you want to grow, you have to be modern. Small family businesses are okay, but you can't drive a Mercedes 300 from them. Among us there still aren't many with expertise in financing and banks, and we really feel the lack. So meanwhile, anyone who starts to grow has to hire a Jew.

As the owner of a sewing shop in Maghar states, "I'm one of the only factories certified as an 'approved factory.' It wasn't easy, but I didn't give up and I hired a lawyer from Tel Aviv who handled the case for me, and in the end I did it."

Additional required information, in the form of professional advice, concerns tax laws and bookkeeping. On the whole, medium-sized businesses hire part-time bookkeepers. Most entrepreneurs tend to employ the services of accounting offices located mainly in the large Arab towns.

THE RELEVANCE OF THE ENTREPRENEURIAL CULTURE

Our survey and interviews reveal that it is impossible to distinguish between cultural traits encouraging entrepreneurship and the structure of opportunities available to the entrepreneur. An entrepreneurial personality, reflected in perseverance, hard work, thrift, self-discipline, and the desire to be self-employed, is a major resource for the establishment of a business. Yet the structure of the Arab economy and the nature of its links with the whole of the Israeli economy emphasize qualities and values which stem from the need to adjust to the socio-economic realities of an ethnic minority. Here weight is given to the ability to identify the pragmatic aspects of the Arab entrepreneurial culture, such as family support and resources, in addition to the entrepreneur's determination to succeed. The story of Nohah, a woman who owns a prosperous sewing shop in Abu Sinan, is an extraordinary one because of the rarity of female entrepreneurs, yet it brings together the different issues that have emerged from our discussion of entrepreneurial culture:

I've been in the field since 1972. I started working at the age of 14 in Kafr Yasif. After two and a half years, I went to work for Gibor in Akko. I worked there for two and a half years too. Zihadi Nohad, the owner of a sewing shop in the village, was looking for seamstresses, so I left Gibor and worked for Nohad for 11 years, two years sewing and nine years in charge of 60 seamstresses. While I was working for Zihadi, I bought a sewing machine and worked at home, in my bedroom, after hours. I worked every day until 11 or 12 at night. Then I left Zihadi and bought two more machines and I set them up in my bedroom and started to work—me, my sister, and another girl from the family. We sewed uniforms for schools in Haifa and Kiryat Bialik [a Jewish town within Haifa metropolitan area]. I got the job from Maruzini from Kiryat Bialik through someone in Kafr Yasif. I worked that way for wages for four months. Then I said I wanted to bring in three more machines. My married sister and I bought them together and started looking for more work. I went to Tel Aviv and Holon, to Beit Romano and Levanda St. I went into one place called Bam-Bam that sells pants and shirts for children. I told him [the owner] what I did. He was honest with me and said he didn't know me but he would give me a small job to try me out. I sewed 200 pieces for him and he was pleased. After that we started to work for him. We were six seamstresses. We worked from the morning until one o'clock at night. My sister's husband would take the clothes and bring the patterns from Tel Aviv three times a week. During this time I was also working for someone from Nazareth Illit.

I worked with my sister's husband for a year, and then we split up and divided the machines between us. After we split up, I borrowed 10,000 shekels from a good friend. It doesn't pay to borrow from the bank because of the adjustment to the index of cost of living and interest, and because you're always in the red. I bought a car, a 1970 model. I brought my younger brother into the sewing shop, and my cousin did all the bookkeeping. The family helped me all the time. The business was in the house, in a bedroom and a closed-off porch. I didn't take any money out of it, except for food. All the income went to buying machines and helping my brother to study. I started looking for more work, until I found a large factory–Trico Fox in Tel Aviv. They didn't know me, but the guy there, his name is Ze'ev, asked me questions and gave me patterns on trial. That's how come I've been working for them regularly for four years already. Aside from that, I also work with Kibbutz Shomrat and other customers in the area.

The shop began to grow. We had 33 girls. I sent my brother to a mechanics course at Shenkar and I went with him. Now he's studying to be a practical engineer in industry and management at Yad Natan, and what he learns helps me a lot with production. The other brothers in the family said "Let's help her out" and gave me 10,000 shekels to buy a car, and later I also asked Trico Fox for a loan, 50,000 shekels to be paid back in seven installments with no interest but linked to the index of cost of living. Meanwhile, we bought a car and formed a company, my brother and I. All the money we make goes into the shop. The people in the village say we're swell, but some don't like what we're doing, like the owners of other sewing shops. But I have a good reputation, and I work very hard. The most important thing in our business is honesty and credibility with the customers. The girls who work for me like me; I pay more and show them a lot of respect. Some come from the village and even the family and some from Judeida–I pick them up and take them back. To succeed you have to work hard. Now I want to produce my own things for stores. I made a go of it because I wanted to get ahead in life, to make money and help my family and my brothers. My family also helps me to succeed.

Arab entrepreneurs have to steer their way between the relative advantages of the Arab sector and the obstacles placed in their path. Particularly prominent is their entrance into niches of the market that do not attract Jewish entrepreneurs or in which they have an edge in terms of production, price, and service. They tend not to take risks regarding investments that do not come from their own pockets, and they prefer to operate at a steady, secure level instead of incurring the insecurity of expansion. They make intensive use of family resources and their wide-reaching social contacts, channeling them for purposes of business development. Arab entrepreneurs combine a reliance on guaranteed Arab markets with great flexibility and determined efforts to break into markets outside their village and area, undertaken after a clearheaded and cautious assessment of their achievements and growth potential. In the initial stage, they seek out small niches of the Jewish market, and then, having earned themselves a reputation, attempt to compete with the large factories in the market. The entrepreneurs attach particular importance to the manner in which they operate in this market, taking care to preserve the values of reliability and skill and, most especially, to honor their commitment to those who lend them support and assistance—the members of their family. In this sense, the face of Arab entrepreneurship is much like that of the Roman god Janus. On the one hand, entrepreneurs are still tied to the traditional system and family commitments. On the other hand, however, they must give

Table 10.2
Aspects of Industrial Entrepreneurial Culture by Industrial Branch

Branch	Niche	Resources	Impending Factors
Food, Printing	•Mainly local, based on demand for special products; •opportunistic entrance & access to fringes of Jewish market	Reliance on: •kinship for capital and labor; •traditional know-how; •local markets	Lack of risk reducing mechanisms and restriction of •raising capital & collateral •physical infrastructure •managerial & marketing personnel
Construction materials, Metals, Wood	Reliance on local market & entrance into Jewish markets via Arab contractors or directly	Reliance on: •kinship for financing & management; •on social relationships for political contacts and technology & on market; •know-how gained from working for wages in Jewish sector; •promotion of contacts with Jewish organizations & elite groups as a level for creating entrepreneurial communications networks	

Table 10.2, continued

| Textiles | Mainly subcontractors, female workers | Reliance on:
•Cheap labor, cheap & available infrastructure;
•know-how from Jewish parent company | |

weight to purely commercial considerations, which are often at odds with their obligations to family and community.

The entrepreneurial culture of the Arab industrialist is influenced by a combination of the structure of opportunities, the cultural features of Arab society, and entrepreneurial strategies. All of these operate within the framework of the interrelations between the Arab and Jewish economies and under changing conditions of economic activity. The structure of opportunities is commonly believed to be affected by unfair discrimination against the Arab entrepreneur in relation to his Jewish counterpart, particularly regarding issues such as credit, grants, support, and the subsidization of government investments in infrastructure. To cope with these circumstances, the entrepreneur must take advantage of the relative advantages available to him. These derive in part from the low operating costs which result from several factors: cheap labor, labor (especially managerial) drawn from the family, tight control of income and outlays, low financing costs, and relatively inexpensive technology. Entrance into the Jewish market requires that customer needs be met most satisfactorily and that competitive advantages be offered, such as low price, convenient credit terms, flexibility in meeting customer needs, high-quality goods, and punctual supply.

Table 10.2 summarizes aspects of the Arab entrepreneurial culture relating to resources and impeding factors in the major industrial branches. Patterns of entrepreneurship are distinguished by branch type, technological level, sources of financing, markets, and so on.

The entrepreneurial culture remains relevant throughout all stages of founding and operating an industrial enterprise. The entrepreneur, supported by his family and motivated by a desire to be self-employed and to achieve financial success, operates in an environment of both security and insecurity. Reliance on the Arab sector alone will result in a relatively small business low on the entrepreneurship scale. Entrance into Jewish markets, however, entails relatively sophisticated business activity. The entrepreneur requires managerial and financial resources and must adopt economic behavior that gives precedence to the need for efficiency, quality, credibility, and low price. All of these considerations operate within a socio-economic system that places the Arab entrepreneur at a disadvantage, thereby imposing a ceiling on his potential success.

Chapter 11

The Israeli Milieu

THE STRUCTURAL VIEWPOINT

Thus far, our analysis of industrial entrepreneurship in Arab settlements in Israel has focused on the micro level—the shop floor—and the meso level—the Israeli-Arab milieu. This chapter examines aspects on the macro level, considering underlying mechanisms affecting Arab industrial entrepreneurship within the national context. Our aim is to explain the larger milieu in which industrial entrepreneurship and production take place because this has substantial influence on the decisions of the entrepreneur. We thus consider the major underlying structural factors affecting branch selection, plant formation, and the pattern and path of industrial entrepreneurship among Israeli Arabs.

Our examination of structural factors in this chapter focusses on the complex of interrelations that produce the processes and mechanisms underlying economic activity in the Israeli economy in general and in the Arab sector in particular. Although these operate on levels beyond the single plant, related factories, or regional systems, they affect the behavior of the individual entrepreneur. Indeed, structural aspects also include structural change, a major prerequisite for economic growth. Structural change can occur in the presence of the following conditions: technological capabilities, specific infrastructures (human capital, research and development, physical infrastructure, financial institutions), the availability of potential entrepreneurs, and a large and sophisticated local market (Justman & Teubal, 1993). A good example of an obvious structural change in the Arab sector are the shifts in employment patterns. During the 1950s, this sector underwent a transition from peasantry to a second labor market in the branches of construction, agriculture, and services in Jewish towns (Rosenfeld, 1978). An additional transition occurred in the 1970s, when this labor force went from being a second labor market to employment in labor-intensive jobs in organized labor markets.

Our main argument is that although there has been a transformation of Arab society and significant changes within Arab industry in Israel, this has occurred within an unchanged structure. Ever since the establishment of the national structure and the definition of core and periphery, and despite changes in the forms of relations between the core and the (Arab) periphery, the relative status of each has not changed. Changes in Arab industry, as shown in Chapter 4, resulted from a process of constructive destruction, in which enterprises associated with the peasant economy vanished and were replaced by enterprises in new branches of production linked to the developing modern Israeli economy. Since the 1960s, however, no new process of constructive destruction has taken place. Although factories have increased in size and have modified production methods, as shown in Chapter 6, Arab industry is still characterized by small plants, simple technology, managerial relations based largely on kinship, and a relatively unsophisticated output.

The textile and clothing industry is a clear case in point. In the current stage of capitalist development in Israel, the constant search for new methods of capital accumulation and expansion has brought about a geographical shift of certain stages of production into Arab settlements—specifically, the routine, standardized, labor-intensive production tasks in the textile and clothing industry. As has been argued in previous chapters, while this shift created an occupational change in Arab settlements (such as an increase in women's participation rates), it has maintained Arab industry at the lower level of production. In fact, although specific aspects of relations and forces of production within the national structure may have changed, the Arab sector has not challenged its peripheral status. Arab industry, as a major representative of the periphery, has indeed increased in size and expanded its national share of the industrial labor force. Yet the type of industry and its degree of importance on the national scale have remained marginal. In structural terms, whereas in the past Arab industry operated under imposed constraints, in the present its growth and integration are largely in line with the needs of core capital. In reality, within Arab industry itself, conservation processes are stronger than processes of change. Consequently, one may argue that given the continued existence and even expansion of small plants in older production branches, the human, physical, and technological infrastructures have not been challenged by any pressure to move toward a fundamental structural change.

Despite what has been argued in this chapter, and in contrast to the deterministic core-periphery view that may derive from the foregoing discussion, certain progressive changes can be seen in the Arab periphery. A number of industrial entrepreneurs have, albeit to a limited extent, actively sought various responses to their marginal position, although such efforts are more widespread in the realms of commerce and trade (Falah, 1993). These responses are part of a process of transformation in which a distinctive change is expressed by achieving the highest level on the entrepreneurial scale. This is exhibited in size and form of organization and operation rather than in the emergence of new branches, and it suggests that changes in the Arab periphery are possible and attainable.

Within the Israeli economy, three major structural factors have affected the nature of Arab industry. The first relates to the underdevelopment of the Arab economy and industry, the second to the fact that Arab settlements constitute an inferior periphery in the Israeli economic space, and the third to the status of the Arab entrepreneur as a member of a national-ethnic minority with different values and norms from the Jewish majority. Each of these factors has placed the Arab entrepreneur at a disadvantage in terms of both the workings of the market and the economic policies of the government, which plays an active role in the Israeli economy. Individually and together, the three factors affect the nature of Arab industrial development in Israel. As a result, the Arab entrepreneur is forced to deal with a long line of constraints, some outside the Arab sector and others inherent to it, which affect the rate of factory development, the establishment of new plants, branch structure, and the patterns of industrial activity at all stages.

THE UNDERDEVELOPMENT OF THE ARAB ECONOMY

The underdevelopment of the Arab economy is linked to three major elements: its specific development history; the nature of integration in the Israeli economy; and the conservation of traditional institutions. With the establishment of the State of Israel, the Arab population became a minority living mostly in agricultural villages that lacked even a minimal modern physical infrastructure. Largely lacking in basic formal education (to say nothing of technical training and experience in a market economy), this sector soon found itself lagging behind the rapidly developing Jewish economy. As we have seen in Chapter 3, the gap between the two sectors grew steadily wider as the Jewish economy, primarily urban, shifted earlier and further toward industrialization. The little industry that existed in Arab settlements was labor intensive, employed low technology, and supplied internal demand.

This state of affairs does not seem encouraging as a starting point toward a modern industrial society. Moreover, the Arab sector developed as a noncapitalist economy undergoing transformation alongside an expanding Jewish capitalist economy. The latter influenced the development processes of the former, with the government as the main instrument of control. To maintain Jewish control over the economy, the Israeli government adopted a number of mechanisms designed to regulate the integration of Israeli Arabs into the society and economy: security regulations, the appropriation of land, a discriminatory development policy, and political co-optation.

Arab industrial plants began to develop rapidly in the 1970s, when the Israeli economy was dominated by large corporations. These corporations, exploiting their economic power, made it difficult for small industrial enterprises to grow and penetrate national markets, while at the same time the needs of the local market and expanded local demand were spurring the growth of Arab industry. This late growth of the Arab sector, occurring at an advanced stage of integration into the Israeli economy, was due primarily to the relative advantages associated with labor-intensive production employing a low level of technology.

Under such conditions, the outcome of the integration mechanisms was the economic marginalization of the Arab sector and industry, the result of a transformation that largely inhibited industrial development. This means that, in general, despite the changes that Arab society has undergone, it has remained structurally marginal to the major advanced sectors within the economy, and Arabs have not gained any dominant position which could accelerate their process of industrial development. This has been reflected in the Arabs providing a share of the labor reproduction for the Jewish-dominated advanced capitalist sector, as shown empirically by Yiftachel (1992).

For the long term, these marginalization processes diminish the chances of the plants, the individuals involved in them, and the settlements in which they are situated to close the economic gap between them and the more advanced elements of the national economy. These elements include modern factories in the same branch but particularly in growth industries; human capital with a high level of training and professional know-how; and core and growth regions in which large investments are made and in which the lion's share of capital accumulation in the national space occurs.

Marginalization processes effectively barred the involvement of Arab entrepreneurs in the institutions supporting modern industrial entrepreneurship. As a result, they were compelled to rely on traditional institutions as support mechanisms for their industrialization and efforts at entrepreneurship. These traditional institutions have proved sufficient for promoting entrepreneurship up to the third level on the model presented in Chapter 6. Beyond this, they are incapable of providing additional support for further industrial growth and highlight the internal forces which promote underdevelopment.

The features of traditional institutions have been presented in preceding chapters. As we have seen, management is typically in the hands of the owners, with ownership based on kinship relations and the owners holding key positions in the plant. This pattern of ownership, along with the small number of partnerships not grounded in kinship relations (Haidar, 1993), makes it difficult for plants both to become economic entities separate from their owners and to expand their capital base (Haidar, 1985). As shown in Table 11.1, ownership patterns in the Arab sector are very different from those in the modern Jewish economy.

Traditionalism also determines the features of the work force, most particularly the limited intersettlement mobility of the female labor market. This places constraints on the range of alternatives available when choosing a place of employment, thereby perpetuating conditions of exploitation. The current wage scale, social benefits, and possibilities for advancement are not likely to motivate skilled workers to remain in their jobs in Arab plants. Ample evidence of this can

Table 11.1
Distribution of Ownership Structure in Israeli and Arab Industry (percentages)

Ownership	Total Israeli industry 5+ employees 1987	Total Arab industry 3+ employees 1992
Private	20	83
Partnership	10	4
Private stockholders	62	12
Public	3	1
Cooperative	5	0
Total	100	100

Sources: Central Bureau of Statistics (1991); Sofer et al. (1993).

be found in the continued stream of skilled and qualified personnel commuting to Jewish-owned factories in the vicinity or in the metropolitan areas (Bar-el, 1993; Yiftachel, 1991).

The fact that capital is not raised from the financial institutions that represent the primary source of capital in the modern economy is an indication of the lack of availability of sizable capital for the Arab industrial entrepreneur. A further feature of the influence of traditional institutions on industrial enterprises in Arab settlements is the attitude toward land as a production factor. In his comparison between traditionalism and modernism, Bar-el (1993) includes this factor in his list of variables expressing traditionalism; other factors are a low level of education, rapid population growth, ownership of residence, a low level of professional training, and a low rate of car ownership indicating a low level of mobility. The patterns of land ownership still maintained in the Arab community preclude the development of a real estate market and make it difficult to reallocate private land to an industrial zone designed to encourage plant expansion.

THE EFFECTS OF PERIPHERIALITY ON ARAB INDUSTRY

The peripheral status of Arab settlements and their population is the product of several elements, including government policies (both spatial and nonspatial in nature), the majority-minority relationship, and the nature of the economic linkages (portrayed by economic enterprises) that exist between the cores of economic activity and the areas of concentration of Arab settlements. The nature of these relations and linkages is affected by discriminatory government policies and the selective operation of market forces. It is within this framework in general, and within the industrial sector in particular, that the position of Arab industry has been determined, whether by choice or necessity, causing it to be seen as part of the marginal pole of Israeli industry. This contention is supported by the features of Arab industry, as presented in the preceding chapters. What we are concerned with here are its structural relations, for they are at the basis of the mechanisms perpetuating the subordinate status of the Arab sector in Israeli industry.

A spatial core-periphery system is characterized by varying concentrations of economic activity, interregional gaps in living standards, and different strategies adopted by the population to deal with these gaps. In Israel, as in most countries, the core regions are identical with the major metropolitan areas. The core has a distinctly urban character, an urban economic base, high levels of industrialization and infrastructure, and convenient access to services and offers a high standard of living. The location, or base, of government offices in the core also serves to attract economic activity, thereby creating a concentration of economic opportunities with an impact on the national space as a whole. This impact then draws capital and population to the Israeli core, ensuring its ongoing economic prosperity. Secondary cores in the spatial hierarchy are below the primary core but above the periphery.

The structure of core-periphery in Israel, based on spatial patterns of differing living standards, has been explained in various ways (Lipshitz, 1986; Shachar & Lipshitz, 1980; Vilkansky, 1980). The periphery is represented primarily by underprivileged neighborhoods, development towns, and Arab settlements (Efrat, 1983). The delineation of core and periphery is based on interregional and interpopulation gaps measured by socio-economic indicators such as per capita income, employment opportunities, years of schooling and level of education, and access to social services and financial institutions.

Arab settlements are characterized by a rural or latent urban economy. In terms of both distance and quality, the accessibility to services and economic opportunities lags far behind that in the core. While linkages with the metropolitan areas of Tel Aviv and Haifa are fairly good, linkages among peripheral regions are significantly poorer. The nature of linkages with the core, however, reflects a high degree of dependency. While this dependency is mutual, those who primarily benefit from it, and from the profits it generates, are the capitalists in the core who represent the large corporations. The cost of the dependency is a relative lowering of the standard of living in the Arab settlements in the Israeli periphery.

Moreover, the Jewish and Arab peripheries are distinguished by functional and social differences. While development towns in the Jewish periphery have attracted factories retreating from the core in a quest for cheaper land and labor, the Arab periphery has not. Instead, the work force in the Arab periphery commutes to the national core and to areas of concentration of wage employment to fill low-paid jobs in standard production and services. By virtue of their inferior status, the Arab settlements also suffer from a lack of social services, which are channeled primarily to the Jewish periphery.

Examination of the shifts in industrial dispersion for the period of 1977-1985 (Ne'eman, 1992) as compared to the period of 1965-1977 (Gradus & Einy, 1981) reveals that the relative weight of those employed in industry in peripheral regions increased, while the relative weight of industrial workers in the central core areas declined. The rise in the periphery can undoubtedly be explained in part by the rapid growth in the size of the work force employed by Arab industry (particularly in the textile and clothing branch) during the 1980s. Arab industry (employing some 12,000; Atrash, 1992) accounted for just over 4 percent of the 280,000 employees of Israeli industry in the early 1990s (Central Bureau of Statistics, 1992). Moreover, during this period the number of Arab plants employing five or more (520 plants; Atrash, 1992) represented 7.7 percent of all such enterprises in Israel (6787; Central Bureau of Statistics, 1991). What this means, however, is that the Arab sector is still lagging behind the rest of the Israeli economy in terms of degree of industrialization.

Branch diversity and level of sophistication are also indicative of the gap between the core and periphery. In 1985, the proportion (in terms of number of enterprises) of rubber and plastics factories in the periphery was similar to that on the national level. In the metalworking branch, the proportion was higher than the national average in the periphery and lower in the core (Ne'eman, 1992). Today, these are not considered the most advanced or sophisticated industrial branches. The significantly heavy weight of the core regions, as opposed to the periphery, is most striking in the more advanced branches, such as electricity, electronics, and machinery. Such factories are exceedingly rare in Arab settlements. Thus, based on the criterion of industrial branch, there is a considerable gap between core and peripheral regions in general; and even within the periphery, enterprises in Arab settlements are lower on the scale of industrial sophistication. Where growth industries have entered peripheral regions, it has been to locate in *kibbutzim* and urban Jewish settlements rather than in Arab villages. Hence, in addition to the quantitative gap, there is also a qualitative one, providing further support for the contention of a core-periphery paradigm.

The peripheraility of Arab industry is demonstrated by its present branch structure. In Arab settlements, there is an obvious quantitative predominance of plants in the branches of food, textiles, construction materials, woodworking, and somewhat less so metalworking. Now considered older and less profitable, some of these were the leading branches in Israeli industry in the 1950s, with textiles and metals as the vanguards of industrial growth in the 1960s, when the government was deeply involved in industrial production (Gradus, Razin, & Krakover, 1993). Today it is hard to find in the Arab sector any plants in the

Table 11.2
Ratio of Branch Specialization for Arab Factories with Three or More Employees

Major Branches		Marginal Branches		Integrating Branches	
Construction materials	4.4	Electricity & electronics	0.04	Rubber & plastics	0.94
Textiles & clothing	1.6	Machinery	0.20		
Food & beverages	1.5	Leather & leather goods	0.20		
Wood & wood products	1.3	Paper & printing	0.40		
		Metals & metals product	0.40		

Note: The figures for Israeli industry are for 1989, those for Arab industry are for 1992. The ratio of branch specialization is the rate of branch distribution in the Arab sector as compared to the parallel rate in Israeli industry as a whole.

Sources: Central Bureau of Statistics (1991); Sofer et al. (1993).

branches of chemicals and electronics, which, together with metals, showed the greatest growth rate in Israeli industry in the 1970s. The branches that led the way in terms of growth in the 1980s and early 1990s were the various fields of computers, telecommunications, electro-optics, aerospace, and other hi-tech industries. Yet these are nonexistent in the Arab sector. Branch predominance, demonstrated again by the ratio of branch specialization for factories (Table 11.2) and for the work force (Table 11.3), is an expression of the qualitative inferiority of Arab industry. The reliance on old and laggard industries that are relatively labor intensive in their production process and display low output-per-worker ratios is a clear indication of the association of Arab industry with the more marginal pole of the Israeli industrial sector.

Since the 1950s, investments in the periphery have been selective in nature. Arab settlements have been passed over, and investments have been directed primarily to development towns and have been based on an extensive system of incentives promoted by the Law for Encouraging Capital Investments (never applied to Arab settlements) and including grants, subsidized loans, and tax and infrastructure benefits. The factories that chose to locate in development towns

Table 11.3
Ratio of Branch Specialization for the Arab Industrial Work Force

Major Branches		Marginal Branches	
Textiles & clothing	4.2	Food & beverages	0.4
Construction materials	3.7	Metals	0.2
		Paper & printing	0.2
Wood & wood products	1.5	Rubber & plastics	0.2
		Electricity & electronics	0.002

Note: The figures for Israeli industry are for 1989, those for Arab industry are for 1992.
The ratio of branch specialization is the rate of branch distribution in the Arab sector
as compared to the parallel rate in Israeli industry as a whole.

Sources: Central Bureau of Statistics (1991); Sofer et al. (1993).

were largely labor-intensive enterprises with initial demands for unskilled labor,
or were involved in the processing of agricultural produce (Razin, 1991). Thus,
from the 1950s to the mid-1970s, the textile and clothing industry—an older
branch—has predominated in the northern and southern regions of the country.
Since the late 1970s, an increasing share of its production has shifted to Arab
settlements. Since 1977, however, with the spatial shift in investment dispersion,
the growth of the northern and southern regions in relation to the total number of
jobs in industry in Israel has remained stagnant (Razin, 1991). Moreover,
factories of the "first generation," characterized by outdated equipment, suffered
from a lack of efficient use of labor and thus from redundancy and, as a result,
remained dependent on government aid. The lack of branch variety and absence
of modern industries did not allow for the employment of the skilled personnel
becoming available in development towns. By the time efforts were being made
to broaden the diversity of industry in development towns, sophisticated plants had
already been established in the center of the country or near metropolitan areas.

While the first-generation branches, particularly textiles and metalworking, have
exhibited a steady decline in growth rate over the past 15 years, hi-tech (third-
generation) industries—particularly electronics, precision instruments, optics,
biotechnology, and, more recently, telecommunications—have shown a constant
rise in the number of employees and outputs for over 10 years. This increase
stems from the relative advantage of the fields of research and development, the
availability of highly qualified scientific personnel, a modern system of higher

education, and local demand, which created an initial market for sophisticated products (Razin, 1991). In the early stages, these branches tended to locate in the metropolitan area of Tel Aviv, joined in the 1980s by Haifa and the central region, concentrated largely around Rehovot and the Weizmann Institute of Science. The advantages of a supply of skilled workers and the availability of professional services gave the metropolitan areas a clear edge. Conversely, the lack of these advantages in the periphery, and especially in Arab settlements, hindered the development of advanced industries in these localities, even in the case of industries which are not bound to specific locations (foot-loose industry).

On the whole, the incentives offered to hi-tech industries to encourage their locating in the periphery did not assist them in dealing with the location disadvantages associated with development towns and Arab settlements. When such plants were established in the periphery—though distinctly not in Arab settlements—it was only in places at commuting distance from the nearest metropolitan center. Furthermore, these enterprises tended to deal primarily with the production and assembly stages of products whose development had been completed (Felsenstein, 1986), while the research and development departments remained in the metropolitan areas of Tel Aviv and Haifa. The factories established in development towns were, in fact, branches or subdivisions of hi-tech companies operating in the core.

It is only in recent years that these factories have been established in more distant localities, such as Migdal Ha'Emeq and Karmiel in Lower Galilee and Tefen in Upper Galilee, but again Arab settlements have been conspicuously absent from this list. If these plants continue to spread into the periphery, the situation in Israel will undoubtedly be similar to that in other parts of the Western world, where hi-tech industries show some tendency to concentrate in new, previously unindustrialized, areas, most situated outside large cities or traditionally industrial centers (Felsenstein, 1986; Swyngedouw, 1989). The establishment of plants in the periphery requires the erecting of industrial parks with an appropriate infrastructure, an initiative generally undertaken with government aid, support, and subsidies. As we have seen in the chapter on land, such an infrastructure does not exist in Arab settlements in Israel, and since the investment required to construct this infrastructure is beyond the means of the Arab entrepreneur, it demands the allocation of government resources.

Third-generation enterprises, the major growth industry in the Israeli economy, have not viewed the Arab settlement as a potential location for their plants. It both lacks the appropriate physical and human infrastructure and does not enjoy the application of the Law for Encouraging Capital Investment and is therefore not considered a priority location for plants. Given the large urban centers which offer labor reserves on all levels, the lack of highly qualified skilled workers is also a severe location disadvantage. This is true not only with respect to the core but also in comparison to development towns with their preferred status. As a result, the Arab settlement on the whole does not benefit from the injection of public or private productive capital, so as a rule its residents must raise local capital both for initial investment and for the later expansion of an industrial plant. Moreover, no Arab entrepreneur has yet established a modern factory in the industrial park of a Jewish settlement.

Thus, on the scale of economic activity in the Israeli economy, the Arab settlement can be defined as belonging to the lower periphery (lower than the Jewish periphery of development towns) according to a range of criteria, and it is therefore characterized by older industry producing low returns per output unit. Furthermore, the peripheral status of the Arab settlement is perpetuated by the continued existence and continued establishment of this sort of industry within its borders.

MINORITY-MAJORITY RELATIONS AND ETHNIC DISCRIMINATION

While the unequal pattern of development in Israel has been based largely on economic factors, it has also followed ethnic lines and reflects the relationship of the minority versus the majority. At the foundation of the emergence and perpetuation of the peripheral status of the Arab sector are forms of activity supported, whether intentionally or not, by government actions. These actions were dictated largely by the changing needs of the majority and include arbitrary regulations imposed by the Israeli government; the establishment of a framework for Jewish-Arab coexistence that acknowledges the friction and tensions between the two populations and accepts the mutual alienation; and the integration of Arabs into the country's life within constraints which, even if not formally imposed, limit Arabs' entrance into certain aspects of economic activity (Benziman & Mansour, 1992). These policies were grounded in an ideology that sought to ensure employment for immigrants as soon as they arrived in the country and thus channeled resources to entrepreneurs in the Jewish sector.

Although a policy of coexistence has been officially championed since the late 1960s, ethnically based discrimination has not disappeared. Even a decade after its adoption, there was no genuine willingness to accept Arabs into government posts. Investments in Arab municipal authorities continued to be low, and the level of infrastructure services continued to lag behind that in the Jewish sector (Benziman & Mansour, 1992). Indeed, discrimination with regard to the level of municipal services still exists and cannot be explained only by the fact that the tax base of local Arab authorities is considerably lower than that of Jewish settlements of similar size. In the industrial context, the result of this discrimination is the lack of an appropriate infrastructure that might encourage industrial development. The lack of this infrastructure is also the product of a government policy which did not impose a legal obligation to submit an outline plan providing for an industrial zone. The government could then have urged the local authority to implement such a plan, thus promoting the actualization of potential entrepreneurship, which is not realized under present conditions.

Industrialization of the Arab sector proceeded at a slow pace. Arab entrepreneurs lacked both experience and funding sources, and their plants were neither big nor strong enough to compete with the large corporations in the Jewish sector, which enjoyed generous government aid. The government even adopted a clear and consistent policy preventing the establishment of advanced Arab industrial enterprises, on the grounds that they represented a security risk (Benziman & Mansour, 1992). Given these constraints and the ongoing transformation of the economy in the Arab sector, Arab industry continued to expand in the traditional branches of food, woodworking, and construction materials, such as concrete blocks and marble polishing. These branches are relatively labor intensive and employ a low level of technology. Expansion relied on mimicking behavior, in which the pattern of a successful plant was copied, so that existing patterns of production and marketing were preserved. The Arab work force found jobs in industry primarily outside Arab settlements. As early as the 1960s, some 50 percent of all Arab workers earned their living outside their settlements (Central Bureau of Statistics, 1961). Because of the low mobility of the female work force, most of these workers were men. Similar rates of employment outside the settlement were obtained more recently (Central Bureau of Statistics, 1991) and are high even in comparison to development towns of similar size. This indicates a lack of economic opportunities within the settlement. Today, as in the past, Arab workers gravitate to Jewish cities (Yiftachel, 1991), particularly to the metropolitan areas which represent the core of economic activity in the Israeli economy.

In Haidar's view (1991), the government played a crucial role in determining the status of Israeli Arabs in the national economy by the manner in which it channeled the major resources it controlled. He contends that government decisions were guided by the notion that "if it's good for the minority, it's probably bad for the majority." Government resources and the manner in which they were allocated to the Arab sector served the purposes of control mechanisms and dependency relations. The Arab sector was totally dependent on government funds for a proper economic infrastructure, especially for industry, in order to create a starting point for modern economic development. Evidence for this contention can be found in the government's delay in connecting Arab settlements to basic infrastructures, so that in the early 1970s only 32 local Arab authorities were connected to the electricity grid. Moreover, the planning policies in mixed Jewish-Arab regions have been shown to be part of the control of the Arab minority in Israel. The outcome of the planning policies contributed to preserving, and even increasing, Arab-Jewish economic disparities (Yiftachel, 1992).

In short, discriminatory attitudes toward the minority and relations of control and dependency have long existed in the Israeli economy, operating to the disadvantage of the Arab sector. At the foundations of the perpetuation of the Arab sector's status as part of the marginal pole of the Israeli economy is a government policy that does not encourage economic development in general, and industrial development in particular, in contrast to a generous policy of government aid in adjacent development towns.

CONCLUSIONS

The question we have raised in this chapter is the place of Arab settlements, their factories, and their entrepreneurs in the Israeli industrial space. Within the context of the structural change taking place in the Israeli economy, and consequently in Israeli industry, is Arab industry afforded significant encouragement for its development?

The Israeli economy is relatively highly centralized and, as such, constitutes a source of political power for the various interest groups allied with government agencies. The close link between Zionist socialist ideology and the national economy strongly influenced the allocation of public resources. Government policy gives preferential treatment to the organizations and individuals it wishes to promote. The features of the Israeli economy, such as centralization, small size, dependence on investments from abroad, and a large defense budget, have led to considerable government involvement in the economy in general and in industry in particular (Aharoni, 1991). The situation that has arisen in Israeli industry is such that the chances of receiving government grants, incentives, and allotments, whether directly or indirectly, are determined to a large extent by the political affiliation or status of a given interest group. If we add the principles of economic development based on national-ideological considerations, which view government involvement as a means of bolstering the Jewish economy, it is easy to understand what this has meant for the Arab sector—relegation to the national periphery.

Aharoni (1991) claims that in a small, centralized economy such as in Israel, the government is capable of affecting every economic enterprise. Whether through direct involvement or its 'long unseen arm,' the government established priorities for the industrialization of development areas, the maintenance of publicly owned industries, and the regulation of a market, most of whose industrial output is concentrated in the hands of a small number of firms. These government policies discriminated between Jews and Arabs. It was not the Arab economy that was to 'upbuild the land.' Arab industry did not receive government recognition and was not included in the category of those entitled to either direct assistance, through support and grants, or indirect aid through the construction of a suitable industrial infrastructure.

The mutual links between the political and the economic systems created severe difficulties for industrial entrepreneurs in the Arab sector. They were not allowed access to production means; nor were they allocated resources. As things stand, the modernization of Arab industry is almost totally dependent on government decisions, and, without assistance, the ability of these plants to progress is seriously limited. As a result, most have remained small in size and have continued to maintain simple production processes. Consequently, Arab industry has preserved its branch composition over the course of time, relying on those branches which are still labor intensive and do not employ advanced technology. These factories have no influence over the economy, which might enable them to acquire more modern technology, nor do they enjoy the benefits and incentives given by the government to growth industries. Furthermore, the Arab entrepreneur does not have access to the economic and political networks under whose influence the patterns of support and investment might be altered. His survival as a manufacturer is dependent on his ability to produce those specialized products which are no longer of any interest to capital owners in the Jewish economy or to operate as a subcontractor for leading firms in labor-intensive branches such as textiles and clothing.

Arab entrepreneurs still maintain the traditional relative advantages that have always made their businesses viable. In the rare cases in which they have risen on the entrepreneurship scale, this has resulted from their significantly breaking out of conservative frameworks and from institutional support. Nevertheless, technological changes and modifications in the organization of production processes have not been introduced in Arab industry to any considerable extent, which continues to rely on reserves of cheap, unskilled labor. The growing trend for a geographical separation between the stages of production, research and development, and management has contributed to the relegation to the Arab periphery of standardized stages of production (the example is the textile and clothing industry). This phenomenon, known as industrial ruralization, has brought about the concentration of older industries in rural regions with large reserves of cheap labor, where the work force is not entirely mobile and operating costs are relatively low.

Arab industry has not achieved a central position in Israeli industry. As a result of its specialization in labor-intensive industries with low returns per worker, its contribution to the country's total industrial production has remained small. This pattern of industrial development continues to be influenced by external decisions taken in the political and economic core of the country. The core continues to control the commerce in raw materials and finished products. Forces of conservation continue to dominate on the level of the plant, the community, the settlement, and even the entire sector. The patterns of production, the concept of finding a specific niche for production, and the linkages between plants and between sectors are all being largely preserved. These processes of no change perpetuate the peripheral status of Arab industry and do not enable it to advance to a position from which it could rise to higher levels of industrial development.

In contrast to the somewhat gloomy view presented in this chapter, the experience of some entrepreneurs suggests that changes in the Arab periphery are possible. Contrary to the passive position taken by most Arab entrepreneurs, a certain (admittedly very small) group of entrepreneurs has been adopting a more active approach. These people have changed the organization of their production (with an accompanying increase in size of operation and productivity), have extended their markets, and have become further integrated in the Israeli economy. Overall, they have managed to leave behind their peripheral status and achieve a better position from which to respond to economic opportunities created in the Israeli economic environment than have most other entrepreneurs.   Their experience pinpoints a number of elements: those needed to attain the higher levels in our entrepreneurial model and to link an enterprise successfully to the larger economy.   The appearance of progressive enterprises emphasizes the presence of different responses in the periphery to the prevailing conditions of polarized-discriminatory development in Israel. Disparity in the Arab periphery is largely a condition of the nature of linkages which are established between the dominant forces in the society (ethnic groups, owners of capital, the state) and the Arab entrepreneurs, who have modified their operations in various ways in order to combine with those forces.

Chapter 12

Conclusions

ISRAELI ARAB ENTREPRENEURSHIP

The Arab entrepreneur is seen in this book as the prime agent of industrialization and regional development in the Arab space in Israel. As such, we have compared him to the Roman god Janus, guardian of the gateways, facing in two directions at the same time. With one face turned to the Arab entrepreneurial environment and the other to the Israeli, the entrepreneur strives to bridge the gap between them in order to facilitate industrial and economic development. He must reconcile two entrepreneurial environments which are dissimilar both in terms of the institutional structure that differentially allocates resources and opportunities to Arab and Jewish enterprises by means of market forces and government policies, and in terms of the scale of values, norms, and patterns by which the environments operate. The Arab entrepreneur must navigate among the constraints and opportunities that derive from three factors. First is his status as a member of an ethnic and national minority whose culture and language are not those of the majority. Second is his position in the national periphery, which dictates conditions of dependency on the Jewish core. Third is the fact that the Arab community is a traditional society which has maintained an underprivileged status throughout its integration in the modern capitalistic economy of Israel, begun in the 1950s. This set of factors operates as a tier structure, keeping the Arab entrepreneur from the centers of decision making and resource allocation in the economic space of Israeli society.

It is thus not difficult to understand why Arab industry to date has been perceived as underdeveloped and suffering from a lack of infrastructures, capital, and enterprise, an image confirmed by earlier studies investigating industrialization of the Arab sector in Israel. Our analysis of Arab industry in the context of the Israeli entrepreneurial environment also reveals its marginal status in the national economy and the failure of Arab enterprises to take their place among the larger and more advanced factories in the country. Nevertheless, our more detailed microanalysis indicates the existence in the Arab sector of a dynamic industrial entrepreneurial spirit which seeks to make the most of any windows of opportunity it discovers.

There is an increased number of Arab entrepreneurs who are ready to work hard, to cope tenaciously with all difficulties, and to make personal sacrifices in order to ensure the success of their enterprises. Yet while these entrepreneurs display considerable flexibility in exploiting the opportunities that present themselves in the course of this process, the means available to them are decidedly limited. These entrepreneurs enjoy wide support from the communities in which they operate. Year after year, they consistently invest the lion's share of the resources available to them in developing their enterprises. Indeed, nearly all the entrepreneurs in our study doubled the investment in their factories over the past five years, even if the amounts involved are relatively low in absolute figures. The majority of them are constantly open to incorporating new methods—organizational, technological, and others—in order to streamline and expand their plants. Most conspicuous is the desire to acquire modern machinery. With regard to marketing, the Arab entrepreneurs strive constantly to expand. Many seek to enter Jewish markets despite the ·stiff competition and the need to vie with monopolistic corporations in the Jewish sector. Furthermore, Arab municipal authorities are increasingly applying pressure to establish industrial zones within their jurisdiction. In this regard, we have recently seen indications for change that will undoubtedly be felt in the years to come.

The deep commitment to entrepreneurship stems from the perception among the Arab public that entrepreneurship is virtually the only means of achieving occupational mobility in the Arab settlement. Settlement workers suffer from a limited supply of occupational opportunities. Moreover, most jobs in Arab settlements offer extremely poor rewards. Wages are low, the professional challenge is meager, and the social benefits afforded workers are generally the minimum level required by law, if not less. While the Jewish labor market offers greater professional challenge, it involves commuting relatively long distances and working in an alien cultural environment under conditions of ethnic discrimination. Most entrepreneurs claimed to have seen entrepreneurship as a way out of the dilemma they faced in choosing between these alternatives. Employment in the Jewish sector is viewed as a chance to gain experience and know-how toward the founding of an industrial enterprise, but it is not viewed as a desirable environment in which to establish a career. As a rule, entrepreneurs prefer to earn a lower income in exchange for a sense of independence and control over their destiny, along with the expectation of higher financial rewards in the long run. This evidence convinced us that elements in Arab regions in Israel may be regarded as active peripheries in which leading industrial entrepreneurs are making constant efforts to reverse basic mechanisms of dependency.

THE ENTREPRENEURSHIP MODEL

The scale of entrepreneurship that evolved from our analysis indicates a number of breakthroughs in the development of Arab industry in Israel. Several of the plants which began small and relied on family resources for capital, labor, and management and on local markets for sales progressed impressively during the 1980s. Today we can delineate an entrepreneurship scale of four or five levels. On the lowest, which is not isolated in the model, are the smallest plants that rely totally on the resources of the household. They are situated in the residence, employ family sources of capital and labor, operate minimal machinery, and sell primarily to members of the *hamula* (clan) and local village residents. These plants are either owned by entrepreneurs who are unable to tap modern sources for purposes of expansion or are new enterprises established on limited family capital. In this case, the owners have not yet earned enough profits to invest in the development needed to bring the plant up to a higher level of entrepreneurship, although they may have the potential to do so in the future.

On the second level, qualitative changes take place in the patterns by which the various infrastructures and resources are exploited. The first obstacle entrepreneurs must overcome is the market. The fact that the plants are located in the national periphery in settlements whose purchasing power is limited, and that raw materials must be purchased from external sources, compels the entrepreneur to maintain contact, if only on a short-term basis, with markets outside the settlement. Furthermore, the entrepreneur must ensure access to such basic infrastructures as an access road, running water, electricity, and sewerage and must acquire at least simple machinery. Unless they fulfill these conditions, entrepreneurs cannot rise to higher levels or increase their annual volume to over NIS100,000 (around $30,000).

The third level may be achieved after additional employees have been hired, with the work force drawn primarily from outside the framework of kinship relations. This requires a more formal organization of labor, expressed in the computerized management of personnel and production and the division of the plant into separate departments. At this level, Arab markets are too small to maintain the enterprise, so that it begins to penetrate Jewish markets. Most cases involve sales to marginal niches or one-time opportunities in the Jewish sector rather than competition for broader markets. Thus, for example, Arab entrepreneurs take advantage of their connections with Arab contractors working on residential projects under the "Build Your Own Home" scheme introduced into Jewish towns in the 1980s.

On the fourth level, the entrepreneur must define his factory as an independent economic entity and adopt the formal managerial practices required of a corporation or public company. Expanded production and the need to penetrate more deeply into Jewish markets demand a higher professional level from the workers (particularly management personnel), investment in more modern machinery, and permanent facilities. Naturally, to guarantee their investment for the long term, entrepreneurs are willing to undertake such reforms only when their factories are located in legally recognized industrial zones.

At the highest level, entrepreneurs begin to compete for institutional markets in the Jewish sector. They must adopt professional and sophisticated managerial practices and invest the sort of large sums which are unavailable without using bank credit, going public, etc. Modern methods of quality control must also be applied to the production process in order to acquire the seal of the Standards Institute and high credibility as a manufacturer.

In 1992, 67 percent of the plants were still at the lower levels of entrepreneurship. The others had grown gradually, through the investment of a large part of their profits in further development, thereby rising to higher entrepreneurship levels. It is important to remember that virtually all of these plants had been established as small, family enterprises characterized by low entrepreneurship levels and had developed steadily as a result of investments and entrepreneurial actions taken by their owners. At present, some 18 percent of the plants are on the two highest levels of entrepreneurship, with one third of all enterprises on the three highest levels. These plants are dealing with the problems of integration in markets beyond the settlement and the adoption of modern work and managerial methods. The model, therefore, confirms our claim of dynamic entrepreneurship on the part of those who have modernized the various aspects of their industrial production. The introduction of modern methods brings with it qualitative changes in the industrial structure and in patterns of behavior, which may pave the way for some of these plants to take their place among the industrial concerns in the Israeli economy. At least two factories already seem to have achieved this status.

Up to the 1950s, Arab industry was characterized by traditional patterns of behavior. The late 1950s to the late 1970s saw the emergence of light industry operating on the fringes of the Israeli economy on the principle of mimicking behavior. The development of most plants began only in the 1970s, once all Arab settlements had been connected to the electricity grid and the water and road systems. A qualitative transformation in Arab industry began in the 1980s, as its factories started their integration into the Israeli economy, although they have remained a marginal element within it.

OBSTACLES TO INDUSTRIALIZATION

Analysis of the mechanisms impeding Arab entrepreneurship and development focuses on the ramifications of the Arab status as a traditional minority operating in the periphery of the socio-economic space in Israel. The fact that industrialization took place when the Israeli economy was controlled by a coalition of government agencies and large corporations dictated the dependency of the periphery on the Jewish core. Industrialization of the periphery occurred as a result either of the relocation of standardized production processes from the core or the establishment of small plants that relied on regional markets in the periphery itself. The minority status of the Arab population occasioned the creation of mechanisms aimed at separating and discriminating between the Arab and Jewish peripheries. The government undertook to settle new immigrants in the periphery, ensuring them full employment, in order to establish Jewish sovereignty over the entire country and guarantee its security. Consequently, the Jewish peripheral settlements were given preferential treatment through a variety of governmental means. Traditional practices of the Arab minority also generate conditions in which internal resources are scarce, making them that much more dependent on the Jewish majority. The structure of these relations between Arabs and Jews presented the Arab entrepreneur with five major series of mechanisms impeding industrial development.

The first relates to the lack of physical infrastructures and industrial zones in Arab settlements. Up until two years ago, the infrastructure for a modern industrial zone had been laid in only one region alone—Upper Western Galilee. In other settlements in which land for industrial zones has been allocated in recent years, the plots are too small and no modern infrastructures have been installed in order to prepare them for their designated use. Under these circumstances, potential entrepreneurs were forced to invest what they considered huge sums of money in constructing a building, access road, and electricity and sewage systems for their plants. This had to be done before production was begun, and thus the entrepreneur was not yet deriving any income from the factory. Such sums are beyond the reach of most Arab entrepreneurs in Israel at this stage of their development. Moreover, most potential entrepreneurs do not own land, which is only rarely offered for sale. Hence, the members of most families in Arab settlements could never be considered even potential entrepreneurs.

Given these conditions, the ground floor beneath the residential home is an ideal incubator for entrepreneurs on the lower levels of entrepreneurship. Here they find a structure connected to at least minimal infrastructures. In most cases, they manage to evade the taxes and licensing fees required of businesses in an industrial zone. They thereby save money and develop their enterprise to the stage at which they will be able to finance the move to an industrial zone when the limited infrastructures in the residential area will no longer suffice.

The marginality of the Arab settlement in the Israeli socio-economic space is reflected in the substantial public funding of industrial parks in the new towns erected near concentrations of Arab settlements and in the subsidization of Jewish firms investing in the construction of plants in these towns. The lack of industrial infrastructures in Arab settlements stands out most conspicuously against this background. As a result, Arab settlements cannot compete with the new towns for the factories retreating from the core into the periphery through the participation of large corporations.

The second series of impeding mechanisms relates to the lack of investment capital. Here, too, the Arab settlement's chances for development are hurt by government policies giving preference to new towns. The Law for Encouraging

Capital Investment entitles factories locating in development towns to loans, grants, and subsidies, and to this date it has rarely been applied to Arab enterprises. Private banks also find it hard to supply the demand for capital among Arab entrepreneurs. Israeli banks operate on a large national scale. As such, they have difficulty displaying sensitivity to the needs of small, high-risk entrepreneurs, most of whom can not provide the necessary collateral for loans. For the past two years, financial frameworks providing loans to small businesses have been introduced in Israel. To date, Arab entrepreneurs have not enjoyed this government aid, although several of them have acquired financing from commercial banks. There is, however, reason to hope that this arrangement will increase the availability of capital for Arab investment.

Nonetheless, this will not solve the problems of entrepreneurs at the lowest levels, most of whom rely on a small assured market in the settlement and chance opportunities to sell to customers outside. Since their income is both small and unstable, these entrepreneurs are wary of the risks involved in taking out loans at the normal interest rates. Lacking bank capital, most entrepreneurs therefore depend for development on the savings of the extended family and on plant profits. Such capital allows for the steady, though relatively slow, growth of plants at the lowest entrepreneurship levels but is insufficient for the rise to higher levels. For this, the enterprise must expand its sources for raising capital in order to allow for the investments needed to streamline production processes and increase the volume of production.

The third series of impeding mechanisms relates to markets. Arab entrepreneurs are presented with a serious dilemma in having to choose between relatively secure markets in their own and neighboring Arab settlements, on the one hand, and growth and development requiring larger and richer but also riskier Jewish markets, on the other. The limited purchasing power of Arab markets and strong competition for them demand entrance into Jewish markets as a prerequisite for the rise to higher levels of entrepreneurship. This process entails two major stages. At the initial stage, the entrepreneur attempts to sell to Jewish markets whenever the opportunity presents itself while holding onto traditional Arab markets. To this end, he applies a wide variety of strategies. At the second stage, the entrepreneur seeks to establish durable markets for himself in the Jewish sector, facing the stiff competition of corporations with monopolistic power in the marketplace. Most entrepreneurs stated that entrance into the Jewish market is extremely difficult and requires their adaptation to a different business culture than that typical of the Arab settlement. In addition, it demands the existence of good quality control, a reputation for reliability, and the overcoming of intercultural barriers on the part of the Jewish customer as well. At the same time, most of the entrepreneurs who did manage to penetrate the Jewish market reported that after the initial difficulties had been tackled, the barriers fell and they were able to compete for these markets on equal terms. Not all entrepreneurs are aware of the requirements for entrance into Jewish markets, and not all of them are willing to take on the risks involved. Nevertheless, in recent years the number of Arab entrepreneurs in the Jewish market has been growing, a phenomenon particularly noticeable in the construction materials, metals, and woodworking branches.

In the textile and clothing branch, where most of the output is sold to Jewish parent companies, no manufacturers have yet succeeded in maintaining independence for any length of time. Most plants continue to operate as subcontractors for Jewish corporations. The majority of subcontractors noted the disadvantage of being distant from the markets and fashion designers. As a result, they cannot predict consumers' taste in the coming season and thus cannot plan independent production accordingly. This finding supports the contention that for entrepreneurs remote from the centers of economic information and decision making, the problems of evaluating information about production conditions, markets, and innovations make it difficult to make the proper decisions. Arab industrialists are indeed remote from these centers by virtue of three factors: their location in the national periphery; their membership in an ethnic and national minority with a different business culture; and their lack of any tradition of participation in a capitalist economy.

The fourth series of impeding mechanisms relates to the management capabilities of the owners and managers of Arab plants. The most prominent feature here is a reliance on semi-formal management behaviors. Because of the dependence on family members who helped raise the capital for the plant, kinship considerations take precedence in the hiring of management personnel. The lack of managerial know-how and capital for investment in the establishment of formal management systems along with commitment to the extended family and traditional social institutions are important factors impeding the rise to the highest levels of entrepreneurship. To do so, entrepreneurs must adopt modern methods of management. The banks also refuse to finance a plant that cannot provide a business forecast and whose books are not kept by a certified public accountant. Furthermore, regularized bookkeeping is required of companies who wish to go public. In the past, this factor was an obstacle to the investment of Jewish capital in Arab enterprises. Today, a small group of large and successful Arab factories is emerging in which the modern managerial methods required of corporations are being adopted. Nevertheless, these methods are still beyond the reach of the majority of plants. In this regard as well, it is not enough to provide professional training for entrepreneurs in order to increase their knowledge of efficient plant management. In addition, conditions must be created which will enable these plants to finance such a managerial infrastructure.

The fifth series of impeding mechanisms relates to the labor reserves for Arab industry. A considerable supply of skilled and educated workers is now available in the Arab sector. Indeed, some of those employed in the Jewish sector are even overqualified. However, Arab industry cannot compete for these workers since it can only pay a minimum wage and cannot offer its employees tenured positions with the accompanying benefits. As a result, it is the relatively less skilled workers who are employed in Arab plants, whose payrolls contain almost no practical engineers, technicians, or other professionals and in which labor turnover

is high.   Under such circumstances, it is difficult for an Arab factory to hire
workers capable of learning and applying new methods in the various aspects of
the plant's activities. Clearly, this factor hinders the plants' ability to confront the
risks and professional challenges involved in introducing innovations.

Our analysis reveals that the conditions of peripheriality, minority affiliation,
and traditionalism, which hinder the Arab labor force's mobility in Jewish
markets, also increase the motivation of potential entrepreneurs to establish their
own businesses as well as their willingness to fight tenaciously and with great
resourcefulness to ensure the success of these businesses. However, these same
conditions also create impeding mechanisms that inhibit industrialization and
development.   In the face of this reality, the entrepreneurs show high
determination in the struggle to develop their enterprises and display remarkable
flexibility in seizing on any opportunity that comes their way and exploiting their
relative advantages both in the internal Arab market and in the Jewish sector.

TOWARD A GENERAL THEORY OF ETHNIC-PERIPHERAL
ENTREPRENEURSHIP

Several preliminary guidelines for framing a theory that might explain the
developmental course of ethnic entrepreneurship under conditions of peripheriality
emerge from our analysis. The basic features underlying such a theory are as
follows:

- Entrepreneurship is the central agent of industrialization and development.
- Entrepreneurship and development demand a structural change in the socio-economic
  space in which the entrepreneur operates.
- Entrepreneurs belonging to an ethnic minority operate simultaneously in at least two
  entrepreneurial environments with differing business cultures—that of the majority and
  that of the minority.
- Both entrepreneurial environments contain mechanisms that preserve the status quo along
  with mechanisms that generate opportunities for industrial and/or commercial
  entrepreneurship.
- Minority entrepreneurs are compelled to cope with distinctive mechanisms of
  preservation that derive from their position of weakness, which is the result of factors
  such as minority status, peripheral position, and lack of experience of modern
  technology. The ability to uncover key barriers to further development may focus the
  political struggle for ethnic integration on feasible goals.
- Minority entrepreneurs are involved in a constant battle to survive in business. Their
  weapons include determination and a willingness to tolerate personal sacrifice, hard
  work, and low income.
- Minority entrepreneurs find it difficult to accept high risk because of their
  underprivileged access to risk-reducing institutions in their entrepreneurial environment.
- Minority entrepreneurs display considerable flexibility and resourcefulness in their
  efforts to seize on any glimmer of opportunity to promote their business. To this end,

they exhibit great willingness to exploit their relative advantages in both the intraethnic market and the interethnic market.

As a rule, entrepreneurs call on kinship relations, the solidarity of the ethnic community, and ethnic customs and traditions in order to exploit their advantage in the internal ethnic market. To gain an advantage in the market outside the ethnic community, entrepreneurs employ considerable flexibility, a willingness to make do with a low profit margin, and the establishment of an ethnic reputation for products identified with their ethnic origin.

The ethnic community tends to mobilize itself to help its individual members to succeed, since it views them as vanguards capable of paving the way toward socio-economic mobility for all. Traditional institutions assist in supporting entrepreneurs as agents of change, and thus entrepreneurship may even strengthen these institutions in the ethnic community. However, at more advanced stages, the traditional institutions can no longer cope with the challenges with which entrepreneur must deal. At this point, there may be a conflict of interests between the entrepreneur and the ethnic community. Entrepreneurs must now turn for support to institutions in the majority sector, and their commitment to the ethnic community may become a burden. It is at this stage that entrepreneurs may become agents of social and structural change in their community.

Our research indicates that despite the subordinate conditions in which minority entrepreneurs operate, their determination enables them to overcome obstacles and occupy niches that present themselves in the national economy. The identification of such niches makes it possible for minority industrialists to present specific demands within the political-economic system for improved competitive conditions, thereby increasing their chances of widening their windows of opportunity in the national economy.

Our analysis thus offers a basis for a more flexible theory, rejecting the sweeping and overgeneralized conclusions of the ethnic enclave theory and the deterministic approach of the core-periphery paradigm. According to the ethnic enclave theory, entrepreneurs and workers enjoy conspicuous advantages when operating in internal ethnic markets, while any attempt to enter an interethnic market incurs obvious disadvantages. Our research shows that entrepreneurs are typically involved in a constant effort to exploit their relative advantages in both markets simultaneously. Thus, for example, skilled workers prefer to work and prepare themselves for entrepreneurship in the interethnic economy but to base their enterprises, in their early stages, on intraethnic capital, labor, and markets. As soon as they begin to rise on the entrepreneurship scale, however, they seek channels to interethnic markets.

As for the core-periphery paradigm, our research underlines the fact that determined entrepreneurship can break through structural obstacles which marginalize ethnic entrepreneurship to the periphery of the socio-economic space and can achieve higher development and economic integration.

In the context of Jewish-Arab relations in Israel in an era of peace, the chances for Arab incorporation in the Israeli economy may have far-reaching ramifications for Arabs' political identity. Such integration might strengthen the identification of Israeli Arabs with the State and enhance their interest in shoring up its economy as a means of ensuring their own prosperity. The creation of thousands of jobs for Arab workers in Arab industry might also limit the occasions for unequal relations between a Jewish employer and Arab employee, which often strengthen the Arab worker's sense of being unfairly treated. It is important to note that the establishment of peace between the State of Israel and the Palestinians on the West Bank and Gaza Strip, and between Israel and the countries of the Arab world, may, on the one hand, impede the process of Arab incorporation in the Israeli economy and, on the other hand, increase the importance of such economic interaction.

Broad international aid may generate large investments in Palestinian regions for the development of infrastructure and industrialization, while labor costs in these areas will continue to be relatively lower than those in the Arab labor market in Israel. As a result, there is a danger that Arab industry in Israel may lose out in the contest with Palestinian industry. The first firms to close down are liable to be the sewing shops operating as subcontractors for corporations in the Jewish economy. Parent companies are likely to find cheaper labor in Palestinian plants, thus dealing a death blow to the largest industry in the Arab-Israeli sector. On the other hand, a decline in the textile and clothing branch in Arab settlements in Israel might speed their industrialization, through a transformation process which may cause an entrance into the more advanced branches of Israeli industry. Such an outcome might result if the peace process brings about rapid growth in the Israeli economy, thereby opening up new opportunities for Arab entrepreneurs.

The closing of the economic gaps between the soon-to-expand Palestinian economy and the Arab sector in Israel may be a double-edged sword for Israeli Arab industry. As new markets open in the Arab world for Israeli Arabs, Arab entrepreneurs may become the agents transferring goods and know-how from the Jewish economy to neighboring Arab markets. In this case, the integration of Arab industry in Israel into the Jewish economy can be expected to decline, with the Arab sector developing strong economic links with the economy of the Palestinian entity and that of neighboring Arab countries. Such a situation may weaken the ties that bind Arabs and Jews in Israeli society. Hence, it is urgent that the government adopt a policy of promoting rapid industrialization and the development of other economic enterprises in the Arab sector in order to close the gaps between Jews and Arabs in Israel and incorporate Arab industry more fully into the broader Israeli economy. Government policies which served to curb industrial entrepreneurship in the Arab sector must now be replaced by a new policy encouraging rapid industrialization of this sector. This development will enable Israeli Arabs to take their place in the Israeli economy and enjoy a high standard of living, will reduce the friction between Jews and Arabs that derives from economic discrimination, and will increase cooperation and mutual interests between Arab industry and the Israeli economy as a whole.

Bibliography

A.C.O.S.T. 1990. *The Enterprise Challenge: Overcoming Barriers to Growth in Small Firms.* Cabinet Office, Advisory Council on Science and Technology: London, H.M.S.O.

Aharoni, I. 1991. *The Political Economy in Israel.* Tel Aviv: Am Oved (Hebrew).

Aldrich, H.E. and Auster, E.R. 1986. Even dwarf stated small Liabilities of age and size and their strategic implications. *Research in Organizational Behavior* 8: 165-198.

Aldrich, H.E. and Waldinger, R. 1990. Ethnicity and entrepreneurship. *Annual Review of Sociology* 16: 111-135.

Armington, C. and Odle, M. 1982. Small business—how many Jobs? *The Brookings Review* 1: 14-17.

Arnon, I. and Raviv, M. 1980. *From Fellah to Farmer.* Publication on Problems of Regional Development, 31, Rehovot: Settlement Study Center.

Atkin, R. 1974. An algebra for patterns on a complex. *International Journal of Man-Machine Studies* 6: 285-307.

Atkin, R. 1981. *Multidimensional Man.* Harmondsworth: Penguin Books.

Atrash, A. 1992. The Arab industry in Israel: branch structure, employment and plant formation. *Economics Quarterly* 152: 112-120 (Hebrew).

Avitzur, S. 1986. *Inventors and Adopters.* Tel Aviv: Keter (Hebrew).

Baily, T. and Waldinger, R. 1991. Primary secondary, and enclave labor markets: a training systems approach. *American Sociological Review* 56: 432-445.

Bar-El, R. 1993. *Economic Development in the Arab Sector.* Tel Aviv: The Jewish-Arab Centre for Economic Development (Hebrew).

Bar-Gal, Y. and Soffer, A. 1976. Changes in minority villages in Israel. *Horizons* No. 2, Department of Geography, University of Haifa (Hebrew).

Benedict, B. 1979. Family firms and firms families: a comparison of Indian, Chinese and Creole firms. In Greenfield, S.M. et al., eds. *Entrepreneurs in Cultural Context.* Albuquerque: University of New Mexico Press.

Ben-Rafael, E. 1982. *The Emergence of Ethnicity: Cultural Groups and Social Conflict in Israel.* Westport, Conn.: Greenwood.

Benziman, U. and Mansour, A. 1992. *Subtenants: The Status of Israeli Arabs and the Policy They Face*. Jerusalem: Keter (Hebrew).

Bergmann, B.R. 1971. The effect on white incomes of discrimination in employment. *Journal of Political Economy* 79: 294-313.

Berler, A. 1974. *Urbanization and Communication*. Publications on Problems of Regional Development, No. 12. Rehovot: Settlement Study Center.

Binks, M. 1979. Finance for expansion in the small firm. *Lloyds Bank Review* 157: 32-43.

Bird, B.J. 1989. *Entrepreneurial Behavior*. Genview, Ill.: Scott, Foresman.

Boissevain, J. et al. 1990. Ethnic entrepreneurs and ethnic strategies. In Waldinger, R. et al., eds. *Ethnic Entrepreneurs*. Webury Park: Sage Publications.

Brockhanse, R.H. 1982. The psychology of the entrepreneurs. *Encyclopedia of Entrepreneurship*. Englewood Cliffs, N.J.: Prentice-Hall.

Burch, J.G. 1986. *Entrepreneurship*. New York: John Wiley and Sons.

Camagni, R. 1991. Local 'milieu', uncertainty and innovation networks: towards a new dynamic theory of economic space. In Camagni, R. ed. *Innovation Networks: Spatial Perspectives*. London: Belhaven Press, pp. 121-144.

Central Bureau of Statistics. 1961. *Statistical Abstract of Israel*. Jerusalem.

Central Bureau of Statistics. 1973. *Statistical Abstract of Israel*. Jerusalem.

Central Bureau of Statistics. 1987. *Statistical Abstract of Israel*. Jerusalem.

Central Bureau of Statistics, 1991. *Statistical Abstract of Israel*. Jerusalem.

Central Bureau of Statistics. 1992. *Statistical Abstract of Israel*. Jerusalem.

Chamley, C. 1983. Entrepreneurial abilities and liabilities in a model of self-selection. *Bell Journal of Economics*: 70-80.

Cohen, A. 1964. *Israel and the Arab world*. Tel Aviv: Sifriat Ha'poalim (Hebrew).

Cole, A.H. 1959. *Business Enterprise in Its Social Setting*. Cambridge, Mass.: Harvard University Press.

Cooper, A.C. and Dunkelberg, W.C. 1986. Entrepreneurship and path to business ownership. *Strategic Management Journal* 7: 53-86.

Czamanski, D.T., Jubran, R., and Khamaisi, R. 1986. *Employment Potential of University Graduates in the Arab Localities in Israel*. Haifa: Center for Urban and Regional Studies, Technion.

Czamanski, D.T. and Taylor, T.K. 1986. Dynamic aspects of entrepreneurship in Arab settlements in Israel. *Horizons* 17-18: 125-144 (Hebrew).

Deek, J. 1976. *The Small Firm Owner-Manager: Entrepreneurial Behavior and the Management Practice*. New York: Praeger.

Department of the Environment. 1988. *Developing Businesses; Good Practice in Urban Regeneration*. London: H.M.S.O.

Druker, P.F. 1985. *Innovation and Entrepreneurship*. London: Heineman.

Efrat, E. 1983. *Geography of Welfare, Social Gap and Inequality*. Tel Aviv: Achiasaf (Hebrew).

Eisenstadt, E.H. 1981. *Social Differentiation and Stratification*. Jerusalem: Magnes Press (Hebrew).

Falah, G. 1993. Trends in the urbanization of Arab settlements in Galilee. *Urban Geography* 14(2): 145-164.

Felsenstein, D. 1986. *The Spatial Organization of High-Technology Industries in Israel*. Jerusalem: The Hebrew University, Institute of Urban and Regional Studies.

Felsenstein, D. 1992. Assessing the employment effectiveness of small business financing schemes: Some evidence from Israel. *Small Business Economics* 4: 273-285.

Felsenstein, D. and Schwartz, D. 1993. Constraints to small business development across the life cycle: some evidence from peripheral areas in Israel. *Entrepreneurship and Regional Development* 5: 227-245.

Gaspar, J. and Gould, P.R. 1981. The Cova da Beira: an applied structural analysis of agriculture and communication. In Pred, A. ed. *Space and Time in Geography: Essays Dedicated to Torsten Hagerstrand.* Lund: C.W.K. Gllerup, pp. 183-214.

Geertz, C. 1963. *Peddlers and Princes: Social Change and Economic Modernization in Two Indonesian Towns.* Chicago: University of Chicago Press.

Ginat, Y. 1983. *Employment as a Factor in Social Change.* The Pinhas Sapir Center for Development. Tel Aviv: Tel Aviv University (Hebrew).

Golani, G. 1967. *The Settlement Geography of the Traditional Villages: The Case of Taiyibe.* Unpublished M.A. dissertation, Technion, Haifa (Hebrew).

Gottheil, F.M. 1972. On the economic development of the Arab region in Israel. In Curtis, M. and Chertoff, M. eds. *Israel: Social Structure and Change.* New Brunswick, N.J.: Transaction Books, pp. 237-248.

Gradus, Y. and Einy, Y. 1981. Trends in core-periphery industrialization gaps in Israel. *Geographical Research Forum* 3: 25-37.

Gradus, Y., Razin, E., and Krakover, S. 1993. *The Industrial Geography of Israel.* London: Routledge.

Grossman, G.M. 1984. International trade, foreign investment, and the formation of the entrepreneurial class. *The American Economic Review* 10: 605-613.

Habash, A. 1973. *Society in Transition: A Social and Political Study of the Arab Community in Israel.* Ann Arbor, Mich.: Xerox University Microfilms.

Haidar, A. 1985. *Economic Entrepreneurial Patterns in the Arab Village in Israel.* Unpublished Ph.D. dissertation, The Hebrew University, Jerusalem (Hebrew).

Haidar, A. 1991. *The Arab Population in the Israeli Economy.* Tel Aviv: International Center for Peace in the Middle East (Hebrew).

Haidar, A. 1993. *Obstacles to Economic Development in the Arab Sector in Israel.* Tel-Aviv: The Jewish-Arab Centre for Economic Development (Hebrew).

Halbert, R.F. and Link, A.N. 1982. *Entrepreneur.* New York: Praeger.

Hamilton, F.E.I. 1986. ed. *Industrialization in Developing and Peripheral Regions.* London: Croom Helm.

Harrison, F. and Myers, C.A. 1959. *Management in the Industrial World.* New York: McGraw-Hill.

Holland, S. 1976. *The Regional Problem.* London: Macmillan.

Hornbeck, J.F. 1989. *Economic Development, Rural Lending Policies and Federal Outreach Programs.* Washington, D.C.: Congressional Research Service.

Jaffa Research Center. 1991. *Arab Cities and Villages in Israel; Statistical Abstract 1990.* Nazareth: Jaffa Publication Series.

Jiobu, R.M. 1988. Ethnic hegemony and the Japanese of California. *American Sociological Review* 53: 353-367.

Justman, M. and Teubal, M. 1993. Technology and economic growth: the structuralist perspective. In Justman, M., Zuscovitch, E., and Teubal, M. eds. *Technological Infrastructure Policy for Renewal Economic Growth.* Jerusalem: The Jerusalem Institute for Israel Studies (Hebrew).

Kanu, J. 1983. *The Land Conflict Affairs in Eretz Israel Between Jews and Arabs*. Givat Haviva, Center for Arab and Afro-Asian Studies (Hebrew).

Kenneth, R. and van Voorish, B. 1980. *Entrepreneurship and Small Business Management*. Allen and Bacon Inc.

Khalidi, R. 1988. *The Arab Economy in Israel: The Dynamics of a Region's Development*. London: Croom Helm.

Khamaisi, R. 1986. Implementation of outline plans in Arab villages. *Horizons* 17-18: 161-172 (Hebrew).

Kimmerling, B. 1983. *Zionism and the Economy*. Cambridge Mass.: Schenkman.

Kipnis, B. and Schnell, I. 1978. Changes in the distribution of Arabs in mixed Jewish-Arab cities in Israel. *Economic Geography* 54(2): 168-180.

Lawton Smith, H., Dickson, K., and Lloyd Smith, S. 1991. There are two sides to every story; innovation and collaboration within networks of large and small firms. *Research Policy* 20: 247-486.

Lewin-Epstein, N. 1990. *The Arab Economy in Israel: Growing Population—Jobs Mismatch*. Discussion Paper No. 14. The Pinhas Sapir Center for Development: Tel-Aviv University.

Lewin-Epstein, N. and Semyonov, M. 1986. Ethnic group mobility in the Israeli Labor market. *American Sociological Review* 51: 342-351.

Lewin-Epstein, N. and Semyonov, M. 1993. *The Arab Minority in Israel's Economy*. Boulder, Colo.: Westview Press.

Lewin-Epstein, N. and Semyonov, M. 1994. Sheltered labor markets, public sector employment, and socioeconomic return to education of Arab in Israel. *American Journal of Sociology* 100(3): 622-651.

Lieberson, S. 1980. *A Piece of the Pie*. Berkeley: University of California Press.

Light, I.H. 1972. *Ethnic Enterprise in America: Business and Welfare Among Chinese, Japanese and Blacks*. Berkeley: University of California Press.

Light, I.H. 1984. Immigrant and ethnic enterprise in North America. *Ethnic and Racial Studies* 7: 195-216.

Light, I. and Bonachich, E. 1988. *Immigrant Entrepreneurs, Koreans in Los Angeles, 1965-1982*. Berkeley: University of California Press.

Linge, G.J.R. 1988. Peripheralisation and industrial change. In Linge, G.J.R. ed. *Peripheralisation and Industrial Change*. London: Croom Helm, pp. 1-21.

Lipshitz, G. 1986. Divergence or convergence in regional inequality—consumption variables versus policy variables: the Israeli case. *Geografiska Annaler* 68B: 13-20.

Lustick, I. 1980. *Arabs in the Jewish State: Israel's Control Over a National Minority*. Austin, Tex.: University of Texas Press.

Markusen, A.R. 1985. *Profit Cycles, Oligopoly and Regional Development*. Cambridge, Mass.: MIT Press.

Markusen, A.R. and Teitz, M.B. 1983. *The World of Small Business; Turbulence and Survival*. Working Paper 408. Berkeley: University of California, Institute of Urban and Regional Development.

Massey, D. 1984. *Spatial Division of Labour*. London: Macmillan.

Massey, D. 1985. New directions in space. In Gregory, D. and Urry, J. eds. *Social Relations and Spatial Structures*. London: Macmillan, pp. 9-19.

Massey, D. and Meegan, R. 1978. Industrial restructuring versus the cities. *Urban Studies* 15: 273-288.

Massey, D. and Meegan, R. 1979. The geography of industrial reorganization. *Progress in Planning* 10: 159-237.

Mathot, G.B.M. 1982. How to get new products to market quicker. *Long Range Planning* 5: 20-30.

McClelland, D.C. 1961. *The Achieving Society*. London: Van Nostrand Company.

Meir, G.M. 1970. *Leading Issues in Economic Development: Studies in International Poverty*. Oxford: Oxford University Press.

Meyer-Brodnitz, M.B. 1969. Latent urbanization in Arab villages in Israel. *Environmental Planning Association Quarterly* 8-9: 4-12 (Hebrew).

Meyer-Brodnitz, M.B. 1983. The dynamics of physical changes in Arab villages in Israel. In Shmueli, A., Soffer, A., and Kliot, N. eds *The Lands of Galilee*. Tel Aviv: Eretz, pp. 745-762 (Hebrew).

Meyer-Brodnitz, M.B. and Czamanski, D.T. 1986a. *Economic Development in the Arab Sector in Israel*. Haifa: Centre for Urban and Regional Studies, Technion (Hebrew).

Meyer-Brodnitz, M.B. and Czamanski, D.T. 1986b. Industrialization of the Arab village in Israel. *Economics Quarterly* 128: 533-546 (Hebrew).

Morris, B. (1987) *The Birth of the Palestinian Refugee Problem, 1947-1949*. Cambridge: Cambridge University Press.

Myrdal, G. 1944. *An American Dilemma: The Negro Problem and Modern Democracy*. New York: Harper.

Nabarro, R., Davies, R., Cobbold, C., and Galley, N. 1986. *Local Enterprise and the Unemployed*. London: Calouste Gulbenkian Foundation.

Nanjundan, S. 1987. Small and Medium enterprises: Some basic development issues. *Industry and Development* 20: 1-50.

Ne'eman, U. 1992. *Review of the Changes in Core-Periphery Industrialization Gaps in Israel*. Seminar paper, Department of Geography, Tel Aviv University (Hebrew).

Norton, R.D. and Rees, J. 1979. The product life cycle and the spatial decentralization of American manufacturing. *Regional Studies* 13: 141-152.

Obregon, A.R. 1974. The marginal pole of the economy and the marginalized labour force. *Economy and Society* 3: 393-428.

Organization for Economic Co-operation and Development (OECD), 1990. *Implementing Change, Entrepreneurship and Local Initiative*. Paris: OECD.

Portes, A. and Bach, R.L. 1985. *Latin Journey, Cuban and Mexican Immigrants in the United States*. Berkeley: University of California Press.

Portes, A. and Jensen, L. 1989. The enclave and the entrants: patterns of ethnic enterprise in Miami before and after Mariel. *American Sociological Review* 54: 929-949.

Pred, A. 1977. *City-Systems in Advanced Economies: Past Growth, Present Processes and Future Development Options*. London: Hutchinson.

Ratti, R. 1992. *Innovation Technologique et Developpement Regional*. Bellinzona: Instituto di Recerche Economiche.

Rauch, T. 1988. An accumulation theory approach to peripheralisation in underdeveloped countries: The examples of Nigeria and Zambia. In Linge, G.J.R. ed. *Peripheralisation and Industrial Change*. London: Croom Helm, pp. 22-36.

Razin, E. 1991. Industrial dispersal policy in Israel. In Surkis, H. et al. eds. *Changes in the Geography of Israel: Core and Periphery*. Jerusalem: Ministry of Education (Hebrew).

Razin, E. and Shachar, A. 1990. The organizational-locational structure of industry in Israel and its effects on national spatial policies. *Geography Research Forum* 10: 1-19.

Rekhess, E. 1977. Israeli Arabs and land appropriation in the Galilee. *Review*, Dayan Centre, Tel Aviv University (Hebrew).

Rekhess, E. 1986. The Arab village in Israel: a renewing national political national centre. *Horizons* 17-18: 145-160 (Hebrew).

Roberts, B. 1978. *Cities of Peasants*. New York: Edward Arnold.

Ronstadt, R. 1984. *Entrepreneurship*. Dover, Mass.: Lord Publications.

Rosenfeld, H. 1964. From peasantry to wage labor and residual peasantry: The transformation of the Arab village. In Manners, R. ed. *Process and Pattern in Culture*. Chicago: Aldine.

Rosenfeld, H. 1978. The class situation of the Arab national minority in Israel. *Comparative Studies in Society and History* 20: 374-407.

Rothwell, R. and Dodgson, M. 1991. External linkages and innovation in small and medium sized enterprises. *R. and D. Management* 21: 125-137.

Sanders, J.M. and Nee, V. 1987. Limits of ethnic solidarity in the ethnic labour economy. *American Sociological Review* 52: 745-767.

Schnell, I. 1980. *Social Areas in Arab Urbanizing Settlements: The Case of Taiyibe*. Unpublished M.A. dissertation, Technion, Haifa (Hebrew).

Schnell, I. 1986. The formation of Arab space in Israel. *Horizons* 17-18: 49-76 (Hebrew).

Schnell, I. 1987. The formation of Arab Settlement Systems in Israel. *Horizons* 19: 65-91 (Hebrew).

Schnell, I. 1990. The Israeli Arabs: the dilemma of social integration in development. *Geographiche Zeitschrift* 78(2): 78-92.

Schnell, I. 1994a. *Israeli Arab Perceptions: Territoriality and Identity*. Aldershot: Avebury.

Schnell, I. 1994b. Urban restructuring in Israeli Arab settlements. *Middle Eastern Studies* 30(2): 330-350.

Schnell, I. forthcoming. Changes in the spatial pattern of unemployment in Israel. *Geojournal*.

Schumpeter, J.A. 1934. *The Theory of Economic Development*. Cambridge: Cambridge University Press.

Schwartz, D. 1986. *The Effects of the Law for Encouraging Capital Investment on Industrial Investment in the Development Towns*. Rehovot: Settlement Study Center (Hebrew).

Segre, A. 1986. Changes in the textile industrial area of Northern Italy. In Hamilton, F.E.I. ed. *Industrialization in Developing and Peripheral Regions*. London: Croom Helm, pp. 136-148.

Semyonov, M. 1988. Bi-ethnic labor markets, mono-ethnic labor markets and socioeconomic inequality. *American Sociological Review* 53: 256-266.

Shachar, A.S. and Lipshitz, G. 1980. The spatial organization of inter-regional migration in Israel. *Studies in the Geography of Israel* 11: 153-177 (Hebrew).

Shamas, A. 1987. Kitch 22, or: the boundary of culture. *Journal 77* 84-85: 24-26 (Hebrew).

Shapiro, A. and Stokols, L. 1982. The social dimensions of entrepreneurship. *Encyclopedia of Entrepreneurship* :72-90.

Shavit, Y. 1992. Arabs in the Israeli economy: A study of the enclave hypothesis. *Israel Social Science Research* 7: 45-66.

Shaw, G. and Williams, A. 1985. The role of industrial estates in peripheral rural areas: The Cornish experience 1973-1981. In Healey, M.J. and Ilbery, B.W. eds. *The Industrialization of the Countryside*. Norwich: Geo Books, pp. 221-241.

Shmueli, A. and Schnell, I. 1980. *Planning Problems in Arab Settlements: Spatial Issues.* The Pinhas Sapir Center for Development Tel Aviv: Tel Aviv University (Hebrew).

Shmueli, A., Schnell, I., and Soffer, A. 1985. *The Little Triangle: Transformation of a Region.* Monograph Series on the Middle East, No. 3. University of Haifa: The Jewish Arab Center and The Institute of Middle Eastern Studies (Hebrew).

Shmueli, A., Schnell, I., and Soffer, A. 1986. Changes in the residential patterns in the settlements of the little triangle 1949-1980. In Soffer, A. ed. *Residential and Internal Migration Patterns Among the Arabs of Israel.* Haifa: Haifa University Press (Hebrew).

Sjaastad, L.A. 1962. The costs and returns of human migration. *Journal of Political Economy* 70: 80-93.

Smoocha, S. 1978. *Israel: Pluralism and Conflicts.* Berkeley: University of California Press.

Smoocha, S. 1984. *The Orientation and Politicisation of the Arab Minority in Israel.* Monograph Series on the Middle East, No. 2. University of Haifa: The Jewish Arab Center and The Institute of Middle Eastern Studies (Hebrew).

Smoocha, S. 1989. *Arabs and Jews in Israel: Conflicting and Shared Attitudes in a Divided Society.* Boulder, Colo.: Westview Press.

Sofer, M., Schnell, I., and Drori, I. 1993. *Arab Industry in Israel.* Research Report. Beit Berl: Institute for Israeli Arab Studies (Hebrew).

Soffer, A. 1983. The changing situation of majority and minority and its spatial expression: the case of the Arab minority in Israel. In Kliot, N. and Waterman, S. eds. *Pluralism and Political Geography.* London: Croom Helm, pp. 80-99.

State of Israel, Ministry of Interior et al. 1989. *Programmatic Outlines for Planning Industrial Zones.* Jerusalem: The Government Printer (Hebrew).

Sunkel, O. 1973. Transnational capitalism and national disintegration in Latin America. *Social and Economic Studies* 22: 132-176.

Swyngedouw, E.A. 1989. Centre-periphery relations and the see-saw of uneven spatial development. *Tijdschrift van de Belg. Ver. Aardr. Studies* 1989(2), 291-317.

Tamari, M. 1991. *Small Firms in Israel.* Tel Aviv: Centre for Social and Economic Progress (Hebrew).

Taylor, M. 1987. Enterprise and the product cycle model; conceptual ambiguities. In van der Knaap, G.A. and Wever, E. eds. *New Technology and Regional Development.* London: Croom Helm, pp. 751-761.

Townroe, P. and Mallalieu, K. 1990. *Entrepreneurial Roles and Entrepreneurial Competence in Regional Economic Development.* Small Business Research Programme. London: E.S.C.R., Small Business Research Initiative.

Utterback, J.M. 1979. The dynamic of product and process innovation in industry. In Hill, C.T. and Utterback, J.M. eds. *Technological Innovation for a Dynamic Economy.* New York: Pergamon, pp. 40-64.

van Geenhuizen, M.S. and Nijkamp, P. 1993. Industrial dynamics, company life histories and core-periphery dilemma. in *An International Conference on Regional Development: The Challenge of the Frontier Conference.* Dead-Sea, Israel. (unpublished paper).

Vernon, R. 1966. International investment and international trade in the product cycle. *Quarterly Journal of Economics* 80: 190-207.

Vesper, K.H. 1980. *New Venture Strategies*. New York: Prentice-Hall.

Vilkansky, R. 1980. *Core and Periphery in the Development of Israel*. Unpublished Ph.D. Dissertation, Technion, Haifa (Hebrew).

Waldinger, R. 1986. *Through the Eye of the Needle: Immigrants and Enterprise in New York's Garment Trades*. New York: New York University Press.

Waldinger, R., Aldrich, H., and Ward, R. 1990. *Ethnic Entrepreneurs*. Newbury Park, Calif.: Sage.

Watad, M. 1966. Unemployment hunts the Arab village. *New Outlook* 9(7).

Webber, M.J. 1984. *Industrial Location*. Beverly Hills, Calif.: Sage.

Wilson, K. and Portes, A. 1980. Immigrant enclaves: an analysis of the labor market experience of Cubans in Miami. *American Journal of Sociology* 86: 305-319.

Wilter, P.H. 1979. *Entrepreneurship–a Comparative and Historical Study*. Norwood, N.J.: Ablex.

Wong, C.C. 1977. Black and Chinese grocery stores in Los-Angeles Black Ghetto. *Urban Life* 5(4): 439-464.

Yiftachel, O. 1991. Industrial development and Arab-Jewish economic gaps in the Galilee region, Israel. *The Professional Geographer* 43(3): 163-179.

Yiftachel, O. 1992. *Planning a Mixed Region in Israel*. Aldershot: Avebury.

Zarhi, S. and Achiezra, A. 1966. *The Economic Conditions of the Arab Minority in Israel*. Arab and Afro-Asian Monograph Series, No. 1. Givat Haviva: Center for Arab and Afro-Asian Studies.

Zureik, E.T. 1979. *Palestinians in Israel: a Study of Internal Colonialism*. London: Routledge and Kegan Paul.

Index

About the Authors

IZHAK SCHNELL is a Social Geographer in the Department of Geography at Tel Aviv University, Israel. He is also the head of Beit-Berl College Supreme Academic Committee. His major fields of interest are in social geography, the experience of space and place, and Arab space in Israel. His work has been published in Hebrew, English, French, and German.

MICHAEL SOFER is an Economic Geographer in the Department of Geography at Tel Aviv University, Israel and the head of the Geography Department at Levinski Teachers College. He is currently involved in research on the industrialization and transformation of rural space.

ISRAEL DRORI is a Social Anthropologist in the Public Policy Program and the Department of Labor Studies at Tel Aviv University. His major fields of interest include organizational culture, industrial organization, and R&D. He has conducted research on development and change in the Caribbean, Central America, Africa, and Arab and Druze settlements in Israel.

ISBN 0-275-94856-0

HARDCOVER BAR CODE